THE TYPEWRITER CENTURY

A Cultural History of Writing Practices

The Typewriter Century

A Cultural History of Writing Practices

MARTYN LYONS

UNIVERSITY OF TORONTO PRESS
Toronto Buffalo London

© University of Toronto Press 2021
Toronto Buffalo London
utorontopress.com

ISBN 978-1-4875-0824-1 (cloth)
ISBN 978-1-4875-2573-6 (paper)
ISBN 978-1-4875-3783-8 (EPUB)
ISBN 978-1-4875-3782-1 (PDF)

Studies in Book and Print Culture

Library and Archives Canada Cataloguing in Publication

Title: The typewriter century : a cultural history of writing practices / Martyn
Lyons.
Names: Lyons, Martyn, author.
Series: Studies in book and print culture.
Description: Series statement: Studies in book and print culture | Includes
bibliographical references and index.
Identifiers: Canadiana (print) 20200304984 | Canadiana (ebook)
20200305018 | ISBN 9781487508241 (hardcover) |
ISBN 9781487525736 (softcover) | ISBN 9781487537838 (EPUB) |
ISBN 9781487537821 (PDF)
Subjects: LCSH: Typewriters – History. | LCSH: Typewriters –
Social aspects. | LCSH: Typewriting – History.
Classification: LCC Z49.A1 L96 2020 | DDC 652.3 – dc23

Chapter opening illustration: AVA Bitter/Shutterstock.com

University of Toronto Press acknowledges the financial assistance to its
publishing program of the Canada Council for the Arts and the Ontario
Arts Council, an agency of the Government of Ontario.

 Canada Council
for the Arts
Conseil des Arts
du Canada

 ONTARIO ARTS COUNCIL
CONSEIL DES ARTS DE L'ONTARIO
an Ontario government agency
un organisme du gouvernement de l'Ontario

Funded by the
Government
of Canada
Financé par le
gouvernement
du Canada
Canada

Contents

List of Illustrations   vii

Acknowledgments   ix

1 Introduction: The Typewriter as an Agent of Change?   3

2 The Birth of the Typosphere   25

3 Modernity and the "Typewriter Girl"   49

4 The Modernist Typewriter   67

5 The Distancing Effect: The Hand, the Eye, the Voice   86

6 The Romantic Typewriter   105

7 Manuscript and Typescript   121

8 Georges Simenon: The Man in the Glass Cage   137

9 Erle Stanley Gardner: The Fiction Factory   155

10 Domesticating the Typewriter   172

11 The End of the Typewriter Century and Post-Digital
Nostalgia   191

Notes   203

Bibliography   239

Index   257

Illustrations

1.1 Len Deighton and his IBM word processor   14
2.1 Malling Hansen's Writing Ball, c. 1874   29
2.2 Sholes and Glidden typewriter, 1874   34
2.3 The Caligraph typewriter   42
2.4 Dvorak keyboard   46
2.5 Remington advertisement for models 10 and 11, 1909   47
4.1 Guillaume Apollinaire, *Salut Monde*   75
4.2 Guillaume Apollinaire, *Lettre-Océan*   77
5.1 Luigi Pirandello dictating to himself   101
6.1 Jack Kerouac, scroll version of *On the Road*   116
7.1 Richmal Crompton, notes on an envelope   126
10.1 Leo Tolstoy dictating at Yasnaya Polyana   176
10.2 Agatha Christie typing at home, 1952   180

Acknowledgments

The idea for this book originated in a museum. On a visit to Sydney's Powerhouse Museum, which is primarily a museum of technology, I had an unpleasant shock. I spotted a very familiar item displayed in a glass cabinet with an explanatory label for the benefit of the uninitiated. It was a typewriter – a bright red Olivetti portable from the 1960s – and it was familiar because I wrote my own doctoral thesis on the same model. I was confronted by the unsettling reality that an object that had once played an important role in my life had become a museum exhibit, a curious survivor of a now extinct species.

It was only later that I came to realize that the real dinosaur was in fact myself. The sight of the Olivetti behind glass was like a vision of myself as historical artefact. My own writing practices have certainly evolved, but slowly. I happily drafted this book and other work before it on a MacBook, but, for some purposes such as writing cheques, I still use a fountain pen, which today is another endangered species. When I used to do this in department stores, it made shop assistants' jaws drop in amazement. Like Paul Auster with his sturdy German-made Olympia typewriter, "I began to look like an enemy of progress, the last pagan holdout in a world of digital converts." But the real point of these comments about my existential mini-crisis is that writing technologies like pens and typewriters have a history of their own, and that their history can come to life only if it is told through the eyes of their users. Such a history of writing materials needs to be told if we are to have a more complete appreciation of writing practices in past societies. A chance encounter with an Olivetti in the Powerhouse Museum had given me a new agenda for the cultural history of writing.

Having acknowledged both the Powerhouse and my MacBook, I need to say a number of sincere thank yous to some real people. For their contributions in the early stages of preparation of this book, I would like to recognize the impeccable work of two research assistants at the University of New South Wales: Jacinta Kelly in the Centre for Modernism Studies, and Baylee Brits from the School of Arts and Media.

I have received valuable assistance from archivists and librarians in a variety of depositories in several countries. These include the friendly staff of the Harry Ransom Center at the University of Austin, Texas, which is responsible for the enormous Erle Stanley Gardner archive, and the staff of the Bodleian Library in Oxford for assisting my consultation of the John le Carré papers. I am especially grateful to Josie Summer for making my visit to the Enid Blyton archive in Newcastle-upon-Tyne an unexpected pleasure in bitterly cold circumstances, and to Laurent Demoulin for his expertise and collegial hospitality as *conservateur* of the Georges Simenon archive in the Chateau de Colonster in Liège, Belgium. I would also like to thank the Special Collections staff at the Brotherton Library in Leeds, for making available the papers of Barbara Taylor Bradford, and Kornelia Cepok, for her assistance and knowledgeable advice on the Richmal Crompton papers at Roehampton University.

Véronique Rohrbach was generous enough to send me a link to her unpublished doctoral thesis, and to share her experience of obtaining access to the relatively remote Georges Simenon archive. Lisa Kuitert supported the publication of an earlier sketch of this study in *Quaerendo,* of which she is editor. Gordon and Sue Lyons allowed me to use the indispensable Pimlico flat on two research trips to Britain. At the University of New South Wales, I acknowledge the financial support of the Faculty of Arts and Social Sciences in the form of two Emeriti research grants.

I presented some of this work to the Book History Group Seminar at the University of Lund in 2014, and I found the subsequent discussion extremely helpful. I am similarly grateful to Alejandro Dujovne and his colleagues for their responses to my presentation at the third Congress of Argentinian book historians in Buenos Aires in 2018. My Sydney colleagues David Miller and Mina Roces read chapter drafts and made helpful suggestions. I am very grateful for their time and critical attention.

THE TYPEWRITER CENTURY

1 Introduction: The Typewriter as an Agent of Change?

Writing Practices and Technological Change

In 2006, when Larry McMurtry accepted the Golden Globe award for co-writing the screenplay of *Brokeback Mountain*, he thanked his typewriter (it was a Hermes 3000). In Colorado, Hunter S. Thompson, author of *Fear and Loathing in Las Vegas* (1972), took his typewriter out into the snow and shot it (and later himself).[1] Clearly the typewriter was not just a soulless machine; it had a persona, to be befriended, cherished, reviled, or murdered. Many writers treated their typewriter like a living creature, as did Paul Auster, who called his Olympia a "fragile, sentient being":[2] "It was simply a tool that allowed me to do my work," he wrote, "but now that it had become an endangered species, one of the last surviving artifacts of twentieth-century *homo scriptorus*, I began to develop a certain affection for it."[3] In this case, obsolescence made the heart grow fonder. According to Barbara Taylor Bradford, "I think of my typewriter as my own psychiatrist. I pour all my hang-ups in there, emptying my head"[4] – the lesson of her confession being that more people should be typing novels instead of going to therapists. Ian Fleming, on the other hand, turned his machine into an object of worship. After writing *Casino Royale* in 1952, Fleming ordered a custom-made gold-plated Royal Quiet Deluxe Portable from a dealer in New York, and asked a friend to smuggle the parts to him in England on the *Queen Elizabeth* to avoid paying customs duty.[5] The "Man with the Golden Typewriter" had elevated his work-machine to the status of a pagan idol in praise of Mammon.

Author and typewriter had a subtle relationship with each other, even if it was often mediated by a female typist, and this book is devoted to exploring it. Catherine Breslin (*Unholy Child*, 1979) called it an "intimate conspiracy."[6] John Steinbeck took a sharp instrument, perhaps a key, and scratched a rough inscription on the back of his portable Hermes. It read "The Beast Within." What did this signify for Steinbeck? We can speculate, along with critic Robert DeMott, that for Steinbeck the typewriter represented the irresistible compulsion to write, an inner drive that he (like so many authors) could not fully dominate.[7] In fact Steinbeck preferred to use pencils, which he laboriously sharpened as part of his pre-writing ritual, but the typewriter could help him focus his ideas. For writers like Steinbeck, the typewriter also signified an important step nearer publication, the finalizing of a draft before submission to an editor. In this moment of completion, the typewriter sent the author mixed messages. The writer could experience a fleeting feeling of elation, soon superseded perhaps by a sense of disappointment, in the realization that he or she had not quite achieved perfection, because finding the Holy Grail was still an elusive goal. Steinbeck's typewriter, like an old and well-worn book, was inscribed with its own "marginalia," suggesting an ambiguous relationship with its owner.

For many writers, the typewriter was much more than just a faithful companion. It actively contributed to shaping the literary opus. The typewriter forced the writer to be precise. As the writer confronted the keyboard, it could crystallize his or her thoughts in a way that the word processor, with its infinite capacity for swift revision, can never achieve. Without the convenience of instantly crossing out an error by hand, and without the luxury of the delete key, the typewriter encouraged the author to be disciplined and even miserly with words, because revision was possible only if the text were completely redrafted. The typewriter thus collaborated with the writer in the creative process.

There were times, nevertheless, when the machine proved a difficult companion and a source of frustration. Ernest Hemingway complained at one point that his machine was "stiff as a frozen whisker."[8] "I suffer so after typing," lamented Australian writer Miles Franklin in 1933.[9] On his travels, Patrick White faced payments to airlines for excess baggage, typewriter included, and endured the inconvenience of lugging his Olympia up Greek mountainsides to visit isolated monasteries.[10] At times the typewriter seemed a burden, but it was an indispensable one. Its influence was inescapable but unpredictable.

The many ways in which different writers reacted to the typewriter, and incorporated it into their work routines, form the subject of this book. It considers their anxieties as well as the emotional connection they sensed as they approached the keyboard. It will examine how they used the machine, and the relationships that developed between their typing and other means of inscription, including both handwritten drafts and dictation. As far as possible, I interrogate writers' reflections on their own work for clues about how they responded to new technology, and about how, when, and where they used their machine, and how it structured or influenced their creativity. The typewriter changed compositional practices and left a profound mark on writing history. The machine offered writers new opportunities, for speed, critical distance, or, in unexpected ways, a revival of orality. At the same time, a new tension emerged between the writer's creative impulse and the limitations of the instrument; there was a lingering suspicion that mechanical writing was not truly compatible with literary work of the highest quality. A few writers resolved this problem with spectacular success, including those who resisted the typewriter, and those who embraced it.

Modernity opened up new possibilities, but it also posed threats to traditional writing practices. Writers faced the challenge of technology transfer with both enthusiasm and scepticism. In the examples I will present in this book, I try to elucidate what writers thought the machine could offer them, and how they imagined it might change their writing. These questions cannot be asked, much less answered, without considering the wide range of writing technologies available in the early twentieth century and the connections between them. The typewriter's impact has to be integrated into a study of the use of handwritten notes and texts drafted in longhand and revised again by hand. The explosion in office machines that occurred in the early twentieth century created a range of dictation and transcription apparatuses, which were seized on by some writers. Marshall McLuhan detected, and implicitly welcomed, a return to orality in this new synthesis of the spoken and the typed word.[11] Dictation, combined with the use of manuscript and typing, completed the full armoury of resources available to the writer. I focus on the inter-relationships between them, the connected roles of voice, handwriting, and typed text, and the relative importance attributed to each, as writers migrated from one medium to another.

New technologies never completely replace old ones, and the typewriter did not obliterate older forms of writing like the ink-pen, just as the invention of printing had never irrevocably silenced manuscript culture. Rather, as Jacques Derrida would say of displaced technologies, their "structural hegemony was reduced."[12] Walter Benjamin, in a celebrated essay on the visual arts, spoke more poetically of the "shrivelling of their aura" in the new age of mass production.[13] Yet the manuscript still continued to radiate a certain "aura" in spite of the increasing commodification of literary works. To cite Derrida again, "As always, there is and there will be co-existence and the structural survival of past models at the very moment when the genesis of new ones is opening up new possibilities."[14] In this process, older technologies, displaced from their former dominant position, are sometimes invested with a privileged or even sacred status. This has to some extent been the fate of the traditional book in the digital age, in spite or perhaps because of prophecies of the demise of the codex, as yet unfulfilled. Meanwhile, adherents of older technologies continue to denigrate innovative methods and their democratizing tendencies. Such denigration was directed at the typewriter: many writers at first found it very difficult to reconcile genuine creativity with a machine so closely associated with mundane bureaucratic tasks.

A flashback to the fate of the quill pen in the nineteenth century illustrates the syndrome in vivid fashion. By the 1830s, the invention of steel pens had effectively destroyed the monopoly enjoyed for centuries by the goose quill. The steel pen offered many benefits: it lasted much longer than the quill, and there was no need to harden the tip (quills were sometimes baked to achieve this). And yet many writers loathed it because it seemed to be the generator of substandard and pedestrian work. In an essay in 1839, French critic Charles-Augustin Sainte-Beuve deplored what he called the "industrialization of literature," arguing that mass production and the mercenary obsession with profit could never produce great art.[15] Sainte-Beuve was admittedly not writing here specifically about the steel pen; he was reacting to a more general trend of which it was a part, namely the vogue for the serialization of fiction in the press, successfully exploited at this time by "industrial" writers such as Eugène Sue and Alexandre Dumas, who was a steel pen convert.

Authors who distinguished themselves from the process of literary "industrialization" remained very attached to their traditional goose quills. Victor Hugo carefully preserved the six quills with which he composed *Les Misérables*.[16] Gustave Flaubert claimed he had hundreds of them and called himself "a quill-man," suggesting that as an author he had a profound personal connection with his familiar writing instruments.[17] Another French writer, Jules Janin, found the steel pen brutal and graceless, unfit for the "sage lenteur" (slow wisdom) required to achieve stylistic perfection. It could never produce masterpieces, because it was the prosaic instrument of bankers and accountants, fit only to compose stupid melodramas and sensational trash.[18] So, too, the typewriter was given a frosty welcome by aesthetes and *literati*. Truman Capote offered a modern parallel when he dismissed Jack Kerouac's work as not writing, but merely typing.[19] A few writers, in contrast, responded positively to new technology. They embraced not only the machine but even the stigma attached to it by some members of the literary elite. Alexandre Dumas, who produced novels on a proto-industrial scale, defied his quillophile bohemian colleagues and adopted the steel pen in 1831. As we shall see, there are many parallels here with the advent of the typewriter, which had its own stigmatizers as well as its eager converts.

In conventional histories of industrialization, the large-scale innovations capture most attention: coal mines, textile factories, railways and the blast furnaces that produced the steel to build them. There is nevertheless a place for technologies that are less spectacular but that directly affect the lives of ordinary people. The bicycle, the sewing machine, and the typewriter are examples of such "everyday machines," as David Arnold calls them in his account of their contribution to modernity in India.[20] Just like these other products, the typewriter made an impact on the daily work of millions of people and in so doing acquired different cultural meanings in different settings. This book is about an "everyday technology" that can take a rightful place in the history of modernization.

Unfortunately, however, the role of the typewriter has been taken for granted. As Catherine Viollet suggested in her pioneering work on the semiology of the machine, it remains a blind spot in the history of writing practices.[21] It has not merely been underestimated; rather, it has become invisible. Historians of writing technologies have devoted many books to the impact of moveable type and Gutenberg's printing press on Western and other cultures; more recently, Matthew Kirschenbaum's prize-winning book illuminated literary responses to the advent of word processing.[22] Between print culture and the computer age, the role of the typewriter has been obscured. It seems to have slipped silently through the cracks. But if we wish to understand fully the material conditions of textual production between the late nineteenth and the middle of the twentieth century, the impact of the typewriter demands our attention.

In a sense, we might think of the typewriter "as an agent of change," a phrase that sends us back to Elizabeth Eisenstein's well-known work on the printing press.[23] For Eisenstein, the invention of the printing press was a revolution that drastically transformed scholarly life and helped to shape important historical movements like the European Renaissance, the Protestant Reformation, and the Scientific Revolution. It would be rash to claim anything as grandiose as this for the humble typewriter. It is important to avoid the technological fallacy according to which new inventions are alone responsible for significant historical change. I do not wish to attract the charge of technological determinism, which has sometimes dogged the Eisenstein thesis of the "Printing Revolution." Writers are individuals – in fact, they form a profession that can probably claim more than its fair share of eccentrics. This makes it impossible to sustain firm generalizations about them. The typewriter affected them but in different and often unpredictable ways. There was nothing uniform about its influence. The typewriter made a difference, but it made a *different* difference, depending on which writer we consider. Because authors are such a motley crew, this book will inevitably have an open-ended quality, at times presenting divergent arguments that appear to lead in different directions. This simply reflects the unconventional and eccentric individuality inherent in the republic of letters. Matthew Kirschenbaum defended the same non-conclusion in his study of the reception of the word processor, and his words are worth endorsing: "Any analysis," he sensibly advised, "that imagines a single technological artifact in a position of authority over something as complex and multi-faceted as the production of a literary text is suspect in my view, and reflects an impoverished understanding of the writer's craft."[24]

The typewriter changed literary production in the sense that it potentially accelerated it, enabling a great increase in writing speed to occur. At the same time, labour could easily be delegated to professional typists. It followed from this that the volume of literary production could expand exponentially. For example, it is hard to imagine how the plethoric output of pulp fiction in its golden age of the 1920s and 1930s could have been possible without the aid of the typewriter. It is much harder to argue that the typewriter influenced literary style itself, although some writers were convinced that the machine actually improved the quality of what they wrote. "The better the typewriter, the better the writing," according to Gary Provost, author of *100 Ways to Improve Your Writing* (1985).[25]

Australian writer Nettie Palmer, on the other hand, argued that the typewriter changed nothing. What really mattered was the brilliance of the author. "When I read a novel," she wrote,

> whose author obviously believes in his characters to the end, clearly foreseeing in broad outline the last page while he writes the first, I feel I am reading something that (but for the accidents of neglect) will live on. And that book may have emerged either from writing or re-writing by the patient pen, or from assembled mechanisms and card-index cupboards culminating in the alert receptive Dictaphone. It shouldn't matter. If the book was great enough, no reader would know.[26]

Readers, to be sure, may not be immediately aware exactly how, when, and where the book they are enjoying was composed, and they may not comprehend what circumstances or financial pressures determined its creation, nor what combination of writing technologies were present at its birth, but this does not mean that these factors are unimportant in shaping the end result. Perhaps Palmer subscribed to an enduring notion of the autonomy of the creative writer, whose imaginative mind would not be compromised by material circumstances. This corresponds to a conventional view of the romantic genius. From this perspective, Descartes would always be Descartes, Shakespeare would always be Shakespeare, regardless of the multiple paths taken by their texts to reach their readers, and ignoring the different forms in which their works have been reincarnated for various reading publics through the centuries. In this book, however, my argument takes issue with Nettie Palmer. I argue that we *do* need to know the conditions of material production if we are fully to understand both creative processes and the reception of literary works. The typewriter influenced literary production, as well as the production of other written forms, by facilitating greater speed and prodigious output and, in a few cases, by promoting a terser style.

It would be rash to assert that the typewriter changed literary style, and very difficult to substantiate that claim as a generalized hypothesis. The question remains open. But whether the typewriter produced leaner, less florid prose or not, it is significant that some writers certainly *thought* the typewriter changed their writing style. Friedrich Nietzsche famously registered that "[o]ur writing tools are also working on our thoughts," and this revelation was eagerly taken up by media theorist Friedrich Kittler to support the idea that the machine *did* change literary style – a thesis he maintained (and overstated) with Germanic certainty.[27] Nietzsche was not alone in perceiving a transformation in his writing and in attributing it to typewriting. T.S. Eliot found that typing led him shorten his sentences and instead write "short, staccato, like modern French prose," although it is not clear which French writers he had in mind, and even less certain that they used a typewriter.[28] As we shall see in more detail in chapter 8, Georges Simenon was absolutely unequivocal about the power of the typewriter to fashion his novels. In 1955, an interviewer on French radio asked him if there was a connection between his style and typewriting, and after some discussion arrived at the conclusion: "So we wouldn't have the same Simenon without the typewriter!" Simenon endorsed this view with some emphasis: "Certainly not."[29] Respect for the creative autonomy of the individual writer should not prevent us from assessing the role and function of the instruments and materials with which the writer was intimately connected.

The history of the typewriter forces us to consider not only the author's imaginative powers but also the material bases of creativity. Authors do not write books; they write texts, and the way those texts become physical objects and the means by which they arrive in a readable form before an audience are crucial elements in creating meaning.[30] In a similar way, historians of written culture emphasize the importance of writing materials and technologies. The support and medium on and through which textual communication operates help us understand its function and its significance. The material presence of the text, together with the instruments that compose it, contributes something to its impact and reception. It is impossible, to take a historical example, to conceive of ancient Sumerian script without recognizing its exclusive dependence on the medium of clay. After the second millennium, the script struggled to compete with the Phoenician alphabet, which could be written on more pliable materials, and it gradually became an esoteric cultural language rather like Latin in modern Europe.[31] The survival and changing functions of Sumerian script were directly connected to the surface on which it was inscribed. Writing technologies and their material support, whether silk, bamboo, palm leaf, parchment, or paper, may have important repercussions for the nature of communication in social, political, and cultural spheres. This is a compelling reason to pay attention to the physical materiality of the writing process.

Friedrich Kittler and the Historians

Friedrich Kittler certainly paid attention to it. His was one of the few voices to recognize the importance of the typewriter, whose story he correctly identified as a "critical lacuna" in technological history.[32] His ideas have exerted considerable influence over media studies experts ever since the appearance of his *Aufschreibesysteme, 1800/1900* in 1985, followed by *Grammophon, Film, Typewriter* in 1986, although it took fourteen years before both these works were available in English.[33] I approach Kittler from the critical perspective of a historian of writing practices, to underline his positive contribution but also to outline the limits of his technological determinism.

In Kittler's view, the new methods of recording sound, vision, and words that appeared at the beginning of the twentieth century profoundly altered human perceptions of the world. He saw the gramophone, film, and the typewriter not as passive instruments, but as technologies that changed the meaning of what they communicated and had the ability to "capture" their subject. For Kittler, communications media control and influence discourse. In a much-quoted statement, he asserted that "media determine our situation."[34] Machines reshape their users, not the other way around.

This formula asserted the significance of the material form of any communication, but it left little scope for human agency. Historians of the book would certainly agree with Kittler that the material form in which any text is embodied contributes to meaning – in fact, this has been one of the fundamental premises of the discipline. Book historians, however, also know that the reader, like the user of any communications technology, also creates meaning. We might even say that only in the act of reading does any written text really come into existence. The autonomy of the reader, then, is another fundamental starting point for the book historian. Kittler, on the other hand, was not concerned primarily with how individual users of the typewriter formed a relationship with their machine, and he never "interrogates the audience," as Jonathan Rose urged book historians to do.[35] Although, for example, Kittler argues that the typewriter ended the male dominance of textual production, he does not refer to any female authors. Typists, both male and female, secretarial and literary, gave the typewriter meaning at the same time as the machine participated in their composition practices.

In Kittler's emphasis on the power of communications media to shape our lives, he took little account of the socio-economic forces that made the typewriter a popular commercial product at a specific historical moment. He was not a historian. Like Michel Foucault in *Les mots et les choses*, he thought in terms of decisive paradigm shifts in human consciousness, and the task of identifying the historical factors that brought them about was not particularly relevant to him. Each rupture brought about a new constellation, a new discourse network. Thus the typewriter was one component of the new discourse network that emerged circa 1900 along with the gramophone and the cinema, representing touch, sound, and sight, but also transforming the realms of the symbolic (the typewriter), the real (the gramophone), and the imaginary (the cinema). Like the epistemological structures analysed by Foucault, Kittler's discourse networks provided a framework for analysing the relationships between one communications medium and another; but they were not grounded in any underlying historical trends. Their arrival was almost solely generated by technological innovations.

Only in one sense did Kittler think like a historian – when he attributed the main causes of technological change to the needs of war. His vision concentrated on the Second German Reich (1871–1918), and so his ideas gained consistency within his focus on a highly militarized society. Yet it is difficult to accept his monolithic view of the origins of technical inventions. Gutenberg's printing press was devised solely for civilian purposes, and the typewriter, as Kittler well knew, was first developed as a prosthetic device for the blind.

Kittler's writing style is provocative, rambling, and opaque. He could stun and antagonize both readers and friends. One speaker at his funeral called his books "Molotov cocktails."[36] An academic reviewer described his work as "a superficial pastiche of dated secondary sources, hearsay, literature and technical explanations."[37] Unfortunately, Kittler rarely recognized the need to support his theoretical musings with empirical evidence. Above all, he cites and returns to his favourite examples of Nietzsche and Kafka, which may be sufficient to provoke hypotheses on the nature of new media, but a history of inscription practices requires a more solid evidential basis.

If his style is alienating and his technological determinism exaggerated, why should we take any further notice of Friedrich Kittler? He is most notable here for his philosophical reading of the distancing effect of mechanized writing. He built on the ideas of Martin Heidegger, who was impressed by the way that mechanized writing relegated the significance of the writer's hand and thus obscured the mark of his or her personality. Heidegger saw the hand as the essence of human identity, so that to interrupt the natural connection between "man," his hand, and his writing altered his very being. The typewriter, Heidegger wrote, "veils the essence of writing and the script. It withdraws from man the essential rank of the hand, without man's experiencing this withdrawal appropriately and recognizing that it had transformed the relation of Being to his essence."[38] For Heidegger, the typewriter brought about a disconnection of hand, eye, and script, so that writing ceased in a sense to be the expression of the individual authorial voice, the inner soul of the artist, and became simply a series of characterless marks on a page. Cultural and literary values had to be reconfigured accordingly.

We can make several objections to this. We could say that handwriting itself had never constituted anything else but marks on a page, and that the pen, too, was a technology that intervened between the writer and the text. We might add that the typewriter never made the author's hands redundant – in fact, manual application was doubly intensified since writers now needed to use *both* hands at once to operate the machine. But it remains true that individual personality is erased in the uniformity of typed text. We can retain Kittler's notion that the typewriter brought about dislocation, distancing the writer from what was written, and imposing on script a new impersonality that removed the individual characteristics of handwriting. Individual typewriters, it is true, may occasionally have their own idiosyncratic features, and in a few detective mysteries the criminal's identity is indeed betrayed by the particular features of his or her typewriter.[39] But such cases are exceptions to the normal impersonality of the typewritten text. The distancing effect may well have influenced the writing style of some authors, including T.S. Eliot, Kafka, and Nietzsche (although he experimented with a typewriter for only a few months).

This is a valuable idea, and it will keep resurfacing in what follows. The distancing effect, however, defines only one possible typewriting scenario. What Kittler did not see was that several others were also possible. These include what I call the "romantic" attachment to the machine, which did not alienate individual authors from their human essence, but rather completed and fulfilled it. There were writers, although Nietzsche was not among them, who were liberated by the typewriter and used it almost as an organic extension of their own bodies. Perhaps this is the most fundamental reason for a historian of writing's reluctance to accept Kittler's perspective. His range was too narrow to encompass more than a very limited variety of typing experiences. He relied on a small number of examples as substitutes for a substantial cast of typewriter users. As a result, he saw only one possible interpretation – namely, the alienating effect of mechanical writing on the individual author. While recognizing this valuable insight, this book prefers to audition a larger group of users and canvas a much wider range of responses to the machine.

The Typewriter Century

The typewriter century ran approximately from the 1880s to the 1980s, that is to say from the time the typewriter first became generally commercially available to the emergence of the word processor as the dominant writing tool in the Western world. The year 1984, to be precise, was the Orwellian moment when Apple released the first Macintosh computer. The Association of American Publishers calculated in the same year that between 40 and 50 per cent of all American literary authors were using a word processor.[40] Two events and two authors neatly bookend the period that forms the main focus of this study.

The typewriter century began with Mark Twain's adoption of the machine in the early 1880s. Twain claimed, "I was the first person in the world to apply the type-machine to literature," and he is often credited as the first author to use a typewriter.[41] Twain guessed the first such novel was his *The Adventures of Tom Sawyer* (1876), but his memory was faulty: it was in fact *Life on the Mississippi* (1883). The truth was that Twain dictated to a stenographer, who, as usual, remained invisible.

The typewriter century ended, at least symbolically, with the first novel to be composed on a word processor. In 1968, British thriller-writer Len Deighton had a huge IBM word processor hoisted through the window of his first-floor apartment on London's South Bank to write *Bomber*, published in 1970 (figure 1.1). The machine weighed close to

Figure 1.1. Len Deighton and his IBM word processor
(Source: Adrian Flowers Archive)

100 kilograms, and a window had to be removed so that it could be installed in his flat by crane. Photographs show Deighton in his work environment, where he appeared almost trapped against the wall by the machinery that surrounded him, like the map of central Europe literally pinned to the wall where he plotted the bombing raids over Nazi Germany that were the focus of his novel.[42] Photographs of the space, however, did not invariably reveal the key presence of Deighton's assistant, Ellenor Handley, who was the one who actually had to learn how to use Deighton's new mechanical writing-machine.

As Matthew Kirschenbaum explains, Deighton had acquired on lease a new IBM MT/ST (Magnetic Tape Selectric Typewriter), known in Europe as the MT72. As yet, this word processor had no screen – it recorded text on magnetic tape, storing it in a state of "suspended inscription," while using IBM's Selectric typewriter as both its input and output device. In playback mode, the text could be edited and manipulated before printing.[43] It was a hybrid, which would soon be superseded. Unless, however, another writer comes forward with a counterclaim, Deighton can be regarded as the absolute pioneer of word-processing fiction writers. His move in that direction signalled the beginning of the end of the typewriter's hegemony.

I take examples from Mark Twain and Friedrich Nietzsche in the mid-nineteenth century, up to living authors such as John le Carré and J.M.G. le Clézio. In between, my cast of characters is populated by late nineteenth-century novelists, modernist poets, realist novelists of the interwar period, pulp fiction writers of the mid-twentieth century, the Beat Generation, and a few late twentieth-century writers and poets. In her original research, Catherine Viollet took examples from the French-speaking world, but we must now extend the geographical sphere of her work, and accordingly I take my examples from the United States, Britain, and Australia as well as France and Belgium. At the same time, I seek to broaden her focus on contemporary practitioners, and I include popular fiction writers.

At certain points in the discussion, I have adopted the findings of specialists in textual genesis. With immense scholarly skill, they scrutinize surviving material versions of mainly canonical works to reconstruct the evolution of a given text. In addition to these valuable insights, I consider what authors themselves have said or written about their own working methods. This approach carries certain risks. Authors are not infallible witnesses, even about themselves; discrepancies sometimes appear between their accounts of their own work and the realities of the creative and the publishing processes. As we shall see in chapter 6, there are discrepancies in the well-known case of Jack Kerouac; and the dangers of taking Georges Simenon's words about himself at face value are exposed in chapter 8. Nevertheless, authors' descriptions of their working methods form an important starting point for my enquiry. Their methods changed over time: they adopted new techniques, or occasionally illness or poor eyesight forced them to resort to dictation, or perhaps success and a larger income in later life allowed them to hire more professional assistance than they could previously afford. In these ways, the relationship between handwriting and typing might change several times over the course of one writer's lifetime.

The subjective opinions of writers are important because I am interested in how they perceived and conceptualized the machine, as well as how it might have influenced the way writers, canonical and otherwise, operated. I aim in a sense for a cultural history of the typewriter, and this must first be based on authors' reactions to it. Usually, their views are most likely to be made public if they have achieved a high level of celebrity. In this case, the media have been interested in their work and their production methods, generating press interviews, biographies, and perhaps autobiographies. The *Paris Review* interviews, back issues of the *Writer's Digest*, advertising publicity for the typewriter, and writers' websites and blogs provide further occasional insights into modes of writing and the place of the typewriter within them. With these sources we can sketch the place of the typewriter in the cultural imaginary of the twentieth century.

In the course of this study, I pay special attention to popular writers in non-canonical genres (romance, crime, children's fiction, etc.). In so doing, I am reluctant to draw a rigid distinction between literary and pulp fiction, or to attribute literary value to any particular genre, individual author, or literary work. This is not my task. In any case, the borderline between literary and genre writers is a hazy one. Many crime writers, like Georges Simenon for instance, also wrote in other genres and wanted to be recognized for this. But pulp fiction writers generally make good case studies because they were professional writers who wrote prolifically, developed a routine, and achieved celebrity. Moreover, they usually did not hide from public attention. Their celebrity guaranteed public interest in their working methods, generating evidence in the form of articles and interviews, and leading to the archival preservation of their papers. Erle Stanley Gardner and Georges Simenon are particularly good subjects in this respect. Other candidates for study include Henry James, Jack Kerouac, John le Carré, Agatha Christie, Richmal Crompton, Enid Blyton, Barbara Taylor Bradford, and the Australian writer of science fiction and westerns Gordon Clive Bleeck. I have chosen these authors, therefore, either because they have provided us with archives to study, or because they spoke explicitly about their methods to the press. Each of them suggests different ways in which the typewriter affected their compositional and professional practices. In the next section, I offer a few remarks about the context in which most of these popular fiction writers worked.

The New World of the Pulp Fiction Writer

Genre fiction authors worked in a new environment in the first few decades of the twentieth century, when the mass market in fiction was in full expansion, and when print culture, although rivalled as a leisure activity by the radio and the cinema, had not yet been eclipsed by television or the electronic media. On the contrary, radio, film, and television offered successful authors new outlets and new sources of income. Cut-throat competition between publishers multiplied the production of cheap popular fiction and reprints of the classics, even though the paper shortages of two world wars interrupted output. At the end of the nineteenth century, France had led the way in creating a mass literary consumer culture based on the sale of cheap fiction, but, after the First World War, Germany and the United States outstripped that country. In 1929, Erich Maria Remarque's *Im Westen nichts Neues* (*All Quiet on the Western Front*) sold over 900,000 copies in its first year, becoming Germany's first genuine bestseller.[44] The commercialization of literature became more intense than ever before. New retail outlets like railway stations, department stores, and book-vending machines dethroned more "noble" sales points like the traditional Parisian Left Bank bookshop. Books were even given away in miniature format to promote cigarette sales.[45] The conservative middle classes reacted with alarm to the transformation of the book into an everyday object of mass consumption. Making literary culture cheaply available to the supposedly naive and gullible masses seemed to be a mixed blessing. Hence, in 1926, Germany introduced a Law for the Protection of Young People against Trash and Filth. Stephen Mogridge, who ran a lending library in a tranquil southern English village, lamented the mad rush for literary novelty. "The quiet lawns of literature," he said, "are trampled by impatient feet."[46] The "problem" of mass consumerism in literature was aggravated by the paperback revolution, which began in Germany with Albatross before being imitated in Britain by Penguin, in the United States by Pocket Books, and belatedly in France by Hachette's *livres de poche*.

Erle Stanley Gardner, Georges Simenon, and Barbara Taylor Bradford are three examples of popular authors from this period, but they are far from alone. Authors such as Simenon enjoyed intense public scrutiny and received impressive quantities of fan mail. Celebrity and media attention thrust them into a new relationship with their readers. In response to the James Bond novels, Ian Fleming's fans wrote freely to correct his imperfect knowledge of women's perfume and his mistakes about the technical use of firearms. If they asked Fleming a question he could not answer, he told them he would ask James Bond about it. Enid Blyton also maintained an epistolary dialogue with her many child readers and cultivated a strong juvenile fan base, which justified her claim that adult criticism could be ignored since this young audience was all that mattered to her. Blyton replied to readers' letters at the rate of about a hundred per week in 1927, and received many more at Christmas.[47] But by 1953, she was receiving about a thousand letters per day, and replying personally to all of them was impossible.[48] In letters and in the magazines that paralleled her literary output, she wrote to children about her house, her garden, and pets, as well as about characters in the books themselves, in a style carefully crafted to exude confidentiality and prefiguring today's bloggers. Blyton organized her fans into clubs, which raised money for charities, promoted her books, and also provided her with free market research. The Busy Bees Club, founded in 1933, had over 300,000 members by 1955. The Famous Five Club, established in 1952, had over 100,000 by 1959.[49] Self-promotion had become a powerful weapon in the celebrity author's armoury, but authors in the public eye needed to be very strategic about what they divulged about themselves.

Blyton apart, the new world of the popular fiction writer looked to America for its models and inspiration. The career of the Australian writer Clive Gordon Bleeck clearly illustrates the progressive Americanization of Australian literary culture. Bleeck never experienced media attention – in fact he still remains virtually unknown – and he did not even write in his own name, using thirteen different pseudonyms for his American magazine publishers. He never gave up his day job with the New South Wales Railways. In the 1950s, then in his forties, he would type out his stories after work in the back room of his family home in the eastern suburbs of Sydney. He wrote 250 novels or novelettes, most of them westerns, but also including crime thrillers, romances, and "space operas" like *Invasion of the Insectoids*. American magazines were his market, and the importance of the western genre ensured that he paid close attention to the United States. His notebooks included press cuttings and technical ranching terms that he studied in order to redeploy them in his western stories. He made one trip to the United States, writing home profusely about his experiences. When an aspiring writer (Miss Thompson) broke through his protective ring of anonymity and asked him for advice on beginning a writing career, Bleeck recommended O. Henry as the best role model for short-story writing. This was a slightly surprising choice (Edgar Allan Poe would have been more predictable, given his preferred genres), but it showed the American direction of his thinking.[50]

The twentieth-century fiction writer had to climb four main rungs on the professional ladder toward fame and fortune. The first of these, the basic entry point, was the purchase of a typewriter. When Australian writer (of New Zealand origin) Jean Devanny had her first story accepted by the *Auckland Weekly News*, an editor wrote to advise her to invest in a typewriter if she intended to continue.[51] According to William Burroughs, "Sinclair Lewis said: 'If you want to be a writer, learn to type.' This advice is scarcely necessary now. So then sit down at your typewriter and write."[52] As the American children's writer Jane Yolen put it, "Handwriting only reminds me of the days before I was a professional."[53] The typewriter, whether rented, leased, or bought outright, was the badge of the writer's profession.

The second step was to jettison the early pseudonyms of a tentative initiation phase and assume one's true mature identity. This might be a gradual process: Agatha Christie began by using pseudonyms, and then used her own name after her first contract with publisher John Lane, who dissuaded her from taking a man's name.[54] But she still wrote a parallel series of novels as Mary Westmacott. Christie spent a long time in limbo, thinking of her writing as a part-time interest, before she fully adopted the role of a professional writer. In Simenon's case, the rite of passage was unequivocal: when he dropped the name "Georges Sim" in 1930, he considered that his apprenticeship was over and his career as a mature writer could begin.

The third step towards professionalism was to hire an agent, but this was a luxury for only the most successful authors. Christie had a long and successful relationship with Edmund Cork; Erle Stanley Gardner eventually needed more than one agent after his radio and television work demanded an extra specialist. Simenon, on the other hand, did not hire an agent at all. In France, this degree of commercialization was not yet the norm, even for a market-oriented writer like Simenon. He handled his own business deals and manufactured his own public personality, which raised new doubts in the mind of the French literary establishment about the compatibility of art and commerce.

A fourth stage in the writer's professional career was reached only by those who had achieved a stratospheric level of celebrity: they formed themselves into a company. The main purpose of this step was to reduce the burden of income tax, enabling them to pay at the corporate rather than the individual rate. In 1954, Agatha Christie, having discharged her enormous tax debts in the United States and Britain, became, on the advice of Edmund Cork, a limited company, turning herself into a salaried employee of Agatha Christie Limited.[55] Simenon, on the other hand, retained personal control of his translation rights, contracts, requests for articles and interviews, and meetings with film and television producers. Roger Stéphane interviewed Simenon in 1963 at his Swiss home at Épalinges, where he had moved not simply for the views but also as a tax exile. Stéphane was impressed by what he discovered: "Georges Simenon demonstrated his extraordinary capacity for work, his production engine. He displayed his wealth. Not like a *nouveau riche*, but like a literary manufacturer. He produced, he was sold. He showed me contracts, translations and their print-runs."[56] Stéphane was given a glimpse of the operations of what we might informally call "Simenon Incorporated."

The Office and the Writer

Within such a broad context, this history of an everyday machine privileges the responses and cultural practices of its users. Those users and their practices, rather than a literary evaluation of their work, remain the principal focus of the chapters that follow. As a result, this study offers both more and less than a literary history. It will be less than a literary history because it does not aspire to a sustained literary critique of any author or work of literature. It is, rather, an essay in cultural history, and it is intended as a contribution to the history of writing practices. At the same time, it is more than a literary history because it recognizes (principally in chapter 2) the importance of the typewriter in the transformation of bureaucratic practices – in the creation of the typist generally as well as the modern author.

I start from the conviction that a history of typewriter usage cannot be complete without some consideration of its introduction into the office, which strongly influenced the ways in which all users constructed the idea of the machine. Its association with mindless mechanical labour originated in the typing pool. Despite appearances to the contrary, the typing pool was not very far removed from the world of the twentieth-century author. Literary production depended on, and was influenced by, the world of the (usually female) professional typist. Examples abound in this study of authors who began life as newspaper reporters, or as employees in large corporate offices, which is where they served their apprenticeship on the machine. Before becoming a best-selling crime writer, Erle Stanley Gardner was a partner in a legal practice, and he transferred his experience there to the literary sphere, even creating his own mini-typing pool of secretaries at his Californian ranch. In 1917, T.S. Eliot was working at the offices of Lloyds Bank in London, and he was immersed for eight hours a day in the new office culture of typists and card indexes. He would become the poet of clerks, typists, and white-collar employees and their empty lives in drab furnished apartments. Agatha Christie trained as a shorthand typist before becoming an author her own right. Innumerable authors relied on the professional services of secretarial agencies. Literary associations with an office background were therefore numerous, and I have saved the best example to last: romance writer Barbara Taylor Bradford started her career at the age of fifteen in the typing pool at the *Yorkshire Evening Post* before working her way up the professional ladder to become fashion editor of *Woman's Own*. We cannot therefore treat literary writers in isolation from the impact of the typewriter on society as a whole; we need to consider the impact of the machine in the office more broadly. The "Typewriter Girl" is important to the story and does not stand outside it; she represented a gendered division of work that carried over into the literary sphere. Male writers depended on female typists – professionals, lovers, wives – to turn drafts into presentable texts. In so doing, they inherited work practices already enshrined in the corporate office world.[57]

The Plan

In a preliminary approach, chapter 2 outlines the technological history of the typewriter, tracing the story of the machine as an invention, from early prosthetic devices like the Writing Ball used by Friedrich Nietzsche, up to the first commercialized Remington No. 1. The invention of the typewriter was a gradual and collaborative process, and the chapter will explore how, in response to the needs of its users, the machine gradually acquired the essential features that later generations took for granted. In setting the scene for what follows, I rely on well-known authorities like Bliven and Wershler-Henry, but I set my sights on a more distant target than they did, encompassing not just the history of the machine but also the study of several eloquent typewriter users. This chapter brings us to the birth of the "typosphere," which is how I refer to the global imagined community of typewriter users (which was also a global *market* of users in manufacturers' eyes) sharing common practices and common problems, even if the context of their working experiences differed from culture to culture.

Chapter 3 addresses the impact of the typewriter on the transformation of the office from the end of the nineteenth into the early decades of the twentieth century. In this phase of the typewriter's cultural history, women were the vanguard of modernity. The typewriter was implicated in the emergence of the "New Woman" and of the "Typewriter Girl" of the early twentieth century. The introduction of the typewriter was accompanied by a new gendered division of labour, which would not be confined to the business world. The figure of the male author delegating text to a female typist was common in the literary world, too, and it still persists. The important role of the female typist in the cultural imaginary of the typewriter is briefly explored through her representation in turn-of-the-century fiction.

Typewriter modernism briefly enters the more familiar territory of literary history in chapter 4, which reviews the contribution of the machine to the development of literary avant-gardes. The new regime of mechanical printing was crucial to the aesthetics of the futurist project, while the typewriter inspired experiments in freer verse forms by modernist poets such as e.e. cummings, T.S. Eliot, and Guillaume Apollinaire. In that chapter, I will assess common metaphors representing the typewriter, especially comparisons with the machine gun and the jazz piano. These associations with modern warfare and modern music were developed both by literary writers and contemporary advertising for the machine. This chapter concludes with a brief essay on the typewriters of Ernest Hemingway, an author who was explicitly conscious of the presence of his machine.

The next three chapters take us to the heart of writers' varied relationships with the typewriter. First, in chapter 5, I consider the distancing effect of the typewriter and its disturbing ability to depersonalize texts, which so impressed Kittler. The typewriter forced writers to reconsider their texts in a new, more critical light. Some found that this distance produced terser, more "telegram-style" language; others, who dictated their text, found it could encourage the exact opposite – in other words, long digressions and expansive prose. This chapter focuses on the example of Henry James.

The romantic typewriter, discussed in chapter 6, operated quite differently from the accentuated textual objectivity achieved by the machine's distancing effect. In fact they were polar opposites. Whereas the alienated author found that the typewriter encouraged deliberation and a critical detachment from one's own creation, the romantic typewriter privileged fluency and a more intuitive style of composition. The instinctive writing of Enid Blyton is a good example, but Jack Kerouac provides the paradigmatic case. Kerouac's typing method was to abandon what he called the inhibition of syntax and to write freely in a trance- or dream-like state, frequently induced by amphetamines.

In theory, the manuscript is private, print is public; print is definitive, but manuscripts contain many possible options. But have writing practices always conformed to this conventional view? After reviewing the survival of manuscript culture in general, chapter 7 examines the relationship between the manuscript and the typescript, using "manuscript" here exclusively to designate texts drafted in longhand. Agatha Christie's notebooks lay bare for us the role of handwritten material in the preparation and elaboration of her intricate plots; John le Carré's typescripts illustrate the interplay of handwriting and typing at a later stage of textual revision.

The next trio of chapters present individual case studies that illustrate many aspects of typewriter culture introduced in previous chapters. All the case studies selected are of popular writers who worked in non-canonical genres. In the case of Georges Simenon, explored in chapter 8, his speed of composition was legendary. Specific rituals surrounded Simenon's writing, and he had a close connection with the paraphernalia of writing – his pencils, pipes, telephone directories, and the typewriter that completed his much-publicized desk furniture. This chapter will investigate the specific tasks he assigned to both handwriting and typing, depending on what genre of fiction he was writing.

Erle Stanley Gardner provides a second major case study, examined in chapter 9. In his most successful period, Gardner proudly accepted the unflattering description of himself as "the Fiction Factory." He had graduated from painful two-finger typing to the employment of a "pool" of several typists over whom he presided at his California ranch. As in the case of Simenon, the typewriter (increasingly combined with the dictation machine) underpinned his prolific output. But, as with Simenon again, his factory-style production methods compromised any chance of acceptance in more respectable literary circles.

These two case studies revolve around crime writers whose approach to life was at times aggressively masculine. In chapter 10, I aim for a more rounded view by investigating the typewriting practices of several women writers whose papers or autobiographical writings are available for study. With the exception of Agatha Christie, they take us beyond the milieu of detective and espionage fiction into other genres, such as popular romance novels (Barbara Taylor Bradford) and children's fiction (Enid Blyton and Richmal Crompton). All of these happen to be English writers, even if Bradford became largely Americanized, which further balances the French (or, more precisely, francophone) and American emphasis in the chapters on Simenon and Gardner, respectively. The ways that women writers used the typewriter did not fundamentally differ from men's typing practices, but this chapter will demonstrate that two things about them were remarkably divergent. First, they had to integrate the typewriter into a domestic environment, which was almost never the case for male writers, who usually retreated to a study to write. Second, women's attitudes toward becoming a professional writer were often different from those of men; the woman typewriter, as we shall see, did not always accept the notion of earning her own living from writing without considerable doubt and hesitation.

In a final chapter, I review the decline and fall of the typewriter empire, as word processors increasingly invaded and then superseded it, as the much-maligned "barbarians" challenged and usurped the Roman imperium. At the same time, I recognize the enduring attachment of some writers to an out-of-date writing technology. Sometimes the typewriter was preferred for rational and practical reasons, because it liberated writers from the Internet or put offices and institutions beyond the reach of electronic surveillance. At other times, the survival of the "analog underground" derives from a counter-cultural impulse rooted in post-digital nostalgia. An objective and historical view of the typewriter's contribution to the history of written culture is long overdue.

2 The Birth of the Typosphere

Introduction

"You don't have to be famous to be brilliant," proclaimed an enterprising television commercial for Škoda cars, challenging the viewer to name the forgotten "inventors" of everyday technologies such as the traffic light and the mobile phone. The advertisement spotlighted inventions that have transformed daily life but whose originators remain completely anonymous. It is a safe bet that if many readers of this book were similarly asked to name the inventor of the typewriter, the answer would not slip immediately off their tongues. And they would be right to hesitate, because the model of the solo inventor is not always appropriate in accounting for the origins of technological change. All the same, traces of a heroic version of events persist. Traditionally, they glorify one individual scientific genius, usually masculine, who experiences a blinding flash of inspiration, a eureka moment, in which he suddenly conceives the future in a new light and changes the world forever. The invention of the typewriter was not as simple as this popular version of technological progress might suggest. Although Christopher Latham Sholes is usually credited with the invention of the typewriter, and many relevant patents bear his name (as well as the names of others), the birth of the typosphere was the result of a complex combination of factors, which transcended his personal history.

Inventions like the typewriter are, first, the results of teamwork, and since this chapter aims at a brief history of the genesis of the machine, it must recognize the multiple parents who brought it into existence. Second, the typewriter did not appear out of the blue but emerged from knowledge and experience gathered through literally dozens of previous attempts since at least the eighteenth century to design and construct writing machines. The typewriter has its own genealogy, since scientific knowledge, like any other body of knowledge, is cumulative and draws on lessons learned by predecessors. Third, the idea of the typewriter did not sprout fully formed like Athena from the tortured brow of Zeus. It required years of gestation, of hard work and trial and error, in which morale inevitably sagged while debts relentlessly mounted. This long period of development was further extended as feedback from the earliest typewriter users was absorbed. Successful discoveries, furthermore, are never made in a vacuum: the rising bureaucratic demand for faster and more accurate documentation in the last third of the nineteenth century was what brought the modern typewriter into being and ensured that it had an impact. That unique historical conjuncture turned what might otherwise have been just another curious mechanism into a viable commercial proposition.

In what follows, I will sketch the prehistory of the typewriter as a prosthetic device, before accounting for the slow and difficult progress made by Sholes and those around him in the 1860s and 1870s. The journey to typewriter modernity was not straightforward; the eventual outcomes emerged from a range of possible options and ideas, some of which failed (who now remembers, for example, the "Scientific" keyboard?). Technological development is multi-directional, and paths not taken are sometimes rejected for reasons that, from today's vantage point, appear random and unpredictable.[1] Necessity was not always the mother of invention; the noiseless typewriter, for example, now seems a particularly *un*necessary invention. It promised office bosses that it would not compete with the telephone, but in practice it was never completely silent: it just gave out muffled thumps instead of clicking and clacking.[2] Ideas that, for one reason or another, did not come to fruition form part of the typewriter's life story, alongside those that did have a lasting impact on the typosphere. As this chapter will show, the "keyboard wars" surrounding the QWERTY layout remind us that technological innovation is subject to unpredictable accidents and that, in the history of modernity, things do not always turn out perfectly in the end.

Prehistory

The prehistory of the typewriter is littered with designs for writing machines that were never built, and some that no one ever intended to build. A few have even disappeared without a trace, like the machine designed in England by Henry Mill, who received a patent from Queen Anne in 1714, and may have been the first typewriter inventor. But his machine has not survived, and it may never have actually been assembled. A succession of subsequent inventors imagined, and sometimes created, a great variety of machines, designed to print on, or perforate, different sizes of paper, usually in capital letters only, with keys of different shapes, sometimes arranged in a line, sometimes in a circle and sometimes in a half-moon. Until 1874, none of them had any broad commercial potential.

The main function of early typewriters was prosthetic: they could be built with keys embossed with Braille and were designed to help the blind. In Italy, Pellegrino Turri constructed a machine in 1808 for the Comtessa Carolina Fantoni de Fivizzono, who had lost her sight as a child but maintained a substantial correspondence. Turri's typewriter printed very legibly in upper case only. Turri made another important contribution; he invented carbon paper.[3] Pierre Foucault produced his "Raphographe" for the same purpose in France in 1850, and one of his creations won a gold medal at the Great Exhibition of 1851 in London. Foucault himself was blind.[4] The typewriter was thus conceived largely as an aid for handicapped writers; others had no need for it, because they had cheap pens at their disposal.

Typewriters, it seemed, could play a role in the social integration of blind people. The blind could not read their own words, but they could find the keys by touch. The machine was thus the "tactile/visual interface" between the blind and the sighted. Typewriters broadened the possibility of communication between blind and sighted people. Together with the Braille alphabet, the typewriter potentially empowered the sight-impaired.[5]

American pioneer Charles Thurber also worked on machines for the blind. His "Patent Printer" of the 1840s had forty-five plunger keys arranged in a circle.[6] As with many other early typewriters, the paper remained stationary while the carriage was rotated until the desired key arrived in the right position. Speed was not an objective for the user of such a machine. But Thurber's cumbersome invention nevertheless hit on something useful: his platen was not flat but cylindrical, and it moved. Alfred Ely Beach, who for some years was editor of the *Scientific American*, built on Thurber's attempts when he designed his own machine, again with a circular arrangement of keys. Patented in 1856, it was explicitly called a "Printing Instrument for the Blind." In Piemonte, Giuseppe Ravizza built several machines, one of which was his Cembalo Scrivano (writing harpsichord). It had a piano-style keyboard with letter keys arranged in alphabetical order. It had a moving carriage and it was conceivably portable.[7] He used an inked ribbon and added a bell to signal the approach of the end of the line. Three of his machines went to the Milan Blind Institute. Remington was to incorporate many of his imaginative additions into their own typewriters.

One nearly universal trait of all these machines was that, not only did they serve the blind, but they themselves were "blind typewriters" – in other words, they were upstroke machines, in which the keys rose to hit the underside of the platen, with the result that the writer, with or without the power of sight, could not see what had been printed until the paper was later removed. This problem of visibility clearly did not arise as long as the main users of the machine were the sight-impaired. The visibility issue was to be resolved in 1894, by which time new customers expected to see what they were typing.

The Danish pastor Hans Malling Hansen produced a Writing Ball, or *Skrivekugle*, in the 1870s (figure 2.1). Like Thurber's machine, it was based on a plunger mechanism, in which concentric keys protruded from a hemispherical base like spikes from a porcupine's back.[8] Hansen was director of the Deaf and Dumb Institute in Copenhagen, but he saw the potential of his machine for the sight-impaired as well. The Writing Ball weighed an impressive 75 kilograms, but it nevertheless acquired a niche market in Europe.[9] Since the keys printed on a convex surface, they did not always produce an even impression. Nevertheless, this was the first ever commercially available typewriter. Its most famous customer was philosopher Friedrich Nietzsche, who ordered one in 1882. Nietzsche was afflicted by migraines and he also suffered from worsening sight, possibly attributable to advancing syphilis, and he was glad of mechanical assistance. He wrote this poem on his Writing Ball, in capital letters because that was all that the machine provided:

THE WRITING BALL IS A THING LIKE ME: MADE OF
                    IRON
YET EASILY TWISTED ON JOURNEYS.
PATIENCE AND TACT ARE REQUIRED IN ABUNDANCE,
AS WELL AS FINE FINGERS, TO USE US.[10]

Nietzsche was already talking of "us" as though he identified himself very closely with his machine. He used the Writing Ball for only a few weeks, but this was enough to persuade him that the machine exerted an influence over his writing. "Our writing tools," he wrote, "are also working on our thoughts." Media theorist Friedrich Kittler argued that, as a result of using the Writing Ball, Nietzsche's writing became less rhetorical and more aphoristic, adopting a "telegram-style."[11] Nietzsche used this phrase himself, although he may not have been connecting it to the typewriter, merely to the effect of his partial blindness. But the two were certainly linked, since the Writing Ball was designed for

Figure 2.1. Malling Hansen's Writing Ball, c. 1874
(Source: Wikipedia Commons)

sight-impaired writers. Unfortunately, in the humidity of his home in Genoa, Nietzsche found that his ink ribbon became wet and sticky, putting his machine out of action. He decided he preferred a "young person" who would work with him.

Early typewriters were slow and cumbersome. Some looked like cotton looms or giant mousetraps. Many had piano keys rather than buttons to press, like Samuel Francis's machine of 1857, built in the United States, and another built by American John Pratt in 1864 in

England, where he moved after the Confederacy, which he supported, had been defeated in the US Civil War. Many were very elaborate toys. As prosthetic devices, however, they had a serious altruistic purpose, although most of them were one-off contraptions built by the inventor himself. Only a very few looked beyond the limited market of the sight-impaired. John Jones's Domestic Writing Machine, which he produced in New York in 1856, printed in both upper and lower case, but it had to be inked by roller, like a hand-driven printing press.[12] Peter Mitterhofer, a Tyrolean carpenter, built a machine in Austria in the 1860s that he imagined might be useful in government offices, but this prescient thought was not pursued by the Habsburg authorities.[13] Conditions were not yet propitious in central Europe, nor was there sufficient demand for a workable machine to make an impact.

In the United States, the situation was already changing. By the 1860s, when Sholes and his colleagues began work to design a new machine, so many inventors both in America and Europe were competing to manufacture a more practical typewriter that accusations of plagiarism were beginning to surface. Ravizza ultimately died a poor man in Italy but lived long enough to see Remington either adopt or steal his ideas, depending on one's perspective. Plagiarism charges arose in a situation where several would-be inventors were working toward similar objectives. This convergence of scientific effort in the late 1860s indicated a growing need for a new, simpler, and faster writing machine.

When Sholes got to work in 1867, carbon paper was already sixty years old. Alexander Bain had produced the inked silk ribbon by 1841, while Thurber had invented the idea of a moving cylindrical carriage. In 1833, Frenchman Xavier Projean's "Plume Ktypographique" (typographical quill) had put the letter types on separate typebars and arranged them in a circular basket. Beach had produced a keyboard with three rows of letters. Sholes's version combined many of these features, but options remained open on the shape of the keyboard, and several possibilities were available for the arrangement of the keys.

Sholes and Others

Christopher Latham Sholes was born in 1819 in a Pennsylvania log house, the son of a cabinet-maker. He was, it has been said, the fifty-second man to invent the typewriter, but he was the first to call it by that name.[14] Sholes's background lay in the printing industry and in regional newspapers. He was editor of the *Wisconsin State Journal* at the age of nineteen, and founded the *Kenosha Daily Telegraph* before moving to Milwaukee in 1860, where he earned his living as a collector of customs dues in the port. Making machines was not his only interest; he was also keenly interested in social reform. He opposed capital punishment. He supported the Free Soil movement, which argued against the introduction of slavery into the western territories. He later read Henry George's book *Progress and Poverty* (1879) and Edward Bellamy's utopian novel *Looking Backwards* (1888), both widely known late nineteenth-century texts dealing with the role of the state, the future of capitalism, the persistence of poverty, and their mutual interrelationships.[15] He saw his invention as a contribution to social progress, and before he died he expressed the conviction that he had brought a great benefit to mankind, and in particular to womankind. A more nuanced discussion of this point will be offered in chapter 3.

Arthur Toye Foulke portrayed Sholes's invention as a triumph of American entrepreneurship – a nationalistic view that obscured the European origins of at least some of its structural components – and he mythologized the role of Sholes himself as "Mr. Typewriter."[16] Foulke imagined Sholes as the Gutenberg of the typewriter, an eccentric inventor who represented the quintessential American pioneer. Sholes's mild and self-effacing personality, however, does not fit comfortably with this image of pioneering audacity. Important as he was, Sholes worked in a team. At Kleinsteuber's machine shop in Milwaukee, where amateur metallurgists gathered, Sholes met some significant colleagues: Carlos Glidden, a lawyer who was chiefly interested in making farm implements but who also contributed significantly to the typewriter's development, as well as Samuel Soule (sometimes written Soulé), who was an early collaborator, and Matthias Schwalbach, a clockmaker and machinist who became Sholes's foreman. Most crucial of all was the role of James Densmore, whom Sholes had first encountered at the *Kenosha Daily Telegraph,* and who financed the work through thick and thin. Both Sholes and Densmore had a common interest in social reform, and Densmore championed a wide range of causes, from free postage and phonetic spelling to better roads.[17] Like Sholes, Densmore was a former newspaperman. He not only underwrote Sholes's work financially, but he also provided a boost to morale and was a rigorous enforcer of quality control.

In the mid-1860s, Sholes was making automatic page-numbering machines, which were patented in 1864 and 1866. He was fascinated by an article in *Scientific American* about Pratt's Pterotype, a machine that required the writer to bring the required letter to the typing point before depressing a key.[18] Sholes thought he could achieve something simpler, and Glidden encouraged him to do so as well as providing initial funding. His first experimental model typed one letter only ("w") and it looked like a telegrapher's Morse code tapper. It suggested the potential value of putting each letter on a separate typebar. From there the team collaborated to produce a full working model in 1867. Densmore continued as the project's investor. He paid Sholes, Glidden, and Soule $2,000 each in return for a one-quarter share of the enterprise. From this point on, Densmore's financial support was indispensable.

Densmore harassed Sholes to make the machine simpler; in order to do so, Sholes applied to his prototypes various features that had already been introduced by previous inventors. His 1868 version was still clumsy – for instance, it relied on a dangling weight to return the carriage. But he made a cylinder that rotated as well as moving from right to left, and his machine allowed typing on normal paper instead of the very thin tissue paper that had hitherto been needed. Glidden and Soule left Sholes to it at this stage, and, from 1868 onwards, only Sholes and Densmore held all the relevant patents. Sholes already thought he had achieved something worthwhile. He wrote confidently to Glidden in 1868: "I am satisfied the machine is now done. The typographical errors would not be made after practice, any more than a false note would be struck by an experienced player."[19] Sholes's prototype could inscribe twenty words per minute, close to the speed of handwriting. Densmore gave it to James Ogilvie Clephane, a Washington shorthand reporter, to test. As a result of the feedback provided, he demanded more improvements from Sholes. The machine was very far from "done"; several years of unrewarding work were still necessary before something convincing could be offered for sale.

During this difficult period, Sholes lost confidence. In a mood of deepening depression, he despaired of ever making the typewriter profitable. "It is too large," he told Densmore, "too cumbrous, too complicated, too expensive, too troublesome for what it achieves."[20] Densmore, although increasingly in debt, continued to believe the machine would pay: "I believe in the invention," he wrote to his brother Amos, "from the top-most corner of my hat to the bottom-most head of the nails in my boot-heels, and it is such an abiding conviction with me that nothing can dissipate it except the dire experience of exhaustive trial and absolute and utter failure."[21]

Schwalbach manufactured button keys, arranged in four tiered rows and in alphabetical order. Glidden, whose interest in the work periodically revived, hit on the novel idea of a long space bar. Sholes installed a treadle to control carriage return, and added a bell to warn of the end of the line. To reduce the risk of keys jamming, he and Densmore adopted a new arrangement, and settled for four rows of keys. Sholes wrote notes to Densmore on the machine to demonstrate his good progress, all of them in capital letters:

THERE IS A TIDE IN THE AFFAIRS OF MEN
WHICH, TAKEN AT THE FLOOD, LEADS ON TO FORTUNE.[22]

In spite of the encouragement of Shakespeare's Brutus, Sholes was to find fortune extremely elusive.

By 1872, Sholes had spent five years on the typewriter, moving to a new building, making new models, dismantling them and devoting time to what we would now call "fixing bugs." Densmore had sunk $10,000 into the project for no return, borrowing from his brothers and others. He was living on nothing but apples and crackers.[23] His friend George Washington Yost suggested pitching the machine to Remington, the gunsmith company, at Ilion, New York. Remington exemplified the American manufacturing system, in which interchangeable parts were mass produced for various appliances at once, including, in this case, firearms and sewing machines. The large-scale production of typewriters was to follow a similar pattern. In 1873, Remington agreed to manufacture an initial 1,000 machines and sell them to Densmore and Yost. Before long, it seemed more practical if Remington both made and marketed the machines, paying Densmore and Yost a royalty of $15 per typewriter. In 1874, the two men set up the Type-Writer Company with an office on Broadway to manage this income. Yost had a salesman's flair but a cavalier attitude toward debt. He took the company deeper into the red and Densmore with it. Meanwhile Sholes, desperate for money and with ten children to support, had not received a cent until Densmore and Yost bought his rights for a lump sum of $6,000. Unfortunately for all concerned, the commercial launch of the world's first typewriter coincided with the middle of an economic depression.

The Remington No. 1, initially known as the "Sholes-Glidden" typewriter, went on sale in 1874 (figure 2.2). The keys struck upwards under the platen, and so the results were at first invisible. A foot pedal returned the carriage in imitation of the treadle-driven sewing machine. The keys were all made of wood, and they produced only upper-case letters. The whole apparatus was encased in black japanned metal, with a grapevine decoration on the legs. It cost $125, well beyond the range of ordinary consumers.

Figure 2.2. Sholes and Glidden typewriter, 1874
(Source: Wikipedia Commons)

Conquering a Reluctant Market

One interested customer was Mark Twain, who bought his first type-writer, a Remington No. 1, out of curiosity in a Boston shop, where he was amazed to observe a typist producing as many as fifty-seven words per minute on it. His enthusiasm was slightly dampened when he realized that she was typing the same phrase repetitively. Twain used a stenographer and never learned to type himself, beyond "the boy stood in the burning deck."[24] He marvelled at the machine's capabilities, but he did so as a layman who remained ignorant of its mysterious technical operations, just as today most computer users have little idea how their machine actually works.[25] "I am trying to get the hang of this new fangled writing machine," he wrote to his brother in 1875, "but am not making a shining success of it." He certainly appreciated its speed and neatness, adding, "I believe it will print faster than I can write. One may lean back in his chair & work it. It piles an awful stack of words on one page. It don't muss things or scatter ink blots around. Of course it saves paper."[26] For Twain, however, the machine was no more than an expensive novelty that he could show off to visitors. His fascinated correspondents nagged him so much for information about it that he told Remington to put them off the scent. "I don't want people to know," he wrote, "that I own this curiosity-breeding little joker."[27] Before long, he was keen to give it away, and made a present of it to his coachman.

Twain was not the only one who was slow to perceive the full utility of the typewriter. None of those present at its birth had a very clear idea of the machine's market. When Sholes read the article in *Scientific American* which first sparked his interest, he claimed that "Legal copying and the writing and delivery of sermons and lectures, not to speak of letters and editorials, will undergo a revolution so remarkable as that effected in books by the invention of printing and the weary process of learning penmanship in schools will be reduced to the acquirement of the art of writing one's own signature and playing on the literary piano [i.e. Pratt's machine] above described, or rather on its improved successors."[28] The first clientele he envisaged thus consisted of lawyers, journalists, and clergymen, while he thought the typewriter might also appeal to court reporters. The potential attraction of the typewriter for creative writers soon dawned on others, such as a writer at the *Milwaukee Sentinel*, which speculated in 1868 that "it will become as important in the literary world as the sewing machine is in the stitchetary world."[29] No one yet envisaged the great demand from business offices that would eventually make the invention profitable.

By 1875, however, Remington was targeting a wider range of customers. The company's advertisement for the Christmas trade in that year is worth quoting in full for an appreciation of the earliest impact of the machine:

A machine is now superseding the pen. It is manufactured by Messrs. E. Remington & Sons of Ilion.

It is the size of a sewing-machine, and is an ornament to an office, study or sitting-room.

It is worked by keys, similar to a piano, and writes from thirty to sixty words per minute – more than twice as fast as the pen – in plain type, just like print.

Anyone who can spell can begin to write with it, and, after two weeks' practice, can write faster than with the pen.

It is worked without effort, and is not liable to get out of order.

It is always ready for use, does not soil the dress or fingers, and makes no litter.

It is certain to become as indispensable in families as the sewing-machine.

Hundreds have come into use in the last few months in banking, insurance, law, and business offices, in the Government departments in Washington, and in private families, giving everywhere the highest satisfaction.

Editors, authors, clergymen – all who are obliged to undergo the drudgery of the pen, will find in the "Type-Writer" the greatest possible relief.

Young persons acquire its use with wonderful ease and interest. It fascinates them, and there is no device comparable to it for teaching children to spell and punctuate.

There is, therefore, no more acceptable instructive or beautiful Christmas present for a boy or girl.

And the benevolent can, by the gift of a "Type-Writer" to a poor, deserving, young woman, put her at once in the way of earning a good living as a copyist or corresponding clerk.

No invention has opened for women so broad and easy an avenue to profitable and suitable employment as the "Type-Writer," and it merits the careful consideration of all thoughtful and charitable persons interested in the subject of work for women.

Mere girls are now earning from $10 to $20 per week with the "Type-Writer" and we can at once secure good situations for one hundred expert writers on it in courtrooms in this city.[30]

No price was given. As well as the "original" market for the typewriter among newspapermen, lawyers, clergymen, and court reporters, Remington now advertised the typewriter's pedagogical utility and its popularity in offices in both the private and public sectors. The advertisement's emphasis on the typewriter's sewing-machine ancestry, as well as the assurance that it would not soil anyone's dress, possibly implied a female clientele; and this clientele now clearly existed in the office as well as in the home.

Businesses prioritized speed and visibility while typing, while portability became a priority for other clienteles, such as housewives, students, or war correspondents. Every worker who needed to submit work to another reader appreciated greater legibility. As *Typewriter*

Topics magazine declared in 1921, "The student in college, the author, the playwright, the lawyer, the journalist all must have their typewriter. This has been fixed by the inexorable law of legibility."[31] A few customers envisaged the typewriter as a prestige item, like King Alfonso XIII of Spain, for whom inventor James Bartlett Hammond built a gold-plated typewriter, with a casing bearing the royal insignia and inlaid with mother-of-pearl.[32] Typewriter manufacturers responded to the requirements of these various consumer groups.

The initial reaction, however, did not match expectations, and the solvency of Remington itself was in doubt. Remington sold only about 4,000 typewriters in the first four years of manufacture.[33] The Remington No. 1 was exhibited at the 1876 Centennial Exposition in Philadelphia and aroused great interest, but nobody bought one.[34] In 1886, Remington sold its typewriter operations to Wyckoff, Seamans & Benedict, which continued to make typewriters at Ilion. Consumer resistance was not overcome until the 1880s, by which time Remington had lost its monopoly. Densmore was then able to pay off his debts and those of the Type-Writer Company, as well as fulfill his obligations to Sholes.

By the 1880s, Sholes was bedridden and slowly dying of tuberculosis. Densmore sent him money when he could. In 1889, Densmore surrendered all his property in the machine to the newly formed Remington Standard Typewriter Company, in return for royalties. He died in 1889, leaving an estate estimated at half a million dollars.[35] His faith had been justified, although after all the debts were repaid it had not made him a very wealthy man. Densmore is sometimes accused of exploiting Sholes, but this cliché of the parasitical financier ignores Densmore's deep financial commitment and the influence of his contagious optimism. In a much earlier letter, Sholes fully acknowledged what he owed to Densmore. This project, he wrote in tribute, "became a living soul only as and after you breathed the breath of life into it. Left to me alone, or anyone else concerned in its early inception, and before this time, it would have passed from the memory of man."[36]

By the end of the 1880s, demand for the typewriter exceeded supply, and sales continued to grow as the retail price fell and improvements were made to the original design. The Remington No. 2 of 1878 introduced a shift key, enabling the writer to use both upper- and lower-case letters, and at the same time the foot treadle was abandoned, severing forever the ancestral link between Remington typewriters and sewing machines. Remington became able to produce typewriter parts by machine, although skilled workers still assembled them by hand. In 1895, Underwood released the first "visible" typewriter, the first typewriter without a masked roller, enabling the writer to see immediately what had been typed. In 1896, Remington added an automatically reversing ribbon. Kidder offered the first "Noiseless Typewriter" for sale in 1917, but this development had little future. It removed one of the typewriter's most characteristic features, the clacking sound of the keys in action, to which many users had grown accustomed (and in some cases, they were even fond of it). In 1941, Remington invented proportional spacing, which gave the text a more even appearance. Previously, narrow letters like "i" had been given the same amount of space as wider letters such as "w"; henceforth each letter had its own appropriate width.

Gradually, then, the major stumbling blocks to the spread of the typosphere were overcome. The issue of portability had been tackled, beginning with George Blickensderfer's first portable typewriter of 1890. The former American president Theodore Roosevelt took a folding portable made by the Standard Typewriter Company with him on safari in 1910.[37] The armies involved on the Western Front in the First World War used hundreds of portable machines. In 1921, Ernest Hemingway's fiancée Hadley Richardson gave him a portable Corona No. 3 as his twenty-second birthday present. This extremely successful model was made of aluminium and weighed only six pounds (less than three kilograms).[38] Portable machines increasingly dominated the market by the 1960s, with Olivetti and Smith-Corona leading the way.

At the same time, mass production reduced retail prices. The Remington No.1, as I have noted, went on sale for $125 in 1874, but before long nobody needed to pay this all at once, as Mark Twain had done. In 1913, the new Oliver typewriter was advertised for $100, but customers were asked to pay a deposit of only $15, and make subsequent payments of 17 cents per day. By this time, too, there was already a thriving second-hand market. In 1913, the Standard Typewriter Exchange in New York was offering various used models for less than $12 each.[39] In 1921, a new folding Corona cost just $50.[40] Typewriter usage had become accessible to all. The teenage Woody Allen bought his Olympia circa 1950 for only $40.

In the year 1913–14, the United States produced $25 million worth of typewriters, of which almost half were exported.[41] Most exports went to Britain, other European countries, and Canada, but by 1921 Mexico had become a significant buyer, while Britain and Europe were becoming much more self-sufficient in typewriter supply.[42] By the eve of the First World War, typewriter design had stabilized. The important question of visibility had been resolved, and both upper and lower cases made equally available. By 1909, Carl Mares already felt it was time to write the history of the typewriter, and he could then assert that "[t]he structure of the typewriter has undergone a complete revolution.

It seems impossible, at this time, to imagine that any further changes of a fundamental nature will take place for years to come."[43] Perhaps Mares was being overly optimistic: he could not foresee the advent of the electric typewriter, which lay well into the future and will be encountered in chapter 11. The typewriter had acquired certain additional features since Sholes's first model. It had a standard keyboard with a shift key, ribbons of standard width, visible writing, a tabulator, and a backspace key. None of this had been automatic at the outset.

Only one problem remained – that of correctibility. Although various mechanisms and substances have been produced to facilitate erasure of the text, none was fully satisfactory, and they all slowed down completion. This issue would never be overcome until the word processor enabled immediate correction as well as the wholesale manipulation of texts. Until then, writers who wanted their texts to have an unblemished appearance had to retype the whole page every time they made an error.

A host of successful companies joined the typewriter market across the world,[44] of which Olivetti proved one of the most enduring. Camillo Olivetti was a Jewish entrepreneur, married to the daughter of a Waldensian pastor who believed in the Protestant ethic of self-improvement. There was a significant American influence on his projects: he personally visited Remington, Royal, and Underwood before taking up typewriter manufacture. Under the supervision of Camillo's son, Adriano, Olivetti produced its first typewriter in 1911; by 1933, the factory in Ivrea (Piemonte) was producing 24,000 typewriters per year, including its very successful portables.[45] During the Fascist period, Camillo withdrew from the business, while Adriano converted to Catholicism and joined the Fascist Party. Adriano absorbed the lessons of Taylorism, which guided his rationalization program, incorporating standardized parts and assembly-line production. In Europe, however, imitation of American models could only go so far. Italy, like many other European countries, had a much smaller domestic market than did the United States, and investment capital was in shorter supply. Adriano Olivetti, furthermore, preferred a paternalistic style of management, which recognized the social responsibilities of the factory owner, and he wished to avoid the authoritarianism he identified with the American production system. After the Second World War, Olivetti became a global company and diversified into computers and calculators. In 1959, Olivetti took control of Underwood. Only at a critical moment in 1964 did it accept the intervention of a financial consortium, thus ceasing to be a family firm.[46]

Olivetti always faced stiff international competition. Adler began operations in Germany in 1898; in the United States, L.C. Smith, which was later to become part of the very successful Smith-Corona brand, was founded as an independent company in 1903, and the Royal brand was introduced in 1906; the Imperial Typewriter Company was founded in Leicester in 1908; the Paillard company began producing its very popular Hermes typewriters in Yverdon, Switzerland, in 1920. After an early phase when the market was wide open and a wide variety of machines was offered, the attributes of all typewriters grew increasingly standardized. The fonts changed, but the keyboard and the size of the carriage were uniform. Paper size, in turn, conformed to a general standard. The A4 sheet, according to Lothar Müller, has been one of the "building blocks of modernity," US-Letter size notwithstanding.[47]

Speed Typing

The speed of the typewriter was what had first impressed Mark Twain so much that he bought one, but, by modern standards, early speeds, like those of early motor cars, were snail-like. The Remington models of the 1870s wrote about thirty words per minute, which did not compete very favourably with the speed of fluent handwriting. In 1907, Underwood claimed a record at eighty-seven words per minute, and lifted this performance to ninety-five words per minute in 1909.[48] Margaret B. Owen, World Champion Typist in 1913, achieved 125 net words per minute over an hour on an Underwood ("net" meaning her recorded speed was adjusted after deductions for errors).[49] Of course, speeds always depended on the nature of the keyboard, and on whether the typist under observation was typing from memory or copying an unfamiliar text. They also depended on the length of the words typed.

Potential speeds increased markedly after touch-typing developed, and after Margaret Longley of Cincinnati, the director of a shorthand and typing institute and a committed supporter of women's suffrage, daringly proposed that typists should use all the fingers of both hands.[50] She outlined her revolutionary "all finger method" in *Remington Typewriter Lessons*, published in 1882. The immediate reaction was unfavourable. An editorial in 1887 in the trade magazine *Cosmopolitan Shorthander* argued that the third finger of each hand was relatively untrained and that it was impractical to expect it to type.[51] Quite independently of Longley, however, Frank E. McGurrin, a court stenographer in Salt Lake City, was promoting an all-finger technique on his Remington No. 1. He not only worked with ten fingers, but he had memorized the keyboard layout and could type blindfolded when he really wanted to show off. McGurrin typed so fast that he claimed the title of "World's Fastest Typist" and challenged all comers to beat him in public contests for a purse of $500. He demonstrated his prowess widely and became invincible on tour.

He fought a significant duel against Louis Taub, a typing instructor from what had formerly been Longley's typing school in Cincinnati. Taub took up McGurrin's challenge in 1888. This was a significant typing duel not only because of the considerable personal investment that each man had made in the contest, but also because each duellist chose a different weapon and used a different technique. Taub, who was doomed to defeat, used the traditional four-finger "hunt-and-peck" method – in other words, find your key and then hit it. At the same time, he typed on a Caligraph machine, which had a double keyboard: it had separate keys for upper- and lower-case characters, making seventy-two keys in all (figure 2.3).[52] McGurrin, in contrast, used a Remington with a single QWERTY layout. The race was in two stages: first came forty-five minutes of dictation, followed by forty-five minutes of copying from a previously unseen text. McGurrin won the first stage because he knew the keyboard layout from memory, and raced further ahead in the second leg because he could type with his eyes on the text without watching the keyboard at all.

McGurrin's victory vindicated his display of bravado. His day in the limelight, however, proved short-lived: later in 1888, he went the way of all sprint champions, defeated in his turn by the even speedier Mae Orr in Toronto. Nevertheless, his victory over Taub was not simply a personal triumph, and it can be interpreted on several levels. First, it was a success for McGurrin's Remington over the Caligraph, signalling doom for the double keyboard, with its individual keys for both capitals and lower-case letters. The Caligraph proved to be a cul-de-sac in the history of typewriter inventions, although this was far from apparent to its contemporaries. A complete typing system was also at stake in the contest, and the outcome was a win for touch-typing over two- or four-fingered method. On another level, it probably advanced the acceptance of the QWERTY keyboard layout, although, we shall see below, this was a mixed blessing.

Following McGurrin's initiative, speed typing became a spectator sport for years to come, and the World Typewriting Championships reportedly drew significant crowds in the years before the First World War.[53] An elaborate set of rules evolved for typewriting contests: words were deemed to constitute five key-strokes, and competitors were penalized for inaccurate margins and uneven spacing, as well as for hitting the wrong key and misspelling a word. Typewriter races did not endure as a competitive sport, because there were significant drawbacks. Competitors had points deducted for making mistakes, which

Figure 2.3. The Caligraph typewriter
(Source: Wikimedia Commons)

meant that judges had to read through a mountain of paper after the race to calculate results. The audience meanwhile was kept waiting, and sometimes went home without knowing who the winner actually was. Typewriter racing did attract considerable publicity for brands like Remington and Underwood. Underwood hired a coach and trained a select racing squad in a special typewriter gym, while developing their own racing typewriters with particularly fast methods of changing paper. Unbeaten champion Rose Fritz (1905–9) achieved a speed of 125 words per minute, and by 1915 the Underwood stable reigned supreme.[54] In spite of Frank McGurrin's brief moment of fame in 1888, female typists soon demonstrated their superiority.

Stenography

Typists had a double identity: they were also stenographers. Shorthand had a long history, emerging first as an aid to recording court proceedings and parliamentary debates. In the hands of law reporters and journalists, it was a predominantly masculine skill in the nineteenth century, and its practitioners treated it as a high-status profession demanding considerable tact and a high degree of confidentiality. In 1888, one instructor warned that stenographers always had to fill in gaps and required extensive "dictionary knowledge" to do so.

Stenography was praised as a "noble and mysterious art," and novices were advised not to look for a job until they could achieve ninety to a hundred words per minute and read their own notes accurately.[55] In court and parliament, shorthand was a means of capturing speeches verbatim in abbreviated writing, and it therefore stood somewhere between the oral and the written.

Many shorthand methods were available. In his partly autobiographical novel *David Copperfield* (1850), Charles Dickens described the difficulty of mastering the Gurney alphabetical system: "the wonderful vagaries that were played by circles; the unaccountable consequences that resulted from marks like flies' legs, the tremendous effects of a curve in a wrong place; not only troubled my waking hours, but reappeared before me in my sleep [...] I had groped my way, blindly, through these difficulties, and had mastered the alphabet, which was an Egyptian Temple in itself." "Every scratch in the scheme," according to the young Copperfield, "was a gnarled oak in the forest of difficulty."[56] Copperfield was hoping to improve his social position and thus win his beloved Dora, but he found transcribing shorthand notes an overwhelming challenge: "As to reading them after I had got them," he admitted, "I might as well have copied the Chinese inscriptions on an immense collection of tea-chests." To woo Dora successfully, he would have to reinvent himself.

Copperfield may not have floundered quite as badly in the hieroglyphics of the Pitman system, which was rapidly becoming dominant. Isaac Pitman was a Baptist and an autodidact, a vegetarian and a teetotaller, with a flair for self-publicity. His phonographic (that is, sound-writing) system, which was based closely on pronunciation, carried all before it in the 1840s. By the 1860s, the majority of British court reporters were trained in the Pitman method.[57] Before long, his system monopolized the field and was adopted in business circles in Britain and the United States. Phonographic writing therefore developed quite independently of typing, but by the 1880s they became twin skills, essential and interdependent attributes of the professional typist. Shorthand was recognized as an important adjunct of the typosphere.

Keyboard Wars

McGurrin's victories did not immediately guarantee the universal adoption of the QWERTY keyboard. For some, all they had shown was that McGurrin was impressively fast and had an entrepreneurial knack for advertising the fact. Perhaps his choice of the QWERTY keyboard was just an accident. Although Remington had adopted the

QWERTY keyboard in 1874, it did not become standard until it was recommended by the Toronto Typewriters' Congress of 1888.[58] Even then, it was not the only possibility available, nor was it inevitable that it should become the standard inclusion, known as the "Universal" keyboard layout. There were several alternatives. The Hammond "Ideal" keyboard, for instance, was shaped in a curve, and had a top row reading DHIATENSOR, a sequence containing letters used in 70 per cent of common English words.[59] In 1893, Blickensderfer created the "Scientific" keyboard, putting the ten most frequently used letters in the bottom row. In the 1970s, the Maltron keyboard presented a more ergonomic, tilted keyboard, with 90 per cent of the commonest English letters on the home row, as the middle of the three alphabetical rows is known.[60] Nevertheless, QWERTY prevailed.

It was even adopted in non-English-speaking areas, with some modifications. In German, it became the QWERTZ keyboard, with additional keys for umlauts and a special "sz" key. In France, it was translated as AZERTY, and in Italy QZERTY, but essentially the core arrangement was based on the one Sholes had created in 1874. Elsewhere, in literary cultures that were not based on the Western alphabet, QWERTY held no sway. This was the case in Russia and other Cyrillic alphabet zones, and the same applied to Hebrew and Arabic typewriters, whose carriages moved in the opposite direction to Western machines to produce text that was read from right to left. Nor was QWERTY relevant to Indic scripts like Bengali, Hindi, Gujarati, and Tamil, even if they are written from left to right. The Thai language, with its forty-four consonants, posed another challenge to typewriter manufacture. The earliest Thai machines had eighty-four keys, until the introduction of a shift key reduced the problem. Even then, some characters were not included and gradually dropped out of use.

A full survey of typewriters in non-Latin scripts is beyond the scope of this book, but the story of Chinese typewriters has attracted recent scholarly attention. Early Chinese typewriters had no keys at all. Following a system first created in China by missionaries, between 2,000 and 5,000 of the commonest characters were set in a flat rectangular bed, while a lever moved the carriage over the characters selected for printing. Hence the Double Pigeon model, which was popular under Chairman Mao, had no keyboard, a wandering platen, and a lever resembling a Morse code tapper, which struck downwards onto the chosen character.[61] To save time and inconvenience, it was useful to juxtapose characters that were commonly combined, such as "American" and "imperialists," or "liberation" and "army."[62] Such combinations assumed a routinized and highly predictable use of language. The proximity of common characters, of course, was exactly the opposite of what Sholes's QWERTY-style dispersal of keys was designed to achieve.

In the 1930s and 1940s, the Chinese-American author Lin Yutang developed an electric Chinese typewriter.[63] He tried to classify Chinese characters according to their size and shape, in order to make it easier for the operator to find and select the desired character. Lin conceived his typewriter as a cultural hybrid like himself – a child born of Western technology and Chinese calligraphic arts. Unfortunately, he exhausted his funding resources and could not obtain a patent until 1952. Western manufacturers showed only lukewarm interest: they assumed that East Asian typists would buy standard typewriters and learn to write in English, making the typewriter a powerful instrument of American globalization.

Sholes had originally put his letter keys in alphabetical order, and traces of this remain today – for instance, in the FGHJKL sequence on the home row. He and Densmore worked on separating some of the often-used keys, to prevent the typebars from bunching and clashing. But their distribution of letters was arbitrary and achieved its aim imperfectly. QWERTY is not necessarily the most convenient layout for touch typists, and it rather resembles a challenging Rachmaninov piano concerto that stretches the finger span of many pianists. Sholes had no intention of making typing speeds any faster. In 1874, touch-typing was unheard of, and designers only had the two- or four-fingered operator in mind. Remington accentuated the random arrangement of keys by moving the letter "r" to the top row, enabling them to perform a neat publicity trick: the word "typewriter" could be produced using exclusively the top row.

The QWERTY keyboard became established even though it was not necessarily the speediest formula. It was open to challenge. In 1932, August Dvorak, then an education professor in the University of Washington at Seattle, patented a quicker keyboard, which time-and-motion studies suggested saved significant time. Dvorak put the five vowels and the five commonest consonants (DHTNS) on the home row (figure 2.4). With vowels concentrated on the left side of the keyboard, and consonants on the right, the typist's right and left hands could work in dialogue with each other, whereas the Universal QWERTY keyboard always puts a greater burden on the left hand. Dvorak maintained that his arrangement enabled typists to compose about 400 common English words without leaving the home row, whereas the QWERTY home row could only manage 100.[64] The typists' fingers did not have to move so far, hurdling letters and rows, and typing speed could be improved by 35 per cent.

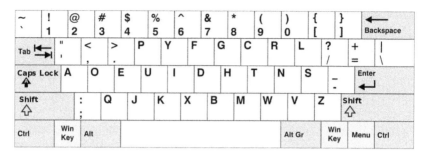

Figure 2.4. Dvorak keyboard (Source: Creative Commons)

QWERTY or Dvorak? The debate continued without resolution for forty years. Dvorak's methodology and findings were questioned. The criteria for the selection of the typists used in his tests were challenged. Furthermore, there was a potential conflict of interest, since the tests on which Dvorak based his claims were conducted by none other than himself and his own masters students, and he had a financial stake in the success of his own keyboard. High school students were given tests based on many one-handed words, which gave the Dvorak keyboard a built-in advantage. Some typing mistakes, of course, were produced by human error rather than the choice of keyboard, but when Dvorak's students claimed to calculate exactly what percentage of errors were caused by human factors, they were unconvincing.[65] Further testing of Dvorak's keyboard carried out by the US Navy, and in 1953 by the Australian Post Office, did not indicate any substantial advantage for either format. The much-vaunted superiority of the Dvorak layout therefore remains debatable.[66]

Dvorak had certainly taken a more systematic approach to the problem than Sholes. Unlike Sholes's arbitrary scattering of common letters, Dvorak could at least claim that his version was based on scientific principles, such as the typist's general comfort using the home row, and the advantage of putting the commonest letters in easy reach. But in spite of its logical superiority, the Dvorak system was never commercialized. QWERTY had its defects, but it had become an ingrained habit, and too many millions of typists had been trained in it for it to be easily jettisoned. It has been called an irrational system, but if millions of typists were competent in QWERTY usage, it was economically very rational to carry on manufacturing typewriters with QWERTY keyboards.[67] The computer keyboard inherited QWERTY in a smooth transition, although there were no mechanical or ergonomic reasons why it should do so. Unlike Macintosh and

Figure 2.5. Remington advertisement for models 10 and 11, 1909
(Source: Wikimedia Commons)

PC computers, QWERTY and Dvorak had no possibility of becoming mutually compatible: typists were exclusively trained in either QWERTY or Dvorak formats. In a standardized environment, it was a choice of one or the other.

QWERTY, then, proved impossible to dislodge. Dvorak protested at the entrenched nature of the opposition. Trying to introduce a new keyboard, he said, was like trying to "reverse the Ten Commandments and the Golden Rule, discard every moral principle, and ridicule motherhood!"[68] The market ruled, even if it could not always be trusted to make the best of all possible choices. Economists interpret the persistence and immutability of the QWERTY keyboard as an example of "path dependence," in which wrong decisions are so deeply embedded that they cannot be changed. As Jared Diamond remarked, we might as well try to change the twelve-hour clock.[69]

The technological development of the typewriter followed a path strewn with casualties – ideas not taken up, directions not taken, innovations that came too late to shake the grip of important vested interests. Outcomes did not automatically stem from optimal choices. We should beware of the fallacy of Voltaire's *Candide*, who naively believed that "all is for the best in the best of all possible worlds." False starts and unpredictable outcomes put the undoubted achievements of the typewriter's inventors into perspective. They were not prophets and could not foresee the precise market that would make their efforts profitable. Among them, Christopher Latham Sholes is usually remembered as the father of the typewriter, and his role is honoured by a monument in Milwaukee, but he was a reticent genius. As a result, posterity has never turned him into a star performer like Edison with his light bulb, Bell with the telephone, or Turing with the computer. He was invisible because the difficult birth of the typosphere was a collective effort. It needed Glidden's occasional insights, Soule's early support, Schwalbach's machinist skills, and above all Densmore's financial backing to succeed. Nor should we forget the improvements added later by Remington's own engineers, prompted by feedback from everyday users of the machine (figure 2.5). The contribution of all these team members is easily forgotten, and so too are the prosthetic machines created by their predecessors, which added something to the incremental process that brought the typewriter into being. The machine came a long way since the early efforts of Sholes and his colleagues, and it acquired many loyal followers on its journey. As we shall see in chapter 11, it continued to generate a powerful sense of nostalgia long into the digital era.

3 Modernity and the "Typewriter Girl"

The Empire of the Typewriter

For its contemporaries, the typewriter signified the triumph of science and the advance of humanity toward a better future. Advertisements for the Oliver typewriter in 1910 proclaimed that "clean, legible, beautiful typewriting is the next great step in human progress."[1] The typewriter indeed played a fundamental role in the second industrial revolution of the late nineteenth century. Along with the telegraph and the telephone, it profoundly altered the nature and pace of communications. This was not merely a revolution in the technology of information media: social, economic, and cultural consequences also followed in its wake. The typewriter was an instrument of imperial control, shaping the imperial archive and facilitating colonial administration. The advent of the typewriter drew the boundaries of a new sexual division of labour, transformed the operations of capitalist enterprises, and changed traditional cultural practices, particularly in the literary field. Most importantly for the subject matter of this chapter, the typewriter ushered in the feminization of the clerical workforce. The typewriter was the herald of modernity, and, in the Western world, modernity had a woman's face.[2] The "Typewriter Girl" became a cultural symbol of the new age.

This chapter will sketch the modernization of office work associated with the typewriter and other new machines, before discussing the Typewriter Girl and all that she signified for the way the typewriter and its usage were configured. We must examine the reasons why so many young women were attracted to shorthand typing as a profession, and what challenges this posed for them, their bosses, and their male co-workers. By the 1920s, the mechanized office had engendered a modern woman who was efficient, capable, professional, and indispensable to the daily transactions of early twentieth-century capitalism. Her work, however, was to become routinized and her skills devalued, as the female typist was gradually relegated to the ranks of the "secretarial proletariat."[3]

The empire of the typewriter reached beyond the boundaries of the modern office, to influence writing practices in other settings, including newspaper reporting and creative writing. Joli Jensen perceived something of its broad compass in her suggestive article of 1988, which traced the ways in which the typewriter was constructed in three very different environments: the clean, aseptic world of the office secretary; the smoke-filled world of the rugged professional journalist; and the bohemian and creative world of the literary author.[4] Perhaps Jensen compartmentalizes these situations too neatly. The worlds she so perceptively characterizes were not rigidly separate but overlapping and very permeable. The fiction writer did not inhabit a world of his or her own, but was often a former journalist. To take one example, Georges Simenon, creator of Inspector Maigret, started his writing apprenticeship at the *Gazette de Liège* before his sixteenth birthday. The typist, in turn, often worked for novelists, either on her own, or as a member of a team employed by a typing agency or a secretarial bureau. Without her, as this book will argue, many fiction writers would have been unable to perform and produce in the way they did.

Besides these more obvious interconnections between the universe of the office and the author's desk, the empire of the typewriter raised some penetrating questions about the nature of literature itself. Foremost among them was the issue of speed: the office promoted and calculated ever-faster speeds of production, but it was far from clear whether fast composition would assist or compromise the creative process in literary writing. Second, the office typewriter spewed forth a form of impersonal and bureaucratic writing, but the impersonality of mechanical writing threatened to efface the personalized mark of the author's individual hand, and many authors resisted this development. In addition, we shall see that in the new empire of the typewriter, instinctive and quasi-automatic textual transmission were the paths to typing success. Some authors reacted with hostility and contempt to such a mechanical writing style; others embraced it as a liberation. The resolution of all these issues was fundamental to the creative process, and they emerged from the new world of the modern office, which began to take shape in the Western world in the last two decades of the nineteenth century.

The New Bureaucratic Era

The pre-modern and pre-typewriter office has sometimes been depicted as a dark Dickensian site where impoverished scribes fought off the cold and wrestled with quill pens to complete their slow drudgery of copying legal documents in fine, copperplate script. This is an exaggeration. Not every employer was as mean-spirited as Ebenezer Scrooge, and steel pens had long since replaced the goose quill. All the same, the clerk still needed to pause frequently to dip his pen in his inkwell. One feature of this stereotyped image was certainly accurate: the pre-typewriter office was an all-male preserve. It was usually a small place, where clerks and employer worked in close proximity and knew each other well. Here the copyists learned the trade, and their high level of literacy and personal loyalty could be rewarded by promotion. By the 1920s, the "typing pool" looked very different: all the workers were women, their bosses were much more remote figures, and the women had few or no career prospects.

The typewriter did not cause this transformation on its own, although it greatly facilitated it. After all, as chapter 2 showed, there had been many attempts to design a writing machine before the 1880s, and they failed to have a profound impact until the circumstances of those late nineteenth-century decades called it forth to prosper and multiply. In that period, the changing nature of industry and government created new demands, and the moment arrived when the typewriter became essential equipment. Businesses grew, administration expanded, service industries proliferated. New machines and new methods of bookkeeping, communication, and data storage were required, and these needs were supplied by new filing systems, calculators, addressing machines, cash registers, telephone exchanges, and typewriters. Banks, insurance companies, and government offices, as well as growing corporations, created a new economy of writing, based on new technologies of classifying, archiving, and transmitting information.[5]

Women were in the forefront of this new bureaucratic era, which dawned first in America, before Europe followed suit. The 1880s saw the take-off of office mechanization in America. The *Penman's Art Journal* already declared in 1887: "Five years ago the typewriter was simply a mechanical curiosity. Today its monotonous click can be heard in almost every well-regulated business establishment in the country."[6] The transformation of the office intensified further in the decades between 1900 and 1920. Women's clerical employment generally survived the return of demobilized soldiers after the First World War. In the United States, women had made up only 2.5 per cent of all clerical workers in 1870, but by 1930 they were in a clear majority within a greatly expanded cohort.[7] This figure embraces all kinds of clerical work, including bookkeeping and accounting. If, within this total, we isolate the work of stenographers and typists, the new female presence was even more striking. By 1930, women made up 95 per cent of all stenographers and typists in the United States.[8] Whereas, in that country, the transformation of the office began in the 1880s, the process happened a little later in Europe. In France, for example, there was already a large female workforce in postal services and telecommunications, but the rise of the female typist can be located in the years just before and after the First World War. In French banks and insurance companies, the number of female employees rose tenfold between 1906 and 1921.[9] In Britain, a similar pattern emerged. Women held 20 per cent of clerical jobs in 1914, but more than 97 per cent by 1931.[10] These are the crude statistics of the "white blouse revolution." Women now formed the human infrastructure of a new technological world. They were pioneers who had stepped beyond the confines of the private and domestic sphere that was, theoretically at least, their natural domain. They left traditional forms of female employment like domestic service, and instead turned clerical work into a new female arena.

New manufacturers sprang up to sustain the emerging market in office machines. By 1909, there were eighty-nine typewriter manufacturers in the United States.[11] At first, America exported to the world, primarily through Britain. Soon Europe developed its own typewriter industry and German machines colonized a large section of the market, with the creation of Adler in 1898. Training courses in shorthand and typing sprang up, often in new commercial colleges where students could study in the evenings. The Young Women's Christian Association (YWCA) was a pioneer in typing education. Possibly the first typing instruction course offered anywhere was introduced by the New York YWCA in 1881; by 1890, there were over 1,300 schools teaching shorthand in the United States.[12]

Shorthand, previously a distinct skill, was now combined with typing to form the double repertoire of the stenographer-typist. As was discussed in the preceding chapter, shorthand had been used from the first half of the nineteenth century to record parliamentary debates and court proceedings, as well as playing a role in business life. Isaac Pitman's shorthand system achieved great success in England by the middle of the nineteenth century, and his method came to monopolize stenography training there.[13] Pitman, however, marketed his system chiefly to young male students in judicial and parliamentary reporting, and was slow to recognize the rise of female stenography in a hitherto masculine domain.[14] This work, like many other forms of office work, was gradually regendered. "Typewriting and shorthand," pronounced the *Phonetic Journal* in 1891, "are twin arts, and young ladies who aspire to succeed in one of them, must make themselves proficient in the other. A typist who cannot write shorthand is very much like a pianist who cannot read music."[15]

The typewriter made changes in office organization and personnel possible, and it is now almost impossible to imagine them without its central presence. The increasingly complex needs of business and administration were decisive in creating a demand during the particular period of 1880–1930, thus inaugurating the "Typewriter Century." For some scholars, the transformation of the office must be connected to the shifting nature of patriarchal, industrial capitalism, although none of them can guarantee that similar changes did not occur at roughly the same time in socialist societies too, or that office work was qualitatively different there.[16]

The office became a regular scenario for fictional drama. Georges Simenon wrote a novel from a female typist's viewpoint, but his *Roman d'une dactylo* (A Typist's Story) was published under a long-forgotten pseudonym and is today almost unfindable.[17] Dashiell Hammett's thriller *The Maltese Falcon* opened in Sam Spade's office, where "[t]he tappity-tap-tap and the thin bell and muffled whir of Effie Perine's typewriting came through the closed door [...] On Spade's desk a limp cigarette smoldered in a brass tray filled with the remains of limp cigarettes."[18] The clacking sound of the typewriter was never very far away in the hard-boiled private-eye fiction of the 1930s and 1940s. The story often opened in an office, ranging from the seedy rooms rented by Sam Spade, to the more luxurious suite that Erle Stanley Gardner provided for Perry Mason's fictional legal practice. In *The Case of the Terrified Typist* (1956), Gardner outlined the structure and hierarchy of an office that largely mirrored his own working arrangements.[19] The fictional office was centre-stage, a scene of tension and conflict, where plots thickened and mysteries deepened. But the office was not merely elevated into a legitimate dramatic setting, it also offered a model for gender relations at work designed, of course, according to the aspirations of male authors and their male protagonists.

In this fictional model, the male hero took solo decisions and retained complete authority. His female assistant was usually a very competent typist and stenographer in her own right but she also had important management skills. She managed her subordinates (in Perry Mason's office, Della Street had several of them), and she managed "upwards" – that is to say, she anticipated her employer's wishes and smoothed his rough edges. She was idealized as a devoted employee, a loyal supporter, and a willing accomplice. She tried to restrain her boss's risky excesses, which could bring him into conflict with the law, usually to no avail in Mason's case, given his innate stubbornness and recklessness.

The outer office was the secretary's domain, where she acted as a gatekeeper, shielding her employer from trivial or bothersome interruptions.

In the case of Effie Perine in *The Maltese Falcon*, she even went as far as looking after his clingy ex-lover and partner's widow, Iva Archer, and keeping her at a distance from Spade. She was his border security, admitting only the most interesting and important callers, perhaps an attractive and mysterious woman, or a male client with a bizarre story that would arouse the curiosity of the private eye and of the reader.

The secretarial agency, which many authors found indispensable, also entered fiction, as in the case of the Cavendish Secretarial and Typewriting Bureau, the origin of Agatha Christie's rather unsatisfactory mystery *The Clocks*. Here eight young women did typing work for various novelists, and were hired out to take shorthand in clients' homes. In contrast to Della Street or Effie Perine, they were treated in derogatory fashion by Christie, even though the leading male character was to marry one of them. Edna Brent, one of the bureau's typists, is generally described as slow-witted, while her co-workers are "not particularly bright" or "probably unreliable," and another is "a born giggler."[20] By the time this novel was written in 1964, the fictional female typist had evolved from a trusted professional into a ditsy scatterbrain. Her role in the social imaginary is pursued in the next section.

The "Typewriter Girl"

The term "secretary" or "secrétaire" once referred to a piece of furniture, but it came to signify a person, almost inevitably a woman. The word "typewriter" evolved in the opposite direction, from person to object.[21] For some time, it denoted the female typist rather than the machine itself, giving rise to double entendres about men with typewriters on their knees, and music-hall jokes of the genre:

> Question: Who was that lady I saw you with last night?
> Reply: That was no lady, that was my typewriter.

The association between the typewriter and the woman was so dominant that, in 1896, *The Phonographic World* called for a new vocabulary to describe the phenomenon, proposing the terms "typess" and "stenographess."[22] Whether this was a serious or perhaps a tongue-in-cheek suggestion, it was in any case unnecessary: the typewriter was already defined as female.

Who were the hordes of women who flooded into New York, Chicago, and other urban centres looking for secretarial training and typing work? Why did the job appeal to them so much, and why were they a good proposition for employers seeking to recruit? They were young and single, above all, usually in their late teens or early twenties. In 1900, for instance, almost two-thirds of stenographer-typists in Chicago were under the age of twenty-four.[23] In Britain, some lower-class girls entered the clerical workforce after leaving school at the age of fourteen.[24] In America, by contrast, stenographer-typists were predominantly middle class, with a secondary education that enabled them to acquire the necessary skills with ease.[25] And they were white: American historians note that women of colour entered the clerical workforce in numbers only in the 1960s. New opportunities thus opened up for certain young women at a time when a source of competent labour was readily available to take advantage of them.

A typing job appealed to young women because, although it drew them away from traditional feminine employment as nurses or educators, it was considered clean and respectable and conformed with middle-class aspirations to gentility. Compared to factory work, the typewriter offered better pay, shorter hours, and an escape from physical drudgery. For Monica Madden in George Gissing's novel *The Odd Women* (1893), learning to type is a step upwards, after working a 13½-hour day in a draper's shop and sleeping in a dormitory with other shopgirls who were all suffering physically from the exhausting work.[26] Even when wages remained static, the supply of female typists kept on coming.[27] Only teaching was comparable in terms of salary, but it required considerably more than a few months' training, and it was not always better paid.

As far as employers were concerned, female typists were cheap, docile, and punctual. They did not smoke, drink heavily, or spit, and they raised the moral tone of the office. They were expected to leave the job when they married, and so they were seen as transient workers, and it would profit enterprises very little to invest in their future. According to the patriarchal assumptions of the nineteenth and early twentieth centuries, only men deserved to earn a "family wage," as sole breadwinners responsible for supporting a wife and children. Women's wages were considered "supplementary" and could never be permitted to rival the male wage. In postwar France, pay rates for women typists were at least 25 per cent lower than the male equivalent.[28]

In spite of the male/female wage differential, young women still found typing jobs appealing. They were a means of escaping parental control and enjoying a new independence underpinned by their very own income. This is just what alarmed conservatives, and philanthropic organizations like the YWCA and the Eleanor Association in Chicago undertook to provide safe lodgings as well as moral guidance for newly arrived young women suddenly exposed to all the temptations of the big city. The Typewriter Girl was an independent woman, and a subject of great interest in the "New Woman" literature of the late nineteenth century. In Grant Allen's fast and sometimes flippant novel *The Type-Writer Girl* (1891), the typist Juliet Appleton is the female protagonist. Appleton was educated at Girton College, one of the first female colleges of Cambridge University, founded in 1869 with a strong intellectual emphasis, and she spent a week in a Bakuninist commune in Sussex.[29] She smoked and rode a bicycle, both almost caricatural indicators of female emancipation. Cooperation between women becomes a dominant theme of the novel.[30] Similarly, Monica Madden attended a typing school imagined by George Gissing with a "bookcase full of works on the Woman-question."[31] The Typewriter Girl was a cultural symbol of female independence, political radicalism, and the rejection of marriage as a necessary or even desirable ambition for a young single woman.

In *The Odd Women*, Rhoda Nunn is an independent woman who rejects marriage, which she regards as synonymous with female enslavement. Such women are "odd" in two senses – because they are eccentric in the sense of socially unconventional, and because of demographic realities. A surplus of women in the population meant that many women would never find a husband: they were "odd" in the sense of being "left over" from the main count, because they would never be part of a couple and were therefore considered socially redundant. Nunn gives up teaching to study shorthand and commercial correspondence. She assists Mary Barfoot, who teaches typewriting and office skills to daughters of the educated middle classes.[32] The typewriter here is a means of emancipation leading to independence and the chance to follow a profession. Class boundaries clearly operated: neither Barfoot nor perhaps Gissing himself contemplated the emancipation of lower-class women.

Commentators feared the "de-sexing" of the female typist. In 1912, British social critic Anthony Ludovici protested against a new form of "white slave traffic," by which he meant the employment of young women as typists.[33] These women, he argued, were forced to "prostitute their beauty" to the typewriter, becoming worn-out, unattractive, and unmarriageable. They were "legions of virgins violated yearly in the modern world by the satyr – the machine" and sacrificed to the god of industrial capitalism.

The Typewriter Girl certainly represented a challenge to conventional views of femininity. Turn-of-the-century novelists questioned whether their typist protagonists were sincere in their rejection of marriage. They asked whether or not conventional romantic fantasies still lurked beneath the intimidating facade of the modern woman. On the whole, they tried to reassure the public that traditional ideals of femininity remained intact, and that women, especially "typewriter girls," were still interested in marriage. Grant Allen's novel asserted that, in spite of the heroine's hard exterior, she was fundamentally searching for heterosexual love. But Allen contrived to confuse gender issues by adopting a female pseudonym.[34] He wrote in the first person, making Juliet Appleton not only the architect of her own fate but also the narrator of her own story. As a female typist, however, she was effectively powerless. Her only real weapon was irony, and there was no romantic outcome for this Juliet. In *The Odd Women*, the formidable Rhoda Nunn does indeed fall in love and, although she does not marry, the author gives her back what he sees as her essential femininity.[35] The possibility that a middle-class woman might continue in professional employment after marriage was never contemplated, either by the female typists or by Gissing himself. The "marriage bar" made a woman's paid work and marriage incompatible for respectable couples in this period. In the 1920s and 1930s, the British civil service explicitly prohibited the employment of married women.[36]

The Typewriter Girl caused anxiety, especially for employers. Would she cope physically with the demands of the job? Was she capable of the hard work, discipline, and concentration required? If so, would she lose her feminine qualities in the process, becoming as hard and "de-sexed" as the machine to which she was invisibly bonded? And furthermore, what effect would she have on the men in the office? Would she distract or seduce them? The typewriter entered a highly eroticized environment, in which forms of sexual harassment of the typist were potentially more likely to disrupt operations than "distracting the men." In Buenos Aires, the stereotypical typist was nicknamed "Milonguita," after a popular 1920 tango about the seduction of a young girl from the suburbs, who ends up singing in a cabaret. She is described as "flor de noche y de placer, flor du lujo y cabaret" (flower of the night and of pleasure, flower of luxury and the cabaret).[37] In other words, the female typist was closely associated with sexual availability and loose morals.

Juliet Appleton in *The Type-Writer Girl* found herself subjected to an oppressive male gaze. Her new employer "perused me up and down with his small pig's-eyes, as if he were buying a horse, scrutinising my face, my figure, my hands, my feet. I felt like a Circassian in an Arab slave-market. I thought he would next proceed to examine my teeth. But he did not."[38] For some, no doubt, the erotic gaze was welcome and reciprocated, the classic modern example of the office Cinderella story being the ambitious Staten Island secretary played by Melanie Griffith in the film *Working Girl* (1988), who informs an investment bank executive (Harrison Ford) that she has "a head for business and a bod for sin." In other periods and contexts, the female typist's desire was more sedately expressed, but the office romance remained a possible incentive to take up typing work. One typewriter manufacturer declared that "Employers Often Marry Their Typewriters."[39] Hermione Waterfield, who worked as a secretary in the British Foreign Office between 1958 and 1961, recalled: "At that stage, I was resigned to being a secretary. Of course at that age [about 28] one always hoped to get married, dreamt of someone to take you out of it all."[40] Waterfield owed her escape to her own efforts rather than to any fantasy hero, and she later became a director of Christie's auctioneers. At the time of her interview, she was still a single woman.

In Erle Stanley Gardner's fictional construction of Mason's legal practice, the sexual chemistry between Perry Mason and Della Street was transparent to readers, especially in the earlier stories. In their fan mail, readers questioned the author about the true nature of the Mason-Street relationship and on his intentions for their future. Gardner considered several outcomes, one of which was marriage and a honeymoon interrupted by a series of mysterious murders. This would have been *The Case of the Hilarious Honeymoon*, which, fortunately, he never wrote.[41] Perhaps he never intended to. "Many readers feel that Della is being short-changed," he wrote to his agent, Thayer Hobson. "Should we let them get married and sleep together?"[42] Mason twice asked Street to marry him, but she turned him down, reluctant to mix business with romance, and certainly unwilling to give up her interesting job, which is what marriage implied for her.[43] Instead, Gardner stumbled on a formula successfully adopted by many of today's television drama series: he decided to maintain the sexual tension in an unresolved state for as long as possible, for this was the best way to keep his readers interested. "I think we should keep teasing them [the readers] as long as we can," he told Hobson.[44] An intra-office marriage, as this example suggests, was problematic, but the erotic potential of the office was not thereby diminished.

One answer was to segregate the sexes in the workplace, thus creating an exclusively female typing pool. When Sun Insurance in Leeds hired its first female typist in 1895, a strategically placed partition screened her from public view.[45] In the British civil service, women workers were separated from men, and their meals were served through a hatch so that they would have no reason to communicate with male workers during recreation and meal times.[46] Typists increasingly came under surveillance. In the United States, under the influence of William Henry Leffingwell, Taylorist principles of scientific management were extended from factories to office work.[47] Fearing that female typists

showed a lack of application, Leffingwell prescribed the constant calculation of typists' output. In companies adopting these modern techniques, first in the United States and then by imitation in Europe,
speedometers were attached to typewriters; desks were pointed away
from the doors so that typists would not be distracted by visitors; and
productivity norms were set and fines or bonuses awarded for those
who fell short or exceeded them.[48] In the Sears Roebuck typing pool,
punctuality was monitored, work assignments were timed from start to
completion, and no talking was allowed between typists.[49] We should
not assume that all typists subordinated themselves without demur to
these new regulatory regimes. All kinds of resistance were still possible, from unionization at one end of the spectrum to more passive
reactions like arriving late or frequent sickness.

Establishing a "rational" work routine and a productive office layout
in a new corporate culture turned typists into pieces of mechanical apparatus. "I continued to click, click, click," said Juliet Appleton, "like
a machine that I was."[50] In this mechanization of the feminine, typists
were denied individuality and initiative, and their bodies, gestures,
and eye contact were closely inspected. They were advised on the correct diet, dress, deportment, and posture – the straight back, the arched
wrists, the eyes focused not on the machine but solely on the text to
be typed. The erotics of the typewriter were strictly policed to eliminate any possibility of the flirtatious glance. The typing pool was under
continuous observation, as in Foucault's interpretation of Bentham's
Panopticon, where the prisoners are kept within permanent view, and
their bodies themselves become the sites where power relationships are
made manifest.[51]

Similar expectations applied to secretaries, including Erle Stanley
Gardner's Della Street. In Gardner's Perry Mason novels, inaugurated
in 1933, he never described the visual appearance of his main characters. Focusing primarily on the plot and the action, he found descrip-
tive writing an unnecessary distraction. He simply wrote that "Della
Street should be loyal, alert and efficient. She should be in love with
her boss, but that love should be relegated to the background during
working hours because of her intense interest in her job."[52] But when
he signed a contract in 1951 to create a Perry Mason newspaper cartoon
strip, he had to decide how the characters looked. His agent, Thayer
Hobson, provided an outline for the cartoonist. He described Della
Street as follows:

Approximately 27, hazel eyes which dominate her face, clear, steady, un-
afraid as though seeing far below the surface.

Trim figure, weight between 109 and 112.

Definitely not a blonde. No actual description of her hair has been given in books, but presumably Chestnut-brown. Wears smartly tailored suits a good deal.

Assured, efficient, good judge of character. Looks at Mason with tender solicitude, ready to back his play on anything.[53]

In the subsequent television series, assiduously micro-managed by Gardner's own production company, this idealized image of smart looks, intelligence, and personal devotion was perfectly portrayed by Barbara Hale.

The Typewriter Girl had displaced men from their leading role in clerical employment. In *The Odd Women*, Mary Barfoot gives an address on the subject of "woman as an invader," in which she rehearses the arguments usually adduced against women replacing men. The female invasion, it was alleged, deprived men of the means to support a family, while working women drove wage levels down, and they were also desexing themselves by not going into nursing or becoming a governess, which remained more suitable avenues of female employment.[54] Women, responds Barfoot, must develop *all* their faculties and push their claims defiantly. "There must be a new type of woman," she proclaims, "active in every sphere of life: a new worker out in the world, a new ruler of the home."[55] The Typewriter Girl was imagined as just such a new woman.

The New Woman figured prominently in the literature and social commentary of the 1890s, but she gave way in the 1920s and 1930s to a new social type – her descendant, the Modern Girl. Like the New Woman, the Modern Girl put a high price on her own autonomy but, unlike the New Woman, she was invariably young and openly feminine. If we risk a broad comparison of social types, we find the Modern Girl was probably less educated than the New Woman of the 1890s, less politically committed, and perhaps less subversive in her attitudes toward romantic love and marriage. In one aspect, however, the Typewriter Girl did not exactly fit the template of the Modern Girl. Whereas the independent Modern Girl of the 1920s was distinguished by her consumption habits and especially her use of cosmetics,[56] the female typist was never allowed the possibility of dressing provocatively – at least, not in the office.

Men were pushed out of many areas of clerical work, but they could still find jobs with career prospects in bookkeeping or accounting, whereas female typewriting was a dead-end job. Certainly, a few women aspired to become a secretary, a term that meant something quite different from a typist, signifying broader responsibilities, which today would be those of an executive's personal assistant. But not everyone could become Perry Mason's Della Street, and the chances of this kind of promotion were few and far between. From the 1920s onwards, the typewriter was increasingly associated with work considered menial, low-paid, and routine. To call this a process of deskilling would be misleading. Typewriting was always a skill requiring training, dexterity, and expertise. As Rhoda Nunn explained to the novice Monica Madden, "One must practice until one can do fifty words a minute, at least. I know one or two people who have reached almost twice that speed. It takes a good six months' work to learn for any profitable use."[57] But the typewriter became increasingly devalued as it was constructed as synonymous with monotonous and repetitive tasks. Women typists had once been pioneers; but they increasingly formed a bureaucratic underclass.

At the outset of the modernization of the office, the female typist posed problems and jolted hitherto stable preconceptions about women's employment. Women, it was subsequently discovered, had "natural" abilities that made them ideal typists. This "discovery" was perhaps a rationalization *ex post facto* of the feminization of clerical work. It functioned as a way of confining female typists within the ghetto of the typing pool. Female fingers were allegedly more agile and nimble than men's, perfectly suited to the work. Harrison's typing manual of 1888 asserted that the typewriter "is especially adapted to feminine fingers. They seem to be made for type-writing. The type-writing involves no hard labour, and no more skill than playing the piano."[58] This writer apparently had a surprisingly low regard for pianists. Women were credited with docility, patience, and great attention to detail, which all seemed assets for a good typist.[59] The early associations of the typewriter with the sewing machine and the piano reinforced this representation of the machine as one that corresponded perfectly with supposedly inborn female talents.

In practice, women typists collaborated in the formulation of new conventions for business correspondence. With minimal resources (they had only one font to play with, and no automatic centring or right justification), they developed new forms of textual layout, which demonstrated the typewriter's ability to reshape correspondence. As Sue Walker has shown on the basis of a study of typing manuals, typists introduced wider margins and more paragraph indentations into the text.[60] In the United States, they adopted a "blocked" layout in which every line began at the left-hand margin. Gradually single-spaced letters began to replace double-spacing. The typewriter, which was less flexible in this domain than handwriting, changed the visual *mise-en-page* of correspondence, and typists pioneered new ways of ordering and structuring the text.

The Typewriter Girl had denoted a modern professional woman, with newfound independence, who could be trusted to be discreet, efficient, and unobtrusive. Mina Harker, in Bram Stoker's *Dracula*, possessed all these attributes, and her talents were crucial in aiding the vampire hunters. *Dracula* was not just a novel of Gothic horror and repressed Victorian sexuality; it also celebrated modern writing and communication technology, including the telegraph, the phonograph, and the typewriter. In *Dracula*, Harker is entrusted by her male superiors with their entire record of papers, diaries, and phonograph messages, which she transcribes and puts into chronological sequence. Her skills in data management and in imposing order on their disparate materials suggest a level of rationality not normally coded as feminine. In fact, working as a typist contaminates her femininity. Van Helsing remarks in the novel, "That wonderful Madam Mina! She has man's brain – a brain that a man should have were he much gifted – and woman's heart."[61] Her efforts help to unearth and destroy the forces of evil, but, temporarily at least, her portable "Traveller's Typewriter" blurs her gender identity. Once Dracula is defeated, she completely regains her feminine identity, since she marries and effectively exchanges her typewriter for a baby.[62]

The ideal typist was smart, attractive, and deferential. Her job was to read the boss's mind and anticipate his wishes before he had even articulated them. She was conservatively dressed, in dark skirt and a white long-sleeved blouse buttoned up to the neckline, and she wore no ostentatious jewellery. Concentrating entirely on the text she was drafting as she touch-typed, her gaze never strayed, her straight posture never crumpled, and she could not on any account be interrupted. She was loyal, accurate, and usually unnoticed. The Victorian ideal of the "angel in the house" had given way to the angel in the office.[63]

The typewriter had helped to create her, it had given her independence and self-respect, but ultimately it had enslaved her. French intellectual Roland Barthes felt pangs of conscience about his role as a typist's slave-driver: "Since I'm often very busy," he told an interviewer,

sometimes I have been forced to give my texts to typists for copying (I don't like doing this very much, but it happens). When I thought about this, it really bothered me. Without standing on a soap-box and making a big speech about it, I'll just say that to me this represented an alienated social relationship: a person, the typist, is confined by their master in an activity I would almost call an enslavement, when writing is precisely the field of liberty and desire. In short, I told myself: "There's only one solution. I really must learn how to type."[64]

And he began practising on an electric typewriter.

Speed, Impersonality, Instinct

The modernization of the office gave women new roles but also established a new gendered division of labour, which was passed on to the literary world. When male novelists hired female typists from secretarial agencies, or asked their wives or lovers to type accurate drafts for them, they were replicating an organization of work that originated in the bureaucratic sphere. The boss's office and the writer's study were not very different in this respect.

It was the mechanical speed of the typewriter that most impressed early observers and users. As noted in chapter 2, this is what struck Mark Twain, when he bought his first typewriter. Rhoda Nunn, as we have also seen, recommended a target for the novice typist of between 50 and 100 words per minute, while highly trained stenographers could reach speeds of 200 words per minute from dictation.[65] Many fiction writers interviewed by Arthur Hoffman, editor of *Adventure* magazine from 1912 to 1927, reported that only a typewriter enabled them to put their thoughts down on paper as fast as their imagination produced them. Writers were asked which writing method presented the least "check" on the creative process or, conversely, which instrument slowed them down or restrained them the most. Out of the 111 authors who answered, 43 reported that they lost ideas because their means of recording them was slower than their imagination, 10 took notes to prevent this loss, and 55 had no trouble with losing ideas. Many of these pulp fiction writers found the speed of the typewriter a great asset. Max Bonter combined the typewriter with shorthand, and typed even faster than he could think, which he admitted tended to result in a "flow of bull."[66] Another interviewee, Robert V. Carr, responded, "When manufacturing literary sausage I naturally want to grind it out rapidly."[67] Many such fiction writers began as journalists, and had become accustomed to fast typing to meet short deadlines, with little time for revision.

This had implications for literary composition. The typewriter clearly made it possible to create at a faster speed. This in turn implied that authors potentially had the time to write more books, so that the typewriter invited not only faster creations but also considerably more of them. Some writers, as will be shown in later chapters, embraced these new possibilities with enthusiasm, churning out fiction at an unprecedented rate. In fact, the enormous output of pulp fiction between the 1920s and the 1940s relied heavily on the typewriter. Other authors, however, with perhaps a more romantic view of literary genius, questioned whether speed and quantity were compatible with true literature. They found rapid results inherently suspect, if not illegitimate, and likely to produce "literary sausage," as Robert Carr described his own work. For them, the typewriter's value would be realized not in the process of composition but rather at the point of submission of their texts to a publisher. Until that point was reached, their writing demanded time, concentrated thought, and careful planning. The new bureaucratic era led them to associate the typewriter with hack writing for purely mercenary reward and of little literary value. They espoused a twentieth-century version of Sainte-Beuve's criticism, levelled a century earlier, of "industrial literature."

The typewriter introduced a form of mechanical writing that severed the traditionally close connection between an author, his or her hand, and pen and paper. The typewritten text was standardized and anonymous. The individuality of the manuscript was lost, the mark of the authorial signature effaced. Of course, evidence existed that every typewriter was, indeed, imperceptibly different from the rest, that it carried its own secret "signature." In "A Case of Identity," Sherlock Holmes solved the mystery by precisely identifying the idiosyncrasies of an individual typewriter.[68] But this was going against the grain: the impersonality of the typewritten text remained a striking feature, and it disturbed contemporaries in the early typewriter decades. Richard Warren Sears even fought against the anonymity of his own company's correspondence, and continued to write business correspondence by hand long after typewriters were easily available.[69] Once drafted, business letters were customarily presented to the executive for his personal signature, and typists adopted the practice of typing their own initials at the bottom of the texts they drafted; apart from this there was no way of identifying the writer except by the typing errors she committed. Pitman and his followers strove to eliminate all typographical errors, but mistakes were made, and they were all that remained to betray the typist's presence, the last vestiges of human intervention on the typed page.[70] With the typewriter, a new distance intervened between the individual author and his or her impersonal text. In this sphere, too, the office revolution had repercussions for literary writers. As chapter 5 will discuss, some writers were disconcerted by the way that typed text distanced themselves from their own work.

Rapid touch-typing opened up further possibilities for all writers by facilitating a more instinctive and fluent style of writing. Typists were trained not to think about what they were actually typing, because any intellectual effort would reduce their speed. Ideally, they were to type without registering the meaning of the text in front of them, rather like Edna Brent in Agatha Christie's *The Clocks*, whose task it was to type the pornographic novel *Naked Love*, but "its painstaking eroticism left her uninterested."[71] In a typing manual of 1959, Marion Lamb advised: "Even experienced typists who have achieved a high degree of automatisation of skill find that they make typing errors when they take a creative interest in what they are typing. The thought essential to composition interferes with typing skill."[72] Under the Isaac Pitman regime, the ideal typist was trained to be blind and invisible, as it were, a passive mediator who was effectively mentally absent from the task in which she was engaged.[73] The prevailing discourse of female passivity vis-à-vis the machine becomes fully legible only in the context of such instructions to the typist to completely efface herself from her own work process.

Typists were encouraged to empty their minds and become channels of uninterrupted communication, creating as far as possible the illusion of unobstructed mediation between author and finished text. It is not surprising that some typists became spiritual mediums, like Henry James's amanuensis Theodora Bosanquet, channelling his messages from beyond the grave. Suitably enough, the shorthand typist Mina Harker in *Dracula* provided the vampire hunters with information under hypnosis. This novel repeatedly puts its female characters into trance-like states like sleepwalking or hallucinatory dream experiences. Harker's mind is no longer her own: it becomes a battlefield where the antagonists fight for control. Dracula exerts a telepathic control over her, while Van Helsing performs counter-hypnosis to make contact with her subconscious knowledge of the enemy.[74] Like an ideal typist, she has effectively "emptied" her mind.

Instinctive writing provided a possible model for creative authors. There were some, as we shall see, who responded very positively to the notion of literary composition that was spontaneous and free-flowing, composing in a continuous stream as though the actual source of inspiration came from somewhere outside the author. This was the case for Enid Blyton, as it was in a more extreme form for Jack Kerouac. On the other hand, many others preferred to see writing as a craft, favouring prose that was polished and fashioned and never entirely innocent.

Our quest for the Typewriter Girl at the heart of the modern twentieth-century office has been guided by sociologists of labour, typewriting instruction manuals, and fictional examples. The rise and decline of the

Typewriter Girl raised significant questions about literary creativity, which echoed far beyond the walls of skyscrapers and newly mechanized offices. These questions, which frame the rest of this book, were confronted and answered, in various ways, by the world of literature. These were questions, first, about the speed of composition: how much speed was possible or desirable in the creation of fine literary works? Second, they included questions about impersonal and bureaucratic writing: where were the author's hand and personal signature now to be located, and could they in fact be best preserved by resisting the empire of the typewriter altogether and continuing to write in longhand? Lastly, the office revolution posed questions about instinctive, spontaneous, and "mindless" writing, which inspired some but disgusted others. The typewriter extended its authority both within Western society and globally in the service of empires; changes within the office were only the beginning of its influence.

4 The Modernist Typewriter

Keys to Modernity

The typewriter was a *modern* machine. It signified progress, a technological triumph that would bring an end to drudgery (even if, in practice, thousands of female typists found that drudgery had many faces).
The typewriter heralded a modern world where transactions could be
accomplished faster and more efficiently than ever before. It had revolutionized the office, and it would also change the nature of other forms
of writing. American poet Hart Crane warned in 1930,"Unless poetry
can absorb the machine, i.e. acclimatize it as naturally and as casually
as trees, cattle, galleons, castles and all other human associations of the
past, then poetry has failed its full contemporary function."[1] The typewriter was an important instrument in formulating the discourses and
practices surrounding the condition of being "modern."

This chapter considers some writers and poets of the early twentieth
century for whom printing technology in general, and the typewriter
in particular, opened up new creative opportunities. It does not aim
to reinterpret modernism as a whole, which would be far beyond my
scope, but rather to underline the importance of printing technology
in the composition of modernist literature. The typewriter assisted literary avant-gardes in breaking with past traditions and in formulating freer modes of expression. The futurists promoted an iconoclastic
program that aimed to abolish the ruling conventions and canons of
art and literature. They were governed by a new aesthetic of the machine, embracing mechanical printing as well as other recent scientific
achievements like the motorcar and the aeroplane. In their wake, poets
of the First World War and the interwar period used the typewriter
to develop a style free of the constraints of rhyme and metre, the line
and the stanza. For them, the typewriter was liberating. Here I briefly

consider Guillaume Apollinaire for his word-pictures, as well as Ezra Pound, e.e. cummings, and T.S. Eliot, who all developed broken and discontinuous verse styles that reflected the modern mechanical age. Gertrude Stein is unfortunately not included here, because she did not use a typewriter – Alice B. Toklas worked as her amanuensis. Ernest Hemingway will be considered last, as a writer whose characteristically bare prose reflected what was often perceived as a common effect of the typewriter: its tendency to eliminate superfluous descriptions and literary flourishes. First, however, I review some common representations of the typewriter. The ways in which the typewriter was imagined and the metaphors deployed to describe and advertise it all reflected its status as an emblem of modernity.

Guns and Pianos

Typewriter users readily drew analogies between the machine and modern weaponry. The speed and sound of a typewriter recalled a machine gun. Perhaps significantly, Remington produced guns and ammunition before it began to manufacture typewriters. Media theorist Friedrich Kittler described the typewriter as a "discursive machine-gun."[2] In the 1920s, Ernest Hemingway, who played a personal role in the First World War as a stretcher bearer on the Italian front, wrote a poem about his typewriter in which its "mechanical staccato" is seen in military terms, as the infantry of the mind advances over difficult terrain, making the typewriter their *mitrailleuse* (machine gun).[3]

Even before the First World War, weaponry analogies were rife. Australian writer Henry Lawson imagined a battleground where writers fought out their own war to the clacking sound of typewriters. One poem, written in 1904, is called "The Firing Line," and the typewriter here might itself be said to be "firing lines."[4] The third stanza reads:

> In the dreadful din of a ghastly fight they are shooting, murdering, men;
> In the smothering silence of ghastly peace we murder with tongue and pen.
> Where is heard the tap of the typewriter – where the track of reform they mine –
> Where they stand to the frame or the linotype – we are all in the firing line.

As the generations succeed each other, Lawson's typewriter becomes the peacetime battleground upon which political machinations take place.

Reversing the metaphor, gangsters of the Prohibition era called their automatic weapons "Chicago typewriters."[5] The Oxford historian A.J.P. Taylor later put it in typically contentious style: "Since then [the 1930s] my style [...] has changed with my writing instruments. With a pen you write words. With a typewriter you write sentences. With an electric typewriter you write paragraphs. In military terms: bow and arrow, musket, machine gun. I try to keep up a continuous fire."[6] Taylor, who was renowned for his aggressive and polemical prose, didn't live long enough to work on word processors. Perhaps this was just as well – his metaphor on the evolution of warfare had already gone quite far enough.

These were gendered analogies – men compared the sound of the typewriter to staccato gunfire, while Remington advertisements claimed that any woman who could play the piano could learn to type. A stereotyped masculine image of the hard-bitten reporter developed, crouched over his typewriter with cigarettes and coffee at hand, "bashing out" his copy. Female associations were quite different: Enid Blyton wrote in her garden with a portable perched on her knee – a pose in which "bashing" would have risked destabilizing the machine. Female typists were touch-typists; untrained men used the hunt-and-peck method.

At the same time, the typewriter's popularity was part of the Jazz Age, and musical metaphors were also used to describe its work. As soon as typewriting machines were designed to stand upright, keyboard action was often compared to playing the piano. As early as 1857, Samuel Francis of New York patented a "literary piano," in which the long black-and-white keys resembled piano ivories.[7] The French poet Denis Roche explained much more recently:

I have never played the piano, so I can't compare. Having said that, when I type very fast, I have a slight impression of piano-playing and I even surprise myself, you know how these pianists [...] draw arabesques with their hands, I don't go that far but sometimes I'm not far off. It's really quite stimulating. The word that comes to mind is spinning around (*virevolter*). I have the impression that my hands are spinning around: "The dance of the spirit in amongst the words."[8]

Musical analogies reflected the feminization of typewriter usage. According to Françoise Sagan (*Bonjour Tristesse*, 1954), "For me, writing means finding a certain rhythm. Which I compare to the rhythms of jazz."[9]

Futurism

The futurist movement worshipped modern technology; its aesthetic project was inspired by the cult of the machine – the motorcar, the aeroplane, the machine gun, and printing technology included. The futurists admired the machine's metallic presence, and the speed and dynamism of its moving parts, especially when the machine itself was designed for mobility, like the locomotive or the motorcar. They responded to the noise of the machine, and that included the noise of a working typewriter, even if it created no more than a whisper in comparison to the cacophony of intensive shelling in the First World War, which futurism also sought to represent artistically. In all their endeavours, futurists made a cult of the modernity of the machine, deploring *passéiste* art forms rendered obsolete by a new fusion of art and technology (the term *passéiste*, or *passatista*, was the futurists' code for anything they found distasteful and wanted to destroy).

The artistic agenda of futurism was immersed in a modern technological environment. Literature, and especially poetry, co-opted technological devices to promote new aesthetic values and strategies. Following the first futurist manifesto, published on the front page of the French daily *Le Figaro* in 1909, the futurists developed the manifesto into a literary genre in its own right, incorporating it in their strategies of self-advertisement.[10] More than fifty futurist manifestos were proclaimed between 1909 and 1915, when Italy entered the First World War.[11] They were framed in extravagant, polemical language, full of hyperbole and unsettling slogans, glorifying war, energy, and raw violence. There were manifestos on painting and music, the *Futurist Manifesto of Lust*, the *Manifesto of Futurist Cooking*, and the all-embracing and grandiose *Futurist Reconstruction of the Universe*, to name but a few. Most relevant for our concerns were Marinetti's texts on the futurists' typographical revolution.

Filippo Tommaso Marinetti, founder and chief spokesman of the futurist movement, envisaged the destruction of libraries, museums, and art galleries, all of them monuments to dead cultures, which now had to give way to futurist conceptions of art. Books and printing were to be revolutionized, too, but in this case not destroyed. Marinetti explained enigmatically that the target of his hatred was "the so-called typographic harmony of the page," which imposed a straitjacket on free expression. The futurist revolution would transform the printed page, which Marinetti wanted to "liberate" from syntax, grammar, and linearity. Instead, new technological sensations would be represented in unconventional and iconoclastic ways. Machines are liberating, the futurists announced, as they declared war on dominant bourgeois aesthetics: "Let us boldly create the 'ugly' in literature and kill solemnity wherever it may be."[12]

Marinetti's *Technical Manifesto of Futurist Literature* (1912) accordingly launched an attack on punctuation and denounced pointless adjectives and adverbs. The slogan of the printing revolution was "words in freedom" (*parole in libertá*). In 1913, Marinetti explained that the aim of his typographical revolution was to overthrow the traditional book, with all its trimmings and decorative features inherited from Renaissance typography, which the futurists consigned to the dustbin of history: "I have initiated a typographic revolution," he wrote,

> directed against the bestial, nauseating sort of book that contains *passéiste* poetry or verse *à la* D'Annunzio[13] – handmade paper that imitates models of the seventeenth century, festooned with helmets, Minervas, Apollos, decorative capitals in red ink with loops and squiggles, vegetables, mythological ribbons for missals, epigraphs and Roman numerals [...] My revolution is directed against the so-called typographical harmony of the page, which is contrary to the flux and reflux, the leaps and bursts of style that run through the page itself.[14]

Normal rules about sequences of vowels and consonants were to be overthrown, and spelling could be instinctively distorted. Writing and printing machines could facilitate free expression. "After the animal kingdom," futurism proclaimed, "the mechanical kingdom begins!"[15]

In practice, the armoury of a new typographical *mise-en-page* was mobilized to give an onomatopoeic representation of modern life and its cacophonous soundscapes. In fact futurism tried to capture the entire range of the senses in textual form. Fortunato Depero's *Luna Park, Esplosione tipografica* (1929), for example, portrayed the noise and confusion of Coney Island amusement park in print, with swirling type in different fonts and sizes describing lines of movement and action, some vertical, some diagonal, some circular, but all subverting horizontal normality.[16] The regulated order of the typed or printed page was abandoned to represent cascades, circuits, coloured lights, the roller-coaster itself, which undulated all over the page, while the motion of the ride was rendered verbally as "salire. scendere. salire. scendere" (going up, going down, going up, going down). Meanwhile a "fontana alfabetica" spouted letters into the air.[17] Depero tried on a single page to produce a complex synthesis of the aural, visual, and verbal. The text had been liberated from the straight line and from the convention of using the same font throughout. The image was no longer to be read from left to right and from top to bottom. It was as open to multiple reading pathways as an abstract painting. The written word had been deconstructed and reassembled to create a jumble of sensory impressions.

For futurists, the typographical unity of the page remained constant, but the line and the paragraph had been eliminated. The result was what Perloff labelled a verbal and visual collage, although Marinetti himself never used that term.[18] The text had exploded, and its fragments littered the page like random pieces of debris. Redundant descriptions were removed, and the language of the onomatopoeic sound poem raced ahead at top speed, tolerating neither pauses nor detours. At the same time, Marinetti hoped to eliminate the subjective authorial voice; instead the verbal-visual collage of futurist poetry emanated from a depersonalized source.

The same desire to synchronize a range of sensory phenomena is found in the experimental theatre of the futurist artist Giacomo Balla. Typography informed his first original work for the stage, designed in 1914. In *Macchina tipografica*, Balla attempted to produce an audio-visual version of a printing machine. He was probably thinking of a loud rotary press in action rather than typewriters, but the difference is only one of scale. Balla was celebrating the beauty and power of all writing machines. Twelve actors performed the score, simultaneously imitating the sound of the printer, thus:

1 settesettesettesette...
2 nennenennenennenenne...
3 vùùùùmmùùvùùùùùsmùùvùù
4 tètètètètètètètètè...
5 miaaaaaanavanò
6 sta-sta-sta-sta
7 lalalalalalalalalalal
8 ftftftftftftftftftft
9 riòriòrièrièriòriòrièriè
10 sescscscscspsspsscscscscscscspssps
11 vevevevevevevevevevev ...
12 nunnnònònunnnònònunnònò

The actors themselves were dressed as anonymous machines, and they performed in front of a backdrop on which the word "tipografia" appeared.[19] For a while, Sergei Diaghilev was tempted to incorporate it into the next Italian program of his Ballets Russes. He thought better of it, probably wisely.[20] As this curious episode suggests, futurist experiments frequently took the form of performance art, and the group staged many such events in theatres and *cafés-concerts*. They endured abuse and the audience threw things at them in disgust, but Marinetti regarded this kind of reaction as a triumph.

The futurists' reconceptualization of the printed page to achieve freer artistic expression reached maximum intensity in the representation of warfare. The movement glorified war and violence, which it saw as a means of purification and the ultimate form of social hygiene. It was also the quintessential fulfilment of virility. War for Marinetti was not merely destruction but an assertion of life itself. "In Tripoli" (1911), he provocatively wrote, "I observed how trivial is the spectacle of lacerated human flesh when compared with the shining and aggressive barrel of a gun scorched by the sun and rapid fire."[21] In 1912–13, Marinetti saw active service at the siege of Adrianople during the First Balkan War. The result of his experience was his oft-performed war poem *Zang Tumb Tumb*. In this work, Marinetti sought an onomatopoeic rendition of shells, bombardment, sounds and images that all launched a stereophonic attack on the senses. Typographical originality would reproduce the sound of battle. Bombs and bullets were rendered as "zong-toomb," "traak-traak" or "pik-pok-poom-toomb." He made free use of assonance, with a series of progressively larger font sizes to create the effect of crescendo. Spelling was entirely phonetic, and plenty of heavy bold type was deployed for greater impact. Marinetti personally performed this work all over Europe, accompanied by hammers and bells.[22]

Marinetti enthusiastically aligned futurism with the emerging Fascist Party and later with Mussolini's regime. The movement's fatal descent into Fascism must temper any critical appreciation of its innovative ideas. David Wright broke ranks with a chorus of fascinated critics when he speculated that Marinetti may have been "on the cusp of nonsense" and that his poetry might represent "the ramblings of a madman."[23] Futurism's Fascist sequel, however, highlights the sinister aspects of its program. There was a clear correspondence between the inherent misogyny of the avant-garde, its cult of male violence, its anti-bourgeois nihilism and faith in the creative powers of war, on one hand, and the values of Fascism, on the other.

"Words in freedom" was nevertheless an important idea, because it liberated the printed page from conventional constraints like punctuation, straight lines, regular margins, and a rigid left-to-right approach. Under futurism, the text had no frame, no headings, and no bottom line. Futurism had expanded the visual potential of the page, turning words and characters into dynamic images. Some of this typographical liberation would flow through into modernist poetry, as the next section will illustrate. It presented a fragmented assortment of phrases and word-images whose lack of logical continuity was echoed in the work of Pound and Eliot. In the process, the avant-garde raised fundamental questions about the definition of poetry. If there were no lines, no rhyme or metre, and no stanzas, what essentially distinguished poetry from prose, on one hand, or from visual art, on the other? The boundaries were fluid, and modernist poets continued to question conventional art forms.

The futurist project produced its own version of the technological fallacy. Marinetti made the machine his muse, but typewriters and printing technology could not alone determine the literary environment. Instead, artists and poets took what they wanted from new technology, absorbing or incorporating it to a greater or lesser extent depending on their own creative ambitions and aesthetic strategies. Technology was appropriated in different ways by different individuals. Potentially, however, early modernism had turned the typewriter from a copying machine into a crucial creative instrument. It undermined traditional composition by accentuating the materiality of the typed text and the "concreteness" of poetic language.

Modernist Poetry

Stéphane Mallarmé's poem "Un coup de dés" (A Throw of the Dice), published posthumously in 1914, is usually seen as a precursor of the free verse of the modernist poets of the interwar period.[24] Mallarmé, unlike Marinetti, was no political radical, and had no affiliation with the advertising industry, from which futurist artists borrowed new visual techniques and a hectoring language (in the 1920s, Depero designed posters and bottles for Milanese aperitif maker Campari). Mallarmé mapped words and blank spaces across the page, defying symmetry and deliberately violating the reading patterns imposed by books and other printed texts. He freely switched from Roman typeface to italic and from one font size to another. There was no left justification, as the poem spread out across the page, forming what Mallarmé called "constellations" of words. A coherent interpretation of the poem as a whole has eluded critics, but perhaps its presence on the page and its unusual layout are more important. It is a disjointed composition, and its very disjointedness is a component of the modern condition.

Others, including Guillaume Apollinaire, took the visualization of poetry in print further, constructing collages of words, images, and images composed of words. His magpie-like habit of assembling disparate and disconnected materials consciously resembled the techniques of the cubist painters. Apollinaire's 1917 collection *Calligrammes* combined verse and imagery. His transformation of words into the shapes of familiar objects was often, as Johanna Drucker points out, a sort of joke, which the poet shared with his readers.[25] In "Il pleut" (It's Raining), the words formed streams of slanting rain drizzling down toward the bottom right-hand corner of the page. "La Cravate et la Montre" formed the words into a tie and a pocket watch, reflecting the poem's title. In the case of the watch, the poetry was quite independent of its innovative format, so that a tension was maintained between word and image. In "Paysage" (Landscape), however, there was greater concordance between typed text and its visual shape:

Figure 4.1. Guillaume Apollinaire, *Salut monde*
(Source: Creative Commons)

CET
ARBRISSEAU
QUI SE PRÉPARE
À FRUCTIFIER
TE
RES
SEM
BLE

(This shrub that is about to bear fruit resembles you.)

In his Eiffel Tower–shaped poem, "Salut monde" (Good Day, World), the fusion of the verbal and the visual was more satisfying (figure 4.1). In this case, a national icon shaped a patriotic, wartime message defying the German enemy: "Good day, world, of which I am the eloquent tongue which pokes out from your mouth, O Paris, and will always poke out at the Germans."

Apollinaire's "Lettre-océan" was a more complicated collage of different elements (figure 4.2). Its subject was the exchange of messages through different media between Apollinaire and his younger brother Albert, who was in Mexico. The page mimics the format of a postcard, with a space for a postage stamp and a Paris postmark. The wireless telegraph is represented with brief texts arranged as radio waves beaming outwards from the Eiffel Tower like the spokes of a wheel.

Apollinaire's *Calligrammes* shared the anarchic form of futurist verse, but with the addition of a dose of humour, which was painfully lacking in futurist productions.[26] Like the futurists, Apollinaire used type to make word-pictures, even if only about one-third of the works in *Calligrammes* incorporated images, and even if not all of them were typed. They inhabited an uncertain border zone between poetry and visual art. *Moi aussi je suis peintre* (I, too, am a painter) was Apollinaire's original title for the collection, before the outbreak of the First World War interrupted his life and work.

The literary avant-garde made creative use of typography. Apollinaire's *Calligrammes* drew on the cubist art of Braque and Picasso and on new typographical forms that were being introduced into posters and other publicity documents by the advertising industry. There was a multimedia dimension to early modernist verse, as illustrated by the ballet *Parade*, written for the Ballets Russes in 1917, which brought together a scenario by Jean Cocteau, Erik Satie's music, Massine's choreography, and sets and costumes made of cardboard and designed by Picasso. The result was a collage of various emblems of modernity, like the skyscraper, ragtime tunes, and the clacking of typewriters. The score included a cue for a typewriter, as well as clinking milk bottles and a foghorn.[27] Cocteau also wanted to include a Morse code tapper and the drone of aeroplanes; to be truly revolutionary, these elements would not just hum along in the background but would be incorporated into the score itself. Decades later in 1950, Leroy Anderson wrote his piece "The Typewriter" for orchestra and typewriter to be played by a percussionist, and it can still be heard on classical music radio stations.[28] The typewriter could make music as well as war, and this notion associated the machine more closely with creative activity rather than purely mechanical tasks.

Modernist writers and poets such as T.S. Eliot, Ezra Pound, and e.e. cummings were closely engaged with the technologies of their time. The typewriter assisted them to break with traditional rhyme and metre; it could create a *mise-en-page* that, for them, resembled a musical score. For theorist Charles Olson, a typed text was not a standardized and impersonal version – it bore the unmistakeable signature of the individual poet. The poetry of e.e. cummings, for example, is immediately recognizable for its lack of punctuation and capitalization and the way that isolated words tumble down the page. In his compositions, the use of blank space was significant, and the typewriter could calculate blankness with fine precision.

Figure 4.2. Guillaume Apollinaire, *Lettre-océan*
(Source: Creative Commons)

Olson believed that the typewriter could render a poem as if it were musical notation, indicating breathing rests and moments of acceleration as well as signalling to readers staging points where they could stop and think. According to Olson, "It is the advantage of the typewriter that, due to its rigidity and its space precisions, it can, for a poet, indicate exactly the breath, the pauses, the suspensions even of syllables, the juxtapositions even of parts of phrases, which he intends. For the first time the poet has the stave and the bar a musician has had."[29]

Olson was mistaken in supposing that any author can dictate how his or her work will be read. Readers have more freedom and independence than Olson recognized to choose their own rhythms and arrive at their own interpretations. Nevertheless, with the help of the typewriter, modernist poets tried to capture the orality of poetry. Poetry, they insisted, was sound, and the typewriter helped to approach new ways of articulating between verbal, visual, and auditory perceptions. It was an essential mediator between composition and performance.

Ezra Pound connected his poetry with eventual oral performance. As he wrote to Hubert Creekmore, a fellow American poet, laying down what sounded like an incontrovertible law: "ALL typographic disposition, placing of words *on* the page, is intended to facilitate the reader's intonation, whether he is reading silently to self or aloud to friends. Given time and technique I might even put down the musical notation of passages or 'breaks into song'."[30] The Chinese ideograms that Pound added to his *Cantos* could hardly be assimilated into the music of his verse, because most of his readers could never pronounce them, but Pound envisaged the rest as a vocal score.

Pound's American publisher, James Laughlin, struck a discordant note (to extend the sonic metaphor) when he reported on his visit to Pound in Italy in 1934. "I watched him working sometimes," he recalled:

> He would assault his typewriter with an incredible vigor. In fact, he had to have two typewriters, because one was always at the repair shop. His typing, which was extremely eccentric, had, I think, a good deal to do with the visual arrangement of some of the pages in the *Cantos* because, in the fury of composition, he couldn't always take time to go all the way back to the left margin; he would slap the carriage and wherever it stopped that determined the indent.[31]

Did Pound's vigour and impatience determine the shape of his poetry by creating inconsistent left-hand margins in this way? There is no doubt that his typing was an explosion of energy. In 1917, he himself depicted his "present existence [as] that of a highly mechanized typing volcano."[32] On the other hand, he gave precise instructions on the layout of his poems to his publisher, which suggested that any idiosyncrasies were in fact under the author's tight control. In 1940, for instance, Pound sent precise instructions to his London publisher, Faber & Faber, about the typesetting of *Cantos LII–LXXI*: "Please follow all EXCENTRICITIES of punctuation," he ordered. "[P]rinter will please keep an even distance between the lines the irregularities are due to my errors of typing/that is to say the UP and DOWN irregularities / the indentations to the right are thought out [...] they are intended to make the matter clearer to the eye."[33] Since Pound admitted here to some "errors of typing," we may suppose that the end result was a combination of random accident and careful calculation. His orders, however, left little scope for the printer's interpretation. Pound's typed text appeared so bizarre to the uninitiated reader that, when he was writing in prison in Pisa after the Second World War, the censor suspected that the typescript of the Pisan Cantos contained secret coded messages.[34]

Cummings similarly explored the typographical effects that a typewriter could produce. For him, the *mise-en-page* was essential, and his poetry depended on mechanical composition to express the required spatial relationships between its various components. In "the sky was candy luminous," cummings demonstrated the use of unconventional spacing, the lack of capitalization that was his trademark, and unexpected indentation:

```
the
 sky
          was
can dy     lu
minous
        edible
spry
  pinks shy
lemons
greens     coo l choc
olate
s.
  un     der,
  a    lo
co
mo
    tive     s pout
            ing
            vi
            o
          lets
```

As Daniel Matore points out, cummings's poetic licence is here under considerable restraint. The left-hand margin anchors the poem, and the concept of the line has been preserved.[35]

Like Pound, cummings objected when typesetters altered his finely calibrated distribution of space and words. Discussing his *No Thanks*, published in 1935 by Golden Eagle Press, he complained that his poems had been translated "out of typewriter language into linotype-ese." Automatic justification ruined his plan for the architecture of the poems, imposing a "neat artificial evenness," which he deplored. "Ah well," he wrote about this dispute, "You should see the army of the Organic marching against Mechanism with 10,000[th]-of-an-inch(or whatever)'hair-spaces'; you should watch me arguing for two and a half hours(or some such) over the distance between the last letter of a certain word and the comma apparently following that letter but actually preceeding [sic] the entire next word."[36] As is evident from the preceding quote, cummings did not usually put a space after commas or brackets. He cast himself and his typewriter as "organic," in contrast to the "mechanical" linotype machine, in a remarkable reversal of the orthodox interpretation of the typewriter's depersonalizing effect. For the prose writers considered in chapter 5, the typed version of their work produced a standardized, even text that took it a step closer to publication. Cummings, however, wrote in his own "typewriter language." For him, the typed version embodied his very personal technique, and it was only at the later stage of the linotype version that uniformity was imposed. His typewriter did not exist to bring an existing text closer to publication; instead, it was the instrument of his creative individuality. The typed text carried his personal signature, and it was only in the hands of the publisher that his ownership of the text and agency as an author were threatened.

T.S. Eliot's use of the typewriter, or rather of various typewriters, has been minutely dissected by Lawrence Rainey to elucidate the textual genesis of *The Waste Land*.[37] Taking into account the colour of the typewriter ribbon on the original typescript, the quality of the paper and its watermarks, Rainey was able to determine where and on what machines Eliot composed the poem in 1921–2. Rainey did not, unfortunately, identify the brand or model of the machines Eliot used. Rainey stressed the novelty of including a female typist as a protagonist of the poem itself, assaulted in her bedsit by a clerk, a "young man carbuncular." The seduction, which the anonymous typist does not resist, leaves her coldly indifferent. At Lloyds Bank, Eliot worked daily with typists. He told his mother in 1919: "I have half a room, two girls and half a typist. I share a typist with someone else"; in the following year he was granted a typist of his own.[38] Typing was part of his everyday existence.

He had started to use a typewriter himself in 1914, and, by 1922, he was composing about a half of his work on a machine.[39]

Eliot, like the other poets mentioned above, paid great attention to the layout and punctuation of his poems. "I only hope," he wrote of *The Waste Land* as he sent it to publishers Boni and Liveright, "the printers are not allowed to bitch the punctuation and the spacing as that is very important for the sense."[40] Eliot felt that the typewriter influenced how he wrote, making his writing more sparse. "Composing on the typewriter," he told his friend and fellow poet Conrad Aiken, "I find that I am sloughing off all my long sentences which I used to dote upon. Short, staccato, like modern French prose. The typewriter makes for lucidity, but I am not sure it encourages subtlety."[41] The typewriter suited the disjointed nature of his poetry. *The Waste Land* consists of unrelated scenes and experiences without coherence or continuity. It has some of the fragmentary or chaotic quality present in futurist productions.

Although I discuss only a few modernist writers above, the work of all of them drew attention to the physical act of composition, in which the location of words on the page was startling and traditional patterns were rejected. In their hands, the poem was a concrete object. Blank space became a vital and dynamic part of the poem, and the typewriter was indispensable to measure it with the desired accuracy. The typewriter helped these writers to challenge their readers.

Ernest Hemingway

Hemingway knew the American modernists in Paris in the 1920s. He was a frequent visitor at Gertrude Stein's apartment, until he decided that menopause had disturbed her mind and that she had become obsessed with patriotism and lesbianism. He befriended Ezra Pound, at least up until the early 1930s, when Pound's fascist sympathies became distasteful to him. Like those writers, he was temporarily involved in the world of the "little reviews," which provided an outlet for experimental literature. In 1924, he became a manuscript scout for Ford Madox Ford's *translatlantic review*, which soon folded.

If the typewriter caused any writer to discard the superfluous and write sparingly, Hemingway's characteristically lean prose style epitomized this. He learned this economy as a journalist. In fact, Hemingway lived a large proportion of his working life reporting in one or another of the twentieth century's many war zones. He started his first job at the *Kansas City Star*, assigned to an enormous room full of typewriter noise.[42] In 1918, he enlisted as a Red Cross ambulance driver and was sent to the Dolomites. On the Italian front, he was badly wounded and returned home a war hero. In 1920, he was employed by the *Toronto Daily Star*, for whom he interviewed Mussolini in 1922 and covered the war between Greece and Turkey, where he contracted malaria. In 1923, he was in the Ruhr covering the French occupation. In 1937–8, he reported on the Spanish Civil War for NANA (the North American News Alliance), and in 1944 he followed Allied forces into Belgium and Germany under contract with *Collier's* magazine. If a war was brewing somewhere, Hemingway and his typewriter found a sponsor to send him there.

Charles Fenton argues that Hemingway's apprenticeship as a journalist turned him into a mature writer and coloured the bare economy of his prose.[43] Unfortunately, Fenton overlooked the importance of Hemingway's writing instruments in his apprenticeship and maturity. Like so many literary critics, Fenton suffered from typewriter blindness. Hemingway used several machines, starting with second-hand models and the machine given to him by the *Kansas City Star*. In 1921, on his twenty-second birthday, his fiancée Hadley Richardson presented him with a new portable Corona No. 3. This was the same folding model that the British Army had used extensively in the First World War.[44] He took it with him to Constantinople in 1922, and it now resides in the Museo Hemingway in Cuba. Later in life, he used a portable Underwood, a Swedish Halda, and various Royal models.

Hemingway's method relied on longhand drafts, which he sometimes produced in a spontaneous flow. He wrote to Scott Fitzgerald about the composition of his story "Out of Season": "When I came in from the unproductive fishing trip I wrote that story right off on the typewriter without punctuation."[45] More frequently, it took longer than this. When a draft was complete, he would set it aside for about three months before taking it up again to revise it. His own typed copy would subsequently be retyped either professionally or by whichever of his wives he was then married to – the only one of his four wives who apparently escaped typing duties was Martha Gellhorn, who was a working journalist in her own right. We also know that he entrusted *The Sun Also Rises* (1926) and *Farewell to Arms* (1929) to his younger sister Sunny to type.[46] To some extent, then, his output was the result of a collaborative effort.

Hemingway was a dedicated reviser of his own texts, and he tended to work slowly. He claimed that he took only six weeks to produce a draft of *The Sun Also Rises*, but this rhythm was not typical.[47] In any case, this estimate was a recollection long after the event, and Hemingway's memory may have exaggerated his speed at the time. Usually, unlike the crime writers to be discussed in later chapters who produced in bulk and at high speed, he insisted on producing small doses of high quality. The typescript of *The Old Man and the Sea*, for example, was composed between March and May 1951. Hemingway often inscribed word counts at the bottom of each page, and, over the sixty-four days he spent on this story, he averaged between only two and three pages per day.[48] He vigorously defended this snail-like pace, protesting to Maxwell Perkins at Scribner's in 1940:

> Worked good last week. Have averaged over five hundred words a day for last 17 days including saturdays and sundays [...] You know there are pricks who are impressed by length. I'll never forget Sinclair Lewis calling To Have etc. [*To Have and To Have Not*] a "thin screaming of only 67,000 words!" May have the number of words wrong. He himself writes a hoarse scream of never less than 120,000. But if I wrote as sloppily and shitily as that freckled prick I could write five thousand words a day year in and year out. My temptation is always to write too much. I keep it under control so as not to have to cut out crap and re-write. Guys who think they are geniuses because they have never learned to say no to a typewriter are a common phenomenon. All you have to do is get a phony style and you can write any amount of words.[49]

He told Perkins later that 400 to 500 words were his daily objective. He aimed to distil the very best essence of his own writing. He told Scott Fitzgerald, "I write one page of masterpiece to ninety one pages of shit. I try to put the shit in the Waste-basket."[50] Hemingway wrote "masterpieces," whereas inferior competitors, like André Malraux, wrote "masterpisses."[51]

Hemingway lived a dangerous life and suffered a series of injuries from accidents, car crashes, and plane crashes, some of them possibly alcohol-related. In 1931, when he was incapacitated by a broken arm, his second wife, Pauline Pfeiffer, offered to take dictation, but Hemingway declined. Anything meant to be read by the eye, he insisted, had to be written by hand and then checked by both eye and ear.[52] His text could of course be checked by eye and ear at the revision stage, but Hemingway replied here as a purist who wanted to control his own original work on the page. He changed his mind later in life, because in 1949 he hired a secretary, Juanita Jensen, from the American Embassy in Havana. When he discovered that she was not at all shocked when he dictated four-letter expletives, he continued the dictation experiment with gusto.[53] In fact, he described his recorder as one of the greatest inventions since penicillin.[54]

Hemingway himself was a dedicated typist who worked on his machine to prepare drafts and his correspondence. In 1939, he posed for some photographs with his Underwood outside the Idaho lodge where he was writing *For Whom the Bell Tolls*.[55] They make a change from the more macho image of the gun-toting Hemingway on big game safaris, which later nourished his public persona. It is not clear for how long Hemingway favoured *plein air* typing. When George Plimpton went to interview him in 1963, he discovered that Hemingway customarily typed standing up at his bookcase.[56] "Writing and travel broaden your ass if not your mind," he wrote in 1950, "and I like to write standing up."[57] He was a very self-conscious typist, constantly referring to his machine as he wrote on it, usually in order to curse it. "Pardon the rotten typewriter," he wrote to his mother, "it's a new one and stiff as a frozen whisker."[58] He called it "the mill," writing in 1922, "Your screed had dragged me to the mill from a bed of pain and I mill like a wild thing."[59] This suggests that his typewriter represented hard labour, but he could nevertheless be a playful typist on occasion, using the "£" and "@" keys for fun in a letter to Dorothy Connable, simply because they were there and had never been used before.[60] He often apologized for the aged machine he was using, the faintness of the ribbon or some other difficulty as he struggled with what he called "the malignancy of the machine."[61]

Occasionally, these problems produced spelling errors or other inaccuracies. Unlike the modernist poets, Hemingway did not make many deliberate mistakes. "I am not trying to pull an ezra on you with fancy spellings," he assured Guy Hicock.[62] Similarly, he told painter Waldo Pierce that his eyes were bad, and if there were errors in his letter he was "not trying to pull a Joyce."[63] He occasionally made up his own words (JezooChrise), and he often wrote in a telegram style, omitting the personal pronoun "I." He repeatedly called himself a "bum typist," and for most of the time he saw the typewriter as a hostile object, but the machine was indispensable to him for correspondence, reporting, and creative work.

The modernist avant-gardes tried to encapsulate different sensory experiences in their poetry. They experimented with ways to represent sound, whether the fury of battle or the discordant confusion of a fairground. When they theorized about their multi-media experiments, they compared poetry to a musical score. The spaces and pauses were precisely calibrated to create poems that looked like diagrams, and they relied on mechanical printing to achieve the desired degree of accuracy. Pound thumped his typewriter with excessive energy, and Hemingway struggled with its "malignancy," but they all took it for granted. They were immersed in new printing technology. Like the jazz piano and the machine gun, the typewriter played its part in the orchestra of modernity.

With the help of the typewriter, the writers considered here achieved a more economical style. The futurists waged war against unnecessary adverbs, while Ezra Pound tried to eliminate all that was superfluous in his verse. The highly condensed Japanese haiku was one of his models (although, of course, seventeenth-century haiku were not typed). Eliot spoke of the typewriter's staccato influence on his style, and Hemingway produced terse, uncomplicated sentences, possibly influenced by his journalism. The machine was inseparable from their creative work.

Several different machines were used to draft Eliot's *The Waste Land* and any single Hemingway novel. Nevertheless, all authors had their own personal relationship with their machine. The typewriter could become a very individualized instrument. Many writers felt that it alienated them from their text, but for cummings the typed poem was profoundly personal and organically grown. He spoke explicitly of his own "typewriter language." The real distortion came later, when the publishers sent his text to the printer, and all his idiosyncratic spellings, spacing, and punctuation were threatened by the homogenizing effect of linotyping and line justification. In the next chapter, a different response is examined, in which authors felt that typing destroyed the same organic connection with their writing that cummings valued so highly, as the typewriter created a distance between authors and their texts.

5 The Distancing Effect: The Hand, the Eye, the Voice

"I, the Undersigned"

There is a curious document in my family archive: it is the deed poll by which, in 1938, my late father, then aged seventeen, changed his name from Edward Silverman to Edward Lyons. The reasons why he did so are still debated in the family, but they do not directly concern us here. The document itself, however, is of interest. It is curious because it carries my father's two signatures, one neatly inscribed beneath the other. In order to validate the deed and to surrender his previous identity, he signed first with his "old" name. To accept his newly chosen self, he signed again with his new name: one person, two signatures, two identities. The act of signing in itself enabled his self-transformation. That moment when he wrote his new signature was the moment that changed his legal identity and made it effective. This example vividly illustrates what Béatrice Fraenkel meant when she argued that the signature is a performative act, just as it also makes clear the close association between an individual identity and his or her handwritten signature.[1] The word "hand" is of course used to signify a part of the body, but it is also used to refer to the writer's handwriting; one wrote in a neat hand, in a legible hand, and above all, one wrote "in one's own hand." Handwriting was an organic extension of the body, and it defined the person.

Typewriter usage must be seen in connection with what it partially superseded – writing by hand. Today the personal handwritten signature is being replaced (or already has been replaced) by fingerprinting, personal identification numbers, electronic signatures, and iris recognition, but the autograph was once the most banal method of recording an individual's presence. Fraenkel has expertly examined how the personal signature first developed in the royal and papal chancelleries of the High Middle Ages to become an accepted sign of identity and of validation.

In sixteenth-century Europe, it began to replace seals and other identificatory signs, like crosses, drawings, and heraldic emblems.[2] Gradually the idea became accepted that the signature was reproducible and therefore that it could be recognized by others as the authentic emanation of a particular individual (although handwriting experts could sometimes be mistaken, as they were in the Dreyfus Affair, when failure to detect a forgery resulted in the imprisonment of an innocent man). Signatures are rooted in the here and now: they come with a specific date and place, and often they are witnessed by others, who in turn inscribe their own marks "in their own hands," all of which can give the act of signing a solemn and ceremonial dimension. The author's hand identified his or her presence, validated a transaction, or authenticated a document. The hand itself was the expression of the self in action.

The typewriter potentially undermined the individuality of personal handwriting. Media theorist Friedrich Kittler argued that the typewriter produced textual anonymity, removing the personal "hand" of the writer. He explicitly traced an evolutionary connection between the typewriter and the printing press, both, in his view, reducing the element of human agency in the writing process.[3] Kittler's view was exaggerated and short-sighted. Like the futurists, he overstated the power of the machine. The widespread availability of the typewriter by no means made handwriting obsolete, any more than the advent of the printing press destroyed scribal culture. Instead, writers adapted each technique at their disposal for different purposes and applied each writing technology to specific phases of composition. According to Kittler, different communication technologies (the cinema, the phonograph, the typewriter) generate their own "discourse networks."[4] The purpose of this chapter is to examine the interrelationships between them. The connections between sight, sound, and text were changed by the typewriter and also by the growing practice of dictation. In examining the interplay between technologies and literary culture, we must assess the varying contributions of the hand, the eye, the machine, and the voice to the creative process.

The typewriter opened up a new distance between the author and the text. German typewriter manufacturer Angelo Beyerlin described this process of disembodiment in detail, thus:

> In writing by hand, the eye must constantly watch the written line and only that. It must attend to the creation of each written line, must measure, direct, and, in short, guide the hand through each movement. For this, the written line, particularly the line being written, must be visible. By contrast, after one presses down briefly on a key, the typewriter creates

in the proper position on the paper a complete letter, which not only is untouched by the writer's hand but is also located in a place entirely apart from where the hands work.[5]

As this chapter will show, many writers experienced a shock when they first faced their own text on the typed page. Some admitted to a *frisson* of anxiety, as there was no longer any immediately visible sign that they were the unique owners of the text they had produced on the machine. The typewriter was responsible for disconnecting eye, hand, and text, and a few were disturbed by the depersonalization of the text imposed by the machine.

The writers discussed in this chapter implicitly assumed a fundamental dichotomy between body and machine, the organic and the mechanical, the personal and the inanimate. They encountered the typewriter as a hostile apparatus, and they struggled against its metallic bulk and its firm resistance. "Keyboards have always intimidated me," Paul Auster admitted.[6] New Zealand author Katherine Mansfield often gave her work to Mattie Putnam, her father's secretary, to be typed, promising in 1907 to "conquer my fox machine if I die in the effort!" The typewriter she was failing to dominate was her American-made Fox Standard, and the fact that she was still sending work to professional typists a few years later suggests that she consistently failed to get the better of it.[7] Only much later did she regularly use her own Corona. The many jokes that circulated about the limited competence of "hunt-and-peck" typists also implied a widespread sense of awkwardness on the machine. Joseph Bailey, television writer and contributor to *Sesame Street*, spoke of himself as a "Biblical typist," meaning that his method amounted to "Seek and Ye Shall Find," and he experienced writing scripts on his IBM as "murder." Hank Nuwer, a contributing editor to *Oui* magazine, described himself candidly as a "hunt and hope" typist, capable of producing 250 wpb (words per beer can). "I have a Royal manual," he said, "and when I punch the keys, they punch me back."[8] Consider American novelist Jack London's account of his exhausting encounters with an early model Blickensderfer, borrowed from his brother-in-law:

> That machine was a wonder. I could weep now as I recollect my wrestlings with it. It must have been a first model in the year one of the typewriter era. Its alphabet was all capitals. It was informed with an evil spirit. It obeyed no known laws of physics, and overthrew the hoary axiom that like things performed to like things produce like results [...]
>
> The keys of that machine had to be hit so hard that to one outside the house it sounded like distant thunder or some one breaking up the

furniture. I had to hit the keys so hard that I strained my first fingers to the elbows, while the ends of my fingers were blisters burst and blistered again. Had it been my machine I'd have operated it with a carpenter's hammer [...]

The worst of it was that I was actually typing manuscripts at the same time as I was trying to master that machine. It was a feat of physical endurance and a brain storm combined.[9]

Mark Seltzer talks of the "radical entanglement" of body with machine, but, in London's case, the encounter rather resembles the violent crashing of waves against immovable rocks.

Yet, as Seltzer has stressed, the dividing line between the breathing, pulsating human being and the cold, silent machine was becoming blurred in the early twentieth century.[10] Taylorist principles of scientific management increasingly treated workers as bloodless machines whose actions could be scientifically analysed, measured, and "programmed" to achieve the most cost-effective results. Bodies and machines were becoming "radically entangled," as people became "mechanized" and defined as operating parts within expanding but soulless organizations. Razor blade tycoon King Gillette described workers as "cogs in the machine, acting in response to the will of a corporate mind as fingers move and write at the direction of the brain."[11] Gillette thus drew a stark parallel between mechanical work and the act of writing.

A number of writers appreciated the intimate connection between body and machine and revelled in the close rapport they experienced with their typewriter in action. This more romantic view of the typewriter will be further examined in the next chapter. In what follows here, the main focus is on those who were primarily impressed by the typewriter's distancing effect. Some tried to counteract this effect and restore something of the fluency they wished to maintain in the composition process. One of these was Henry James, whom I will discuss in this chapter as an example of an author who dictated his novels to typists. Through dictation, he hoped to recover some of the automatic flow of literary composition and defeat the alienating effect of the typewriter. Before turning to James's working methods, I will present evidence from many different writers to illustrate the new discipline imposed by the typewriter.

A New Objectivity

Responses to the typewriter were never uniform. For all those writers who drafted their texts first by hand and then later typed out a fair copy, there were just as many who preferred to type a first draft and subsequently correct it by hand, leaving someone else – presumably a publisher's copy editor – to decipher the mixture afterwards. Belgian writer and film director François Weyergans was one of the latter. "I quite like to type on the machine first of all," he said, "and rewrite by hand afterwards. I prefer to type stupidities on the machine first, then correct in longhand then retype on the machine."[12] When Australian novelist Xavier Herbert submitted the revised manuscript of his novel *Capricornia* (1938), it was a "patchwork of typed and handwritten pages," according to his biographer.[13] Herbert had been condensing a million-word epic, and the script showed all the signs of cutting and pasting, and revisions made in different media at different stages. Herbert evidently composed both in longhand and with typewriter.

Private correspondence in particular seemed to demand handwriting, since it was conceived as an individual, personal form of communication and not normally intended for publication. A few writers felt a residual guilt about typing personal letters: what was gained in legibility was lost in terms of intimacy. Australian author Miles Franklin started using a typewriter for her personal correspondence as well as her professional work in 1912. She apologized to her friend Eve O'Sullivan for sending a typed letter from Chicago: "I wonder [...] if you will forgive me for writing with the machine. I hope so for I never write with anything else now, but as I write my personal letters on my own machine it is just as private as if I wrote by pen. I keep two machines one is in my office and one in my bedroom and if I get away anywhere that I have to use a pen I feel aggrieved."[14] She continued to be on the defensive about writing personal letters on a typewriter in a later letter to Rose Scott:

> This has been the end of a series of several great days for me so I will take time and tell you all about it if you will let me write on the machine. I have forgotten all except how to sign my name by hand, and as I have a lame right shoulder writing with a pen is a laborious business with me. As I write myself it is just as personal as a pen. It is not a dictated letter.[15]

Franklin was keen to explain that since she, and not a hired typist, was writing the letter, it was just as authentically personal as handwriting. Her shoulder pain, which made handwriting difficult for her, is a reminder of how the material act of handwriting sometimes called for a physical investment of the body that matched or even exceeded the demands of typing. It required not just the use of a hand and a wrist, but an unnatural body posture, a manual grip, finely judged but continuous pressure on the page, and a simultaneous effort to keep the paper still on the writing surface.

Compared to handwriting, the typewriter imposed a new discipline. It distanced the author from the text in a new way, breaking the organic tie that some writers felt existed between themselves, their hand, their writing implement, and their paper. East German writer Uwe Johnson reported that "the machine-typed characters prevent me from considering what I've written as something as familiar as my own writing."[16] This distancing effect was especially striking with the earliest commercial typewriters, in which the writer typed "blind" because the roller was masked. Since the paper was under cover, writers could not immediately see the text they had composed. Until the first visible-page typewriter was designed by Underwood in 1897, the author had to wait to see the text emerge from the machine.[17] The Australian writer (of New Zealand origin) Jean Devanny told of how she lifted the cover after every two or three words to see how she was progressing.[18] This invisibility implied an unprecedented disengagement of the writer from the text.

Dislocation was complete when the text actually *did* appear, five or six lines later. It was tidy and standardized, fit for immediate duplication, often shocking in its neatness and regularity. "It don't muss things or scatter ink blots around," Mark Twain had characteristically remarked.[19] Every line was uniformly straight and its size completely regular, and the spaces between each character were absolutely identical. Of course, the writer could not yet change the font or font size, and lines could not be centred or right-justified; nor could the typewriter spell check.[20] Still, mechanical production removed traces of the text's idiosyncratic human origins. To Martin Heidegger, the typewriter effaced the presence of the writer.[21]

Typewritten text acquired a new objectivity, which could create anxiety. German novelist Hermann Hesse bought his first typewriter in 1908, and he appreciated the fact that it put much less strain on his wrists than writing longhand. At the same time, he was disturbed by the immediate confrontation with his own writing in print, noting, "the coldness of type, which starts to look like printer's proofs, means that you come face to face with yourself in a severe, critical, ironic, even hostile way. Your writing turns you into something alien and forces you to make a critical judgement."[22] In manuscript form, he suspected that his work appeared better than it really was, but there was no hiding from the truth of the typed page. It forced him to approach his own texts as a distant other, casting a more ruthless eye over a text he might previously have treated with greater self-indulgence. A handwritten text could seem comforting and familiar, but the impersonality of type destroyed the narcissistic effect resulting from too much intimacy with one's own handwriting.

The act of typing gradually imposed a phase of correction and reformulation, as the text was put into more publishable form. A typescript seemed to make blemishes and mistakes glaringly conspicuous. This is what Isaac Pitman's typewriter manuals called "the candour of the typewriter."[23] Australian poet Les Murray composed first in his head or by hand, but then typing intervened, as he explained to his interviewer: "One more retype the next day will often solve hiatuses and infelicities you didn't even realize were there. Misgivings, too. Sometimes only the appearance of near-finality will let you see something's wrong in a poem and that it needs recasting. You've been too hotly in the aura of it to notice, perhaps."[24] This "near-finality" of the typed text was presumably what the French writer Serge Doubrovsky called, apologizing for the oxymoron, its "provisionally definitive status."[25] Paul Auster finds the task of retyping work tedious but worthwhile, commenting that "[t]yping allows me to experience the book in a new way [...] I call it 'reading with my fingers,' and it's amazing how many errors your fingers will find that your eyes never noticed. Repetitions, awkward constructions, choppy rhythms. It never fails. I think I'm finished with the book and then I begin to type and I realize there's more work to be done."[26] Forcing himself to retype was ultimately rewarding.

Correcting a typed text posed challenges. The typewriter was never suitable for complicated corrections, like moving a paragraph, or expanding or moving a sentence. Minor errors could be obliterated by typing an "X" over the mistake, or by erasing text with Tipp-Ex or dabbing on erasing fluid. But Tipp-Ex left a white mark, and erasing fluid, if not carefully manipulated, tended to overflow into adjacent letters. Many writers responded to the challenge of correctability by attaching new text to their pages. They pasted, stapled, or pinned new sections or half-pages over the originals, greatly increasing both the thickness of the document and its improvised look. A few were encouraged by the aura of completeness of the typed text to try to produce the most perfect version possible, even if this implied many retypings until an error-free text was achieved. Michel Butor, French author of *Le nouveau roman*, confessed that some pages of his books had been retyped fifty times over in order to eliminate all blemishes.[27] Similarly, French writer and poet Bernard Noël strove to type text bearing no trace of any mistakes or corrections. Pages with errors had to be discarded, and then, he said, "I stand before a distant thing, distant from me, in which no hand has intervened, where it has left no trace [...] When I write on the machine, I cross things out mentally, so it's invisible."[28] Whether the writing was hyper-corrected, as in these examples, or it appeared as a rough first draft, it produced an "exteriorization" of the text, removing it from the close, personal motion of the writer's hand.

The typewriter thus forced writers to consider their texts in a new, more critical light. By the 1920s, publishers began to insist on typescript rather than manuscript submission, for reasons of legibility and because of the ease of copying and the enormous costs to be saved on typesetting.[29] In spite of this, some writers could drive their publisher to distraction, including Australian novelist and Nobel Prize winner Patrick White, who produced finely typed crowded pages on almost transparent paper. According to his biographer, White condensed his script in order to save money on postage. For White, too, typing out his novel *Riders in the Chariot* (1961) offered an entirely new perspective. He reported thus on the distancing effect of his portable Olivetti: "One suddenly sees how to unknot situations which eluded one in a handwritten manuscript; yet one could not have launched into a typescript in the beginning – or I couldn't have."[30] The use of the impersonal "one" here was no doubt quite instinctive, but it was entirely appropriate to describe the depersonalizing of the typed text and its separation from its individual creator.

Authors were very conscious that the act of typing transformed their style. Two-finger typing prevented French-Mauritian novelist J.-M.G. Le Clézio from achieving a real flow in composition, but he found this beneficial: "Since I have never managed to type properly, I have to do it, from beginning to end, with two fingers. Also, out of laziness, I end up leaving out words and adjectives, here and there. That's how I improve my style, without wanting to."[31] Kittler claimed something similar for the writing of Kafka's *The Trial* and T.S. Eliot's *The Waste Land*. On the typewriter, Eliot found himself "sloughing off all my long sentences which I used to dote on" and instead writing "short, staccato, like modern French prose."[32] Whether one accepts Kittler's arguments fully or not, there is evidence to suggest that the typewriter could induce a leaner and a sparer literary style. The empire of the machine already extended to shaping prose and poetry themselves.

Henry James

The process of composition was very important to Henry James, who relied heavily on his Remington, even though he preferred not to use it himself. He wrote in a language he called "Remingtonese" and found the clicking sound of the Remington reassuring. When, on his deathbed, he famously called for a Remington to be brought into the room, it was to hear its comforting sound, not to use it himself.[33] Most of what we know about James's later writing practices was recorded by his long-time amanuensis, Theodora Bosanquet, who wrote a memoir about her experience and had literary ambitions of her own, which she fulfilled after James's death.[34]

James had a regular writing routine, which varied a little depending on where he was living. He would write in the mornings before breakfast, then have a mid-morning lunch and then write again for up to five or six hours. After that, he would make social calls, go out on a gondola if he was in Venice, have an ice cream in a café if he was in Siena, or perhaps go for a cycle ride in Kent. After dinner, he would read and answer correspondence.[35] After the death of both his parents in 1881, James moved permanently to Europe and eventually settled in Lamb House in Rye. James kept in touch with his relatives in and around Boston, but his European orientation is well known. His Europe, however, was very circumscribed. It was effectively limited to London and the South Coast of England, Paris, Rome, Florence, and Venice. Rye remained his base, where he would dictate in the mornings in the Garden Room, "striding incessantly up and down the room," as fellow novelist Edith Wharton remembered, and go out for a walk in the afternoon.[36] It was here that most of his later work took shape.

The Portrait of a Lady (1881) had made James famous, but he was never a best-selling author. His attempts in the 1890s to make a name as a playwright failed. He composed fiction too slowly for commercial success. It was another five years after *The Portrait of a Lady* before he published another major novel (*The Princess Casamassima* and *Bostonians*, both in 1885–6). In the meantime, James relied on fees for book reviews and short pieces for periodicals like *Scribner's Magazine*, *Cornhill Magazine*, and the *Atlantic Monthly*. In the 1880s, James had used professional typists for particular copying jobs, but it is not clear whether or not he used a typewriter himself.[37] He certainly maintained a voluminous correspondence throughout his life, especially with his brother William and other family members in Massachusetts. As he composed *What Maisie Knew* in 1897, he experienced a recurrence of the wrist pain that had afflicted him at least once before in 1890. On these occasions, he could produce only "rudely-formed cuneiform characters," as he told Grace Norton.[38] He bought a typewriter and hired a stenographer. His first clerk, William McAlpine, had been a shorthand reporter before working part-time for James. James dictated letters to McAlpine, who took them down in shorthand. But James found this was too time-consuming, and he began to dictate directly to the typist, eliminating the intermediate shorthand phase. He was embarrassed to send typed letters and apologized to his friends for their "fierce legibility."[39] This was his way of recoiling from the typewriter's distancing effect. Indeed, James preferred to keep the typewriter literally at a distance, and to establish more fluent production by means of dictation.

James continued to use both longhand and occasional typing to compose letters. Burne-Jones's portrait of James, which now hangs in Lamb House in Rye, shows him in 1894 using a quill. This was a painterly affectation, since James used a pen for personal letters. By 1898, he was complaining that he was "reduced" to dictating letters to his typist. He wrote to Charles Eliot Norton: "Many people, I think, in these conservative climes, take it extremely ill to be addressed in Remingtonese. They won't, in short, have a typewritten letter on any terms; and that very mature child of nature, my old friend Rhoda Broughton, assured me the other day that if I should presume to send *her* one, she would return it to me indignantly and unopened."[40] Typing destroyed intimacy, but, in order to fulfill all his commitments, James had to resort to the use of the "cold-blooded characters" produced on the Remington.[41]

William McAlpine worked for James for three years, but the author wanted something more. "My pressing want," he wrote to his brother William in 1898, "is some sound, sane, irreproachable young type-writing and bicycling 'secretary-companion,' the expense of whom would be practically a hundred-fold made up by increase and facilitation of paying work. But though I consider the post enviable, it is difficult to fill. The young typists are mainly barbarians – and the civilized, here, are not typists."[42] In 1901, he approached Miss Petherbridge's secretarial bureau, hoping they could provide him with a woman typist who would cost less than McAlpine. His brief was a demanding one: he wanted someone prepared to live in Rye and accept all the limitations that implied. He hired Mary Weld, daughter of a British judge in India, educated at Cheltenham Ladies' College and finishing school in Berlin.[43] Between 1901 and 1904, he would dictate *The Ambassadors*, *The Wings of the Dove*, and *The Golden Bowl* to Weld.

For the well-educated Mary Weld, the work resembled drudgery. She wrote that *The Wings of the Dove* required 194 days of dictation, and the fact that she counted them all suggests that, although she would later compliment James, she did not always enjoy them.[44] Neither McAlpine nor Weld had a good understanding of what they were typing. James composed *The Turn of the Screw* with the intention of frightening the reader, but, according to James, McAlpine had been completely unresponsive: "I might have been dictating statistics. I would dictate some phrase that I thought was blood-curdling: he would quietly take this down, look up at me and in a dry voice, say 'What next?'"[45] Typists, as we saw in chapter 3, were trained to dissociate themselves from the content they were typing, and apparently McAlpine had no difficulty in making himself impervious to James's text. As for Weld, she was far from being a fan of Henry James. She confessed in her diary that the only thing of his that she had ever read was *What Maisie Knew*, and that she had never discovered exactly what it was that Maisie *did* know.[46] While James was on a trip to the United States in 1904–5, Weld got married and left her employment. "Among the faults of my previous amanuenses," James later told Theodora Bosanquet, " – not by any means the *only* fault – was their apparent lack of comprehension of what I was driving at."[47]

Not until 1907 did James find twenty-seven-year-old Bosanquet – his third amanuensis and the one who best met the author's needs. Or perhaps *she* found him. Bosanquet, like Weld, had been educated at Cheltenham Ladies' College and worked at Petheridge's secretarial bureau, specializing in indexing. She was working on an index for the Report of the Royal Commission on Coast Erosion in the bureau's office (a task that sounds prosaic in the extreme) when she overheard something much more interesting going on nearby: chapters of *The Ambassadors* were being dictated. Bosanquet followed up on this, discovered that James was looking for an assistant, and secured employment as his typist, but only after she had spent time practising on a Remington, the author's favoured machine. Although she found her first interview with James overwhelming, she "wanted nothing but to be allowed to go to Rye and work his typewriter."[48] When he hired her, James presented her with a brand new Remington. She was not a stenographer, but this was no handicap, since James by now preferred to dictate directly to a typist. James was very happy with her efforts and called her the "Remington priestess."[49] He told his brother he had found

> [a] new, excellent amanuensis [...], a young, boyish Miss Bosanquet, who is worth all the other (females) that I have had put together and who confirms me in the perception, afresh – after eight months without such an agent – that for certain, for most kinds of diligence and production, the intervention of the agent is, to my perverse constitution, an intense aid and a true economy! There is no comparison![50]

She, at least, would not be dismissed as a "barbarian," as James had stigmatized the typing race in general. Bosanquet remained with James until his death (and, indeed, kept in contact with him beyond the grave).

Henry James relied on his typewriter, but, by dictating his novels to a typist, he compensated for the sudden shock that the machine's "fierce legibility" could produce. If the typewriter brought about an unravelling of the organic connection between hand, eye, and text, James tried to recover lost fluency by composing with his voice. As Seltzer expressed it, "[i]f the typewriter [...] *dis*articulates the links between mind, eye, hand and paper, these links are *re*articulated in the dictatorial orality that 'automatically' translates speech into writing."[51] This claim could apply to Henry James. He employed Bosanquet from 1907 onwards to type to his own dictation. Most of his later novels (after *The Ambassadors* in 1903) were dictated to Bosanquet in the Garden Room at Lamb House, where James lived between 1898 and his death in 1916.[52] James did not refer to a rough draft – he composed precisely and deliberately as he strolled up and down the room, verbally indicating commas and full stops and spelling out difficult words to Bosanquet. "The slow stream of his deliberate speech played over me without ceasing," she wrote.[53] James, who was spurred into action by the click of the Remington, could now compose only by dictation, producing prose with what McLuhan called "a free, incantatory quality."[54] He needed the typewriter's clatter in the background: when he temporarily exchanged his Remington for a much quieter Oliver, his inspiration dried up.[55]

Even the plans he designed for his novels were "talked out," as Bosanquet made clear in her diary; in other words, James wrestled with problems aloud, and the typist recorded these verbal notes.[56] There were many pauses during his dictation, and James warned his typists that they should find some means of occupying themselves during his hiatuses. McAlpine would smoke; Weld had her crocheting; Bosanquet read a book, which James would sometimes comment on.[57] Weld waxed lyrical about the musical quality of James's dictating voice: "He dictated beautifully. He had a melodious voice and in some way he seemed to be able to tell if I was falling behind. Typewriting for him was exactly like accompanying a singer on the piano." His long sentences "seemed to spread out across the page like the beautiful and rambling architecture of this medieval town."[58] The rambling could be a problem, but for Weld, it was a "wonderful experience," and any hesitation of speech was entirely absent in James's fluent delivery.[59]

Although James was hyper-conscious of the intermediary who stood (or sat) between himself and the finished text, he had an unusual problem. As he carefully fashioned his sentences, the practice of verbal composition held an inherent temptation for him. He tended to take diversions and add interpolations. He liked to embroider the narrative too much for his own liking. "I know," he once confessed to Bosanquet, "that I'm too diffuse when I'm dictating."[60] Dictation encouraged him to digress and to overqualify statements and descriptions. It facilitated literary flourishes; it generated circumlocutions and repetitions, as in oral speech; it spawned the more frequent use of colloquial expressions, such as "so to speak" or "as it were." As James orally revised his complete works for their New York edition, the text gained fluency but lost some tautness as it increasingly resembled conversational prose. His style became "more and more like free, involved, unanswered talk," in Bosanquet's account, and James explained to her that the text was "much more effectively and unceasingly *pulled* out of me in speech than in writing."[61] Matthew Schilleman examined a passage in detail from *Four Meetings* (which had first appeared in *Scribner's Monthly* in 1877) and estimated that, when James revised it by dictation, it tripled in length.[62]

To achieve brevity, he needed to write silently by hand. Plays and short stories, which had to be finished by a certain deadline or kept within certain word limits, had to be drafted this way. If he started dictating them, the short story was likely to become a novella and grow into what *Harper's Monthly Magazine* would consider an unpublishable length. For example, one story entitled "The Pupil" was rejected by *Atlantic Monthly* in 1890, probably because it was too long. James protested to the editor, Horace Scudder, that he had "boiled it down repeatedly" but repentantly promised to work "back to an intenser brevity" in future.[63] James was one of the most typewriter-conscious novelists of his age. He found the process of dictating to a typist conducive to his concern for formal prose construction, reaching for the exquisite production of "affect" in his readers. Unlike Le Clézio and others already mentioned, however, he did not use the typewriter to achieve a more economical style. On the contrary, dictation led his prose on unforeseen and over-expansive detours. Psychologist Howard Gardner has analysed different cognitive styles of dictation and identified wordiness as one of them.[64] Dictation, Gardner realized, enabled faster output, and created closer synchrony between thought and word, but it had disadvantages. Among them he listed the dictator's difficulty in estimating the length of the text, and the tendency toward colloquial and repetitive language. This accurately describes James's style in dictation to Bosanquet.

James was dictating, Fabio Vericat suggests, from an imaginary text, although when he revised his works for the New York edition, he was dictating from and elaborating on a previously published text.[65] James' technique made it clear that both reading and writing were verbal performances. Even for the silent reader, the text has a rhythm and a "sound." As a dictator, James was fully aware of the acoustic properties of his own writing.

Theodora Bosanquet proved to be much more than a mere scribe. She also acted as James's editor when the need arose. For example, in 1916 she revised part of his preface to Rupert Brooke's *Letter from America*, because a libel suit was threatening over it, just at the moment when James was incapacitated by his first stroke. The fact that she carried out this task successfully implies that she knew his style well and was quite able to reproduce it convincingly in his absence.[66] After his death, she again ventriloquized James's posthumous voice during her experiments with psychic research and "automatic writing." Bosanquet had literary ideas of her own and began her publishing career after James died. She hoped for a post-mortem relationship in which James would recognize her own abilities.

The typewriter played a crucial role in Henry James's creative process. It influenced not just how he worked but the style in which he wrote. He always preferred longhand for private correspondence, but he needed to find other methods to accelerate production of the reviews, articles, short stories, and prefaces that guaranteed him an income – the writing he called his "mercenary" writing. As he relied increasingly on his Remington, he avoided the distancing effect of the typewriter by resorting to oral composition. Revisions, too, consisted of oral interpolations into an earlier draft. He would not be taken aback, as Hermann Hesse had been, by the cold formality of typed prose. Instead, dictation renewed a close bond between his mind and the text. It gave him more fluency, even if he paid for this in terms of verbosity. Helped by the medium of his typist/editor, he aspired to a closer, more natural bond with the final version of his work.

The Return of the Voice

The move made by several twentieth-century authors toward dictation was a return to ancient and medieval practices of composition, after centuries in which oral reading had declined and writers lost the use of their voice in the creative act. Before these interesting trends developed in the Middle Ages, reading aloud and dictation were the norms. The "author" was the person who uttered the text; that individual spoke to a "writer," who was the one who actually held the writing instruments. Classical dictation, however, had drawbacks, as the first-century Roman rhetorician and pedagogue Quintilian explained:

> From my disapprobation of carelessness in writing, it is clearly enough seen what I think of the fine fancy of dictation; for in the use of the pen, the hand of the writer, however rapid, as it cannot keep pace with the celerity of his thoughts, allows them some respite; but he to whom we dictate urges us on, and we feel ashamed at times to hesitate, or stop, or alter, as if we were afraid to have a witness of our weakness. Hence it happens, that not only inelegant and casual expressions, but sometimes unsuitable ones, escape us, while our sole anxiety is to make our discourse connected; expressions which partake neither of the accuracy of the writer nor of the animation of the speaker; while, if the person who takes down what is

dictated, prove, from slowness in writing, or from inaccuracy in reading, a hindrance, as it were, to us, the course of our thought is obstructed, and all the fire that had been conceived in our mind is dispelled by delay, or, sometimes, by anger at the offender [...] In short, to mention once for all the strongest argument against dictation, privacy is rendered impossible by it; and that a spot free from witnesses, and the deepest possible silence, are the most desirable for persons engaged in writing, no one can doubt.[67]

In spite of this rather tortuous translation, Quintilian's opinion is clear. He felt that dictating to a writer might encourage undue speed, which in turn could produce sloppy prose. The dictator needed to take care in the presence of the scribe. But the silent, individual work that he envisaged here was highly unusual in his own day.

Scholars claim that, from about the seventh century onwards, individual silent reading became more common and gradually started to rival the communal, verbalized reading that characterized much of monastic life.[68] Silent writing followed in the wake of silent reading. After a process of cultural change that took centuries to complete, private reading and writing became conventional practices in Western culture. They increasingly came to be seen as perfectly compatible with sincere personal devotion and conducive to education and self-development. In more modern times, individual reading and writing are regarded as essential sites of critical thinking. This is not to say that reading aloud disappeared. It has never completely done so, but it became reserved for particular occasions, notably those connected with collective religious worship and middle-class family sociability. Silent reading and private writing, however, became dominant practices.

Although the cultural circumstances of the typewriter century were quite different from those of classical Rome or early medieval Europe, that machine brought about a paradoxical revival of oral communication in the composition of texts. Dictating to another person reintroduced a vocal element into prose. Theodora Bosanquet, always an intermediary between speech and writing, felt that Henry James dictated almost as if he were enacting the dramatic scenes of a fictional drama on stage, with himself taking every role.[69] James, we might say, like Mark Twain before him, was one of the great dictators. Twain had found that dictating to a female typist changed the end result because a female presence deterred him from including a number of profanities. In 1904, he felt that dictation would "save time and language [...] the kind of language that soothes vexation."[70]

In the photo archive of Italian publisher Mondadori is a photo montage of Sicilian playwright Luigi Pirandello at work (figure 5.1).

Figure 5.1. Luigi Pirandello dictating to himself
(Source: agk images/Fototeca Gilardi)

Although the photograph cannot be precisely dated, it was probably taken circa 1930. The photo shows Pirandello sitting and working intently at his Underwood portable. Standing behind him and to his right is another man whose outline is hazy. He overlooks Pirandello's work and points an authoritative index finger at the machine. This second, pointing figure is none other than Pirandello dictating to himself. This contrived montage of "auto-dictation" suggests that, even if a writer worked alone, he might be imagining that he was taking dictation from his own inner voice. Whether real or imaginary, the dictator was turning up everywhere.

Marshall McLuhan welcomed this resurrection of orality. Since the advent of print culture, he argued, human sense perceptions had been thrown into disequilibrium. *Homo typographicus* relied increasingly on sight, while his or her aural and tactile abilities correspondingly shrivelled.[71] Print forced human thinking into linear patterns, as humanity became alienated from its natural sensual self. Humankind, McLuhan argued, needed to rediscover the value of touch and hearing, reconnect with its acoustic potential, and achieve a new reintegration of all the human faculties. If the typewriter could bring the voice back into play, this would be one step in the right direction – that is, McLuhan thought, away from the rigid compartmentalization of eye, ear, and hand, and back to a form of neurological wholeness and harmony.

Unfortunately, McLuhan overstretched his argument in promoting the typewriter's influence. He went so far as to suggest that typed text ordered the reader's pace and rhythm in a new way. He asserted that typed text gave clear indications of where the reader should draw breath and, since each blank space or interval was exactly measured by the machine, the typewriter had quantified "acoustic space." The poetry of e.e. cummings was a good example, according to McLuhan: it used the typewriter to give poetry a musical score. "The typewriter," he concluded, "brought writing and speech and publication into close association."[72]

In practice there is nothing in a text, however punctuated, whether manuscript or typed, that tells its reader exactly where to draw breath. The musical analogy introduced by McLuhan was not illuminating. The musical notation of an orchestral score does not instruct, say, a French horn player how to regulate his or her breathing, just as the pace of any composition is a matter for the conductor's own interpretation. It is a fallacy to assume that any text or musical score is able to impose a fixed interpretation on the reader or musician. Authors' intentions are often thwarted by the autonomy and critical resistance of their readers. We might add a further point: although dictation may adopt some of the informalities of everyday speech, it does not resemble conversation because it does not invite a verbal response. Dictation is always a monologue. As Honeycutt wisely points out, dictation is not speech; rather, it is special form of writing.[73]

Quintilian had mentioned the risk that the author might vent his frustrations on his scribe. And he had concluded that the very presence of a scribe compromised the author's privacy. Henry James, on the other hand, liked to have a typist present as his novel came alive. He commented on his typists' reactions, he took note of what they were doing while he paused for thought, and he seems to have needed the reassuring clicking of their machine in the background as he spoke. Unlike Quintilian, perhaps, he was not nostalgic about lost opportunities to compose in solitude. The situation of such an author entirely changed when new technology mechanized the dictation process. The importance of the voice was not thereby diminished, but it could now be recorded, and Quintilian's hope for authorial privacy could be fulfilled. Dictaphones and transcribing machines removed the necessity for author and typist to be in the same room, or even in the same hemisphere. Mechanization enabled the complete geographical separation of writer and typist.

We can glimpse what this meant in practice by considering the dictation practices of American crime writer Erle Stanley Gardner. Gardner's working methods are considered in much more detail in chapter 9, and here I focus only on his well-documented dictation practices and their problems. Dictating machines enabled Gardner to write as he travelled. When he camped out in the Californian desert, which he loved to do, he recorded text on wax cylinders and posted them by express mail to one of his secretaries in Los Angeles. As technology evolved in the 1950s and 1960s, audograph machines enabled him to record text on small vinyl discs, which could be replayed by his typists on transcribing machines. But there were always technical problems to overcome. Gardner complained, for example, that he could not tell if his recording had been successful or not until the whole recording was played back, which posed problems because, he added, "once a story has been dictated it is thereafter impossible to recapture the spirit."[74] An additional risk was that material could be lost, as happened in 1966, when Gardner realized that "I have dictated a lot of story material which has gone down the drain."[75] He partly solved this problem through the precaution of dictating to two machines simultaneously.

By the 1960s, Gardner was using an IBM dictating machine, which recorded on reusable plastic Time-Master belts (or Dictabelts). The belts cost sixty-five cents each, and each held about fourteen minutes of dictation, producing approximately 340 typewritten lines.[76] It is easy to speculate that these technological arrangements influenced the shape of Gardner's novels. Dictation technology enabled Gardner to write faster, and to draft several stories at once. It completely detached him from the typing process, in which several secretaries typed different novels and stories simultaneously. But alongside the freedom this process gave him came a new subservience to the Time-Master belts. It must have been very tempting to finish a section of a chapter, or a complete chapter, on a single recording belt. Since Gardner was in the habit of giving different discs or belts to different typists at once, it would make sense to finish each one at a natural break in the narrative. If this supposition is correct, the technical means at Gardner's disposal may have influenced the structure of his stories.

Gardner found that dictating at speed imposed a great mental strain. "The nerve strain is," he remarked, "greater [than dictating to shorthand], because a man speeds up his mental process and, in the course of a day, simply turns out more work than would be the case if he were relying on shorthand."[77] In those days, he later remembered, recorded voices were "garbled and mushy," and so the dictator had to make a special effort to pronounce every syllable distinctly. "It was no wonder," he said, "that secretaries faced with these mechanical monstrosities hated their very guts."[78] This is not to overlook the physical strain on Gardner's own voice – he repeatedly suffered from throat problems from the late 1950s onwards.

Clearly, dictation practices had moved on considerably since Henry James's lifetime. Erle Stanley Gardner exploited recording devices and transcription machines to speed up production, but there was a cost for this. It damaged his health, the sound quality was poor, and there was always a danger of losing copy completely. In the speed of composition, Quintilian's warnings about casual and inelegant expressions were not redundant; more likely they were as pertinent as ever. Nor were the changes that technology had brought necessarily the same as those heralded by Marshall McLuhan. Had dictating machines brought writing and speech any closer? In material terms, at least, the physical distance between the author and the typed text was now infinitely extended. But the distance between the author and the text cannot be measured solely in terms of physical mileage; it was also inherent in the author's disconcerted reaction to the transformation of his or her work into impersonal, uniform typing. The authors considered in this chapter registered the cold detachment of the typed text; they knew the anxiety of print. Other authors had a more imaginative or poetic view of their rapport with the machine, and their conceptions will be examined in the following chapter.

6 The Romantic Typewriter

The Romantic Typewriter

Australian novelist Nancy Cato (*All the Rivers Run*, 1958) enjoyed the fluency of typing. "When I get to the typewriter," she said, "it just comes straight out through my fingers."[1] Cato imagined a process in which words flowed naturally through her body into the machine, without any interruption from her own thoughts or any careful premeditation. In stark contrast to what some writers called "banging something out" on the typewriter, Cato envisaged typing as a smooth and seamless operation. She experienced a creative force, which in her imagination she did not entirely control. This sense that the act of writing was not under the writer's conscious control was a characteristic of the romantic typewriter, which I will discuss in this chapter. The phrase "the romantic typewriter" has a double meaning: first, it designates the person who is writing, and second it categorizes his or her romantic vision of how the machine influences the creative process. I refer to "romantic" in this context to denote instinctive and spontaneous composition, in the same way, for instance, that historians discuss the concept of romantic chess.[2] Romantic chess players resemble romantic typewriters because they made their moves by inspiration, favouring speed and sacrificing pieces rather than proceeding through dull positional play or spending time in longer-term strategic planning.

The romantic typewriter operated quite differently from the accentuated textual objectivity achieved by the machine's distancing effect. In fact, they were polar opposites. Whereas the alienated author found that the typewriter encouraged precision, deliberation, and a critical detachment from one's own creation, the romantic typewriter privileged fluency and a more intuitive style of composition. Two authors in particular will be examined to illustrate this romantic association of the machine with a spontaneous form of writing: Enid Blyton and Jack Kerouac. At first sight, they seem an outrageously improbable duo. Blyton, on one hand, was a former Kindergarten teacher and a prim suburban mother who played golf and enjoyed a good game of draughts (checkers). Kerouac, in contrast, lived a bohemian life, wrote under the influence of stimulants, and had many sexual relationships, most of them with women.[3] Blyton was by nature sedentary, while Kerouac was constantly on the move across America or south to Mexico, either by car or hitchhiking. Although they inhabited different worlds, both shared a belief in a spontaneous, uninhibited writing process in which the typewriter played a key role. Typists, as we have seen, were trained to turn themselves into automatons at the keyboard, blocking any conscious thought that might interrupt the transcription process. Blyton and Kerouac turned this imperative for self-effacement into a virtue. For them, creative writing was a romantic project because it released energies buried within themselves. Before considering these two cases, I will briefly discuss the vogue at the turn of the century for "automatic writing."

Automatic Writing

Strange powers could be attributed to the typewriter. In the 1890s, there was a brief obsession with automatic writing – that is, writing produced by the typewriter of its own free will, or possibly through a medium as the result of communication with spirits or an extra-terrestrial being. Researchers locked a typewriter in an empty room to observe how it would respond to invisible stimuli. James Gillespie Blaine, an American politician who died in 1893, enjoyed a posthumous typewritten life. A letter from Blaine, by then deceased, published in the form of a pamphlet in 1896, was allegedly dictated to a Yost typewriter by supernatural forces "independent of all human contact or human presence near the machine. It was done under the supervision of G.W.N. Yost, inventor of the Yost typewriter, on one of his own machines, which was placed in a cabinet that was perfectly dark."[4] Nine folios of correct copy, it was alleged, issued from this self-activating machine every hour. Presumably readers had to stretch their powers of imagination to conceive how the ghostly author not only typed the text but also changed the paper regularly. If they were unduly cynical, they might also wonder how a ghostly script emerging at the rate of nine sheets per hour could, in the physical absence of its author, boil itself down to a short, five-page printed pamphlet.

John Kendrick Bangs's 1899 novella *The Enchanted Type-Writer* also featured "ghostly writing" of this kind. He imagined a voice from Hades communicating with the world of the living through the remote operation of a typewriter. Bangs, however, kept his tongue firmly in his cheek, playing on popular fantasies about ghostly writing for humorous effect. His novel is based on conversations between a narrator and James Boswell (Samuel Johnson's biographer), who acts as a guide and reporter on society news in Hades in his role as editor of the *Stygian Gazette*. The fictional typewriter itself, recently rescued from the narrator's attic and given a thorough overhaul, springs into action in the middle of the night of its own accord. It miraculously reloads itself with paper and enters a dialogue in which it prints answers to the narrator's questions – for example, about facilities for playing golf in hell.[5]

In such fantasies, the typewriter could produce text without the need of a human operator. It was envisaged as a medium between dead authors and living shorthand typists. Louise Owen, as an example, was private secretary to Lord Northcliffe (the owner of the *Daily Mail*, the *Daily Mirror*, and the *Times*) for over twenty years. After his death in 1922, she received messages dictated by him in séances. In his messages to Owen from beyond the grave, Northcliffe expressed support for the League of Nations and hobnobbed with other celebrities and authors. Owen cast herself as the privileged representative of Northcliffe and guardian of his posthumous reputation, and even embarked on futile litigation against the executors of his will – an exploit that, sadly, bankrupted her.[6]

There was increasing scientific interest in the 1890s in telepathy, hypnosis, and "automatic writing" – that is to say, messages dictated to mediums by the dead, recorded either by hand or sometimes on a typewriter. Henry James's brother William as well as James's assistant Theodora Bosanquet were interested in the analysis of such phenomena carried out by the Society for Psychical Research, founded in Cambridge, England, in 1882. After Henry James's death, Bosanquet became an "automatist," receiving James's posthumous dictation to her in a trance. Bosanquet thus transmitted James's desire to begin a new kind of relationship with her after his death, less professional perhaps and more affectionate than it had been during his lifetime, and she also craved his respect for her own career as a writer. Bosanquet went on to publish books in her own right on Paul Valéry and Harriet Martineau, as well as a memoir on James himself, and she acted for many years as the editor of *Time and Tide*. She was a successful "automatist" who was very far from being a passive agent in the literary world.[7] As a typing medium, she did not passively transmit James's words, but channelled them through the filter of her own aspirations.

The magical typewriter was the target of scientific research, but also undoubtedly attracted a number of charlatans. Mark Twain was another who followed up his fascination with telepathy to become a member of the Society for Psychical Research. He wrote in 1884, "I have grown so accustomed to considering that all my powerful impulses come to me from somebody else, that I often feel like a mere amanuensis when I sit down to write a letter under the coercion of a strong impulse: I consider that the other person is supplying the thoughts to me, and that I am merely writing from dictation."[8] Like other romantic typewriters, Twain apparently felt that the source of his creative urge lay somewhere outside himself.

The notion of the magical typewriter, whether exploited by humourists or analysed by scientists, raises the broader question of the agency or passivity of the writer. It suggested the possibility of writing conducted by the machine alone, or at least writing by an absent or invisible author. Perhaps this was not as fanciful as it seems. It corresponded to the way trainee typists were taught to empty their minds. In their case, the intervention of the conscious mind was viewed as a handicap to typing speed and efficiency. Their physical presence was needed, but they were encouraged to be "absent" mentally. The magical typewriter similarly relegated the intellect of the author or medium to a subordinate position: he or she simply received impulses from a remote source and faithfully transmitted them.

In this instinctive writing mode, the typewriter was no longer merely a mechanical prosthetic gadget. Instead, it became an organic limb of the writer's body. Alex Haley, author of *Roots*, sensed that his machine was an important part of his own body when he reported that "I feel the typewriter is an extension of myself, a conduit between my head and the paper."[9] In contrast to the alienating effect encountered in chapter 5, the writer here perceives the typewriter as something fused with himself. The machine is being literally incorporated – it becomes body, transformed into a dynamic and responsive part of the writer's physical being. American writer Maurice Zolotow spoke in similar terms: "By now," he said, "a typewriter is an extension of my arm." He went on to attribute creative power to the machine itself: "When my fingers touch the keyboard it sets off sentences, *almost by itself*."[10] The romantic typewriter was thus "embodied": it was both physically connected to the writer and at the same time credited with autonomous abilities of its own. The same notion of instinctive typing can be further pursued through the two case studies of Enid Blyton and Jack Kerouac.

Enid Blyton's "Undermind"

Enid Blyton was a compulsive writer. "All through my teens," she recalled, "I wrote and wrote and wrote – everything I could think of! Poems, articles, stories, even a novel. I couldn't stop writing and loved every minute of it."[11] Her output, accordingly, was prolific. She is best known for three major series: the Famous Five series, launched in 1942, was aimed at the nine-to-thirteen age group; the Secret Seven series, which began in 1949, targeted eight and nine year olds; while Noddy, who was also born in 1949, catered for an even younger readership. These were only three of the many series of children's books she produced, not to mention her boarding school stories, magazine work, and nature reports. By 1945, she already had 167 titles to her name,[12] and she continued to produce about twenty books per year during the late 1940s. Altogether her output has been estimated at over 800 titles.[13] Only in the late 1950s did her pace slacken. She lost impetus, according to her daughter, when her life became secure, prosperous, and less stressful.[14] By that time, her work had come under attack from librarians and educators, who accused it first of racism and xenophobia and then of sexism. At the same time, commentators castigated her allegedly stunted imagination and limited vocabulary, designed to satisfy but never stretch the horizons of her child readers. Noddy, according to Colin Welch in an article in *Encounter* in 1958, was a "witless, spiritless, snivelling, sneaking doll [in which] the children of England are expected to find themselves reflected."[15] Her plots, suggested another journalist, "make *Beano* read like Tolstoy," referring to a popular children's comic of the 1950s and beyond.[16]

These controversies completely distracted Sheila Ray, who was perhaps Blyton's best biographer,[17] but they deterred neither Blyton nor her readers. She defiantly refused to pay attention to any critic over the age of twelve.[18] Allegations of political incorrectness and stylistic anemia need not detain us here. Blyton's global sales continued to climb, reaching 400 million by the end of the twentieth century, according to her former agent.[19] In 2008, forty years after her death, she was voted Britain's best-loved writer, ahead of Roald Dahl, J.K. Rowling, and Jane Austen.[20] This level of success was partly the result of careful marketing, always controlled by Blyton herself in her lifetime, as she shrewdly used her children's clubs to maintain readers' interest and personally controlled the extensive merchandising surrounding the Noddy brand of toothbrushes, soap, stationery, pyjamas, and other products. Her success also owed a considerable debt to high-quality illustrations, particularly those of the Dutch illustrator Harmsen van der Beek, whose drawings of Noddy and his clique became indelibly identified with the series. By the 1950s, four-colour rotogravure printing could provide vivid colour images to sell Noddy in hardback.

Blyton had a global reach, but she remained a very English author, whose world was effectively circumscribed by the home counties and the Dorset coast where both she and the Famous Five used to go on holiday. She dealt with literally dozens of different publishers, the most important of them being English companies like Hodder and Stoughton, Methuen, Newnes, and Sampson Low. No matter which publisher issued her work, she maintained her personal holograph on the spine. She wrote, moreover, on an English-made Imperial typewriter, using a "Good Companion" model, named after the novel by English writer J.B. Priestley. At first, she used the typewriter of her first husband, Hugh Pollock, and, reversing the conventional pattern, employed him as her typist.[21] But she bought her own machine in 1927 and taught herself to type at speed.[22] By March of that year, she could note in her diary: "Am as quick almost at typing as I was at writing now."[23] She used the machine for all purposes, including responding to her voluminous correspondence from young readers, although she normally preferred to write to them in longhand.[24] By 1930, she was typing so much that she suffered from what she called rheumatism in her right index finger and she was forced to interrupt her frenetic activity at the keyboard.[25]

The typewriter enabled her to maintain a rate of production that was not just prolific but also continuous, and to embrace many different tasks at once. Blyton edited the weekly magazine *Enid Blyton's Sunny Stories* from 1937 to 1952, providing the content for over 800 issues. She then produced the *Enid Blyton Magazine* until 1959, which she wrote single-handedly. The intervening adventures of the Famous Five, the Secret Seven, and the birth of her own two daughters failed to stem the unrelenting flow. According to her agent George Greenfield, Blyton could produce 10,000 words per day, which meant that she was capable of finishing a Famous Five novel within a week.[26] In her autobiography, Blyton claimed that she could write a 60,000-word book in four days if she was locked up in a room with a typewriter and had nothing else to do.[27] Her personal diaries reveal a writing pace that was less extreme than this, but that was nevertheless impressive and consistent. In May 1934, for example, she recorded drafting between 6,000 and 8,000 words per day.[28] She regarded 5,000 or 6,000 words as a very satisfactory daily achievement, but this did not include responding to over 100 readers' letters daily.[29] Even this speed was hard to credit: one disbelieving librarian accused Blyton of using ghost writers, but was pursued in court and forced to make a public apology.[30]

This was the overall context of Blyton's achievements, in which she developed an instinctive or automatic form of writing on the typewriter. Inspiration, she explained, came to her very easily: "Where I am lucky is that I have such easy access to my imagination [...] I do not have to 'wait for inspiration' as so many do. I have merely to 'open the sluice gates' and out it pours with no effort."[31] The ideas for new stories seemed to her to come almost from nowhere, independent of her own volition. They came

> flooding into my mind. I distinguished them from my ordinary thinking. In my ordinary thinking I thought what I wanted to think – but in these "thoughts" I wasn't thinking as usual at all. They seemed to come from somewhere else, not myself.
>
> They were stories, of course. They came as they do now, out of nowhere – out of my imagination, or from my "sub-conscious." Out of whatever or wherever it is that writers, composers and poets get the thoughts and melodies and rhythms that flood into their conscious minds.[32]

Sometimes, the creative impulse seemed to come from outside herself, as she suppressed her own conscious rationality, but often she referred to a subconscious stream of thought emanating from within.

Blyton's conceptualization of her own imaginative processes emerged from her correspondence with a New Zealand psychologist, Peter McKellar of the University of Otago, with whom Blyton exchanged several letters between 1953 and 1957. As she described the sequence of events to McKellar, Blyton "saw" a cinematic image of the scenes she was about to narrate. She wrote, "I shut my eyes for a few minutes, with my portable typewriter on my knee; I make my mind a blank and wait – and then, as clearly as I would see real children my characters stand before me in my mind's eye [...] The story is enacted almost as if I had a private cinema screen there."[33] She could even see, she told McKellar, if one of the characters needed a haircut.[34] Then she would begin, almost automatically, as she described it: "That's enough for me. My hands go down on my typewriter keys and I begin. The first sentence comes straight into my mind, I don't have to think of it – I don't have to think of anything."[35] The rest would unravel "like cotton from a reel."[36]

Blyton's eidetic imagery was multi-dimensional: she claimed it was not merely visual but also enriched by the sound and smell of what she saw in her mental cinema. Blyton, as author, had only to record the image and, for this, the speed of the typewriter was essential. "I am merely a sightseer," she declared, "a reporter, an interpreter, whatever you like to call me."[37] This rather disingenuous disclaimer corresponded to the romantic view of typewriting in which composition was immediate, spontaneous, and innocent of any intellectual effort to structure or plan the outcome. To achieve this, Blyton needed her typewriter: "You want to know about typing – I always type, for quickness, but I can of course write a story by hand just as well. But typing keeps up with my imagination better. The story evolves so quickly when I write a book. I could probably dictate just as well, but I'd have to bother with a machine and records then and that would 'break the spell'!"[38]

Composing on the typewriter in a trance-like state (or under a "spell") was what McKellar called deploying "hypnogenic imagery."[39] Blyton herself referred to reaching into her own "undermind." She professed to need "no fumbling, no planning, no labouring, no agonizing waiting for inspiration. Let me sit down and shut my eyes for two minutes [...] reach down into my 'undermind' – and out flow my characters, complete in every detail, my setting, the adventure, the jokes, the humour, the emotion that colours a story."[40] Her undermind, however, was mobilized only for prose fiction. Poetry demanded a different category of thought, since formal requirements of rhyme and metre had to be met. Her autobiography, too, was certainly not the result of any colourful dream. On the contrary, it was carefully calculated as a publicity exercise to delight and impress her young readership. Writing a play was another genre that engaged a different part of Blyton's brain. She wrote in one diary entry: "Thought out my play," which suggests an exercise far removed from instinctive writing.[41] Romantic typing was confined to composing children's fiction.

Typing in this fashion led Blyton to claim that she never knew in advance how a story was going to develop. "When I begin a completely new book with new characters," she told McKellar, "I have no idea at all what the characters will be, where the story will happen, or what adventures or events will occur."[42] The ideas raced ahead of her, and the typewriter struggled to keep pace. "I am in the happy position," Blyton explained, "of writing and reading a new story at one and the same time!"[43] This style of creativity had its drawbacks. The writing was uncontrolled and unedited. Blyton seemed unable to select and filter elements from her mental cinema screen. The romantic typewriter had only a limited capacity for self-criticism and always tended to produce raw and undigested material.

Furthermore, according to McKellar's theories, the unconscious mind contains a record of past experiences and perceptions. Thus when Blyton summoned her undermind, she was drawing on a data bank of her unconscious memories. The same memories were likely to resurface more than once, with the result that she continually re-fashioned familiar material. At times, therefore, Blyton seemed repetitive or guilty of plagiarising herself. In fact, her data bank of personal memories was not a rich one. She had lived a relatively sheltered life and did not have a wide experience of the world on which to draw. She claimed in her autobiography that "I have been to many countries," but this can be discounted as blarney.[44] In 1930, she had taken a Mediterranean cruise that docked briefly in Lisbon, Madeira, and Casablanca, and she made a short trip to New York in 1948 on the *Queen Elizabeth*, but otherwise her overseas experience was zero. Family holidays in Swanage (Studland Bay) or Bognor Regis were the norm. Born in East Dulwich in suburban London, she lived for many years in the "stockbroker belt" of Buckinghamshire, and this was the cosy but narrow world in which golliwogs roamed the woods and fairies appeared at the bottom of the garden.

It is uncanny, however, that, in spite of the automatic nature of Blyton's fiction writing, and her ability to release stories and characters at a great rate into her typewriter, she still observed exactly the appropriate word limit for the story she was creating. Perhaps there was a certain amount of self-delusion in Blyton's denial that she never planned a story. As David Rudd has pointed out, she needed to know before she started whether she was going to embark on a Famous Five story, a St Clare's story, or a story like *The Faraway Tree*. Some preliminary decisions had to be made, and a minimal amount of information had to be assembled in the author's mind before she could begin.[45] For instance, she presumably had to have a target age group in mind. Blyton, however, firmly resisted the notion that planning a story might help her. This, to her, was a recipe for dull, uninspired work. She envisaged herself as an author responding to forces that she did not consciously control, but she invariably produced stories of just the right length for the occasion. To this extent, she remained a true professional.

She insisted that she had to start with her mind a blank and put aside any conscious thoughts. She could then write in a trance-like state, ignoring any interruptions, which would break the "spell." The typewriter on her lap was essential to achieve the speed and spontaneous flow of writing she was accustomed to produce. This anti-intellectual approach to typing echoed the instructions drummed into young typists throughout the typewriter century. Just as in the case of the romantic typewriter, the intervention of conscious thought might produce inferior work.

Kerouac and His Scrolls

The paradigmatic case of the romantic typewriter at work remains Jack Kerouac on his Underwood Standard. Kerouac despised the painstaking technique and what he called the "craftiness" of writers such as Henry James. Instead, he tried to achieve spontaneity and fluidity of composition, with or without the assistance of drugs. In *The Essentials of Spontaneous Prose*, which he wrote after *On the Road*, he rejected punctuation in sentences "already arbitrarily riddled by false colons and timid usually needless commas."[46] He recommended no pause for thought, no conscious selection of the appropriate expression, but instead "the infantile pile-up of scatological buildup words till satisfaction is gained." He aimed at a furious style of writing, with no agonizing over the structure of each sentence, no endless prose-polishing of the kind often associated with that archetype of fastidiousness, Gustave Flaubert. Kerouac's typing method was to abandon what he called the inhibition of syntax, and to write freely in a trance- or dream-like state. He compared the writer to a jazz saxophonist, who simply blew an improvised section until running out of breath. The ideal to which Kerouac aspired was not always easy for him to achieve. He struggled to get started on his panoramic American novel *On the Road* and made several false starts before eventually unleashing a frenzied torrent of prose.[47]

What is interesting here is that Kerouac could fulfill his vision of spontaneity only on a typewriter. It is clear in *Atop an Underwood*, in which Kerouac discussed his writing apprenticeship, that for him writing and typing became synonymous at a very early age. By the age of eleven, he was using an old typewriter in his father's printing office, and his father's work as an itinerant Linotypist no doubt provided a valuable early introduction to printing technology.[48] At Columbia University, he ran a one-man typing agency and typed the manuscript of a textbook for his French professor.[49] He then foresaw his future life as a fiction writer, inspired by bursts of great passion, fuelled by several packets of cigarettes, even though at this stage he was not even a smoker.[50] As a writer, he spoke of building up momentum, as what he called "the locomotive in his chest" accelerated to full speed.[51] Far from detaching him from his text, Kerouac's typewriter made him "red-hot," sensing "the flow of smooth thrumming power."[52] The speed and spontaneity he could achieve at the keyboard were the means to the true, confessional writing he hoped to produce.

In 1941, Kerouac had his own typewriter – probably a rented machine – which enabled him to write stories at night while he was working in Hartford, Connecticut. At the bottom of each page, he triumphantly typed "jk," a claim of ownership suggesting that, in his case, no discon-nection was perceived between the typed page and the author's hand.[53] In his piece "Today," Kerouac described the anguish he felt when he had to return his rented Underwood because he could not afford to pay for another month. "Hell, they're taking away everything," he wrote. "Even myself." As he descended into poverty, he sacrificed food and cigarettes in order to pay for a typewriter, his priority item. "You see," he wrote, "my heart resides in a typewriter, and I don't have a heart unless there's a typewriter somewhere nearby, with a chair in front of it and some blank sheets of paper."[54] It never seemed to occur to Kerouac that he could write with a pen instead. In 1954, he wrote to Allen Ginsberg that he was "downright incapacitated without a typewriter."[55]

The typewriter (together with stimulants) gave him the discipline to compose from inspiration and at great speed. He was already a "speed typist" (in several senses), with or without Benzedrine ("benny"), am-phetamine, or other stimulants, and his writing aesthetic required speed at all costs. Just as the contestants in the World Typing Championships had been handicapped by the need to stop typing and change their paper, so, too, Kerouac sought a solution to this undesirable interrup-tion to his interminable flow. He found the answer in his typing scrolls. John Clellon Holmes recalled Kerouac's moment of decision, when he announced: "You know what I am going to do? I'm going to get me a roll of shelf paper, feed it into the typewriter, and just write it down as fast as I can, exactly like it happened, all in a rush, to hell with these phony architectures – and worry about it later."[56] Kerouac's typed scroll had an important role in his creative process, and this needs to be elucidated.

Kerouac had been planning his major work *On the Road* since 1948, and according to his biographer he was producing an average of 1,500 words per day in November of that year.[57] To produce a typed version of the whole novel, however, required space, discipline, a typewriter, and some stimulants. In spite of Kerouac's pronouncements about speed, this was not necessarily fast writing: "I will have to get used to writing slower than before," he wrote, "... twice as slow. *On the Road* is rich, moves along richly, with a great deal of depth in every line."[58] Kerouac certainly wanted momentum behind his writing, but he was also keen to capture the details of every experience, every memory, as the journey proceeded. The typed scroll was itself a journey, a fitting symbol of the road trip at the core of the novel. As it rolled out continu-ously from the typewriter, it resembled the unfolding of the road itself under the car's wheels.

In April 1951, he completed a scroll version of *On the Road* (figure 6.1). He told his close friend Neal Cassady that the full draft of 125,000

Figure 6.1. Jack Kerouac's scroll version of *On the Road*
(Source: Wikipedia Commons)

words had taken him three weeks to write out.[59] The scroll contained 120 feet of continuous prose, according to Kerouac's biographer,[60] and this seemed to be confirmed by Beat poet and admirer Allen Ginsberg.[61] The details surrounding this typescript, however, have been disputed. It is not clear what kind of paper Kerouac originally used, and different versions exist of how he put together the enormous scroll he eventually submitted to Viking.[62] According to Ann Charters, he used architects' paper and then taped the sheets of *On the Road* together to make a continuous scroll.[63] In a 1959 television interview, Kerouac himself explained that he had assembled the scroll with tape.[64] The typed text had no margins and no paragraph breaks, but it did have punctuation. In this form, it was unfit to publish.

Kerouac had not assumed that the scroll would be his final version of the text. It was just one stage in the compositional process. As he had told Holmes in the letter quoted above, he wanted to put everything down rapidly on paper "and worry about it later" – a phrase that explicitly foreshadowed later editing and revision. Kerouac wrote to Frank Morley that Harcourt Brace had rejected the manuscript, but Farrar, Straus and Young had reacted to it slightly more warmly. "They didn't altogether reject it," he reported, "but suggested revising. Then when I started revising it, I realized I'd rather write the whole thing all over again, which I'm about to do."[65] Kerouac began rewriting the novel in longhand and then retyping it. He edited it into paragraphs and transferred it to US Letter–size pages.[66] *On the Road* was eventually published by Viking in 1957. It made Kerouac famous.

The technique of scroll typing fulfilled Kerouac's desire to compose instinctively and at speed, uninterrupted by pauses imposed by the need to change the paper in his machine. He needed to write fast and in a sustained burst supported by amphetamines, although he found the effort mentally draining and physically exhausting. The typed scroll, however, was not the final achievement, simply one necessary phase in the writing process. Kerouac's technique was never set in concrete. He continued to experiment with different writing methods. For *Doctor Sax* (1959), which he actually finished in 1952, he combined pencilled notes and taped dictations as well as typing. In this work he developed what he called "wild form," signifying a rupture with traditional linear narrative. He approached the trance-like state of writing that we have already encountered several times in this chapter. "You just have to [...] slap it all down," he wrote, "shamelessly, willy-nilly, rapidly until sometimes I got so inspired I lost consciousness [of what] I was writing."[67]

Kerouac used similar, but not identical, practices to compose *The Subterraneans*, describing an affair and the breakdown of a relationship, written in the heated aftermath of Kerouac's own break-up with Alene Lee. This time he felt closer to the spontaneous style he was seeking. He typed this novel in his mother's kitchen in the space of three all-night sittings in October 1953, aided by amphetamines.[68] His original text used dashes to indicate where the reader should take a breath. Kerouac believed the text should be structured "in rhythms of rhetorical exhalation," and only the typewriter could reproduce the precise breathing rhythm he required.[69] "My prose," he later explained, "is a series of rhythmic expostulations of speech visually separated for the convenience of the reader's eyes by dashes, by vigorous, definite dashes, which can be seen coming as you read."[70] Kerouac's ideas about writing and speech patterns appear to echo McLuhan's dictum about the typewriter heralding a return to orality, except that McLuhan's *Understanding Media* had not yet been published.[71] By the time of his interview with the *Paris Review* in 1968, however, Kerouac was certainly aware of McLuhan's idea.[72]

Kerouac's publisher insisted on revising the punctuation of *The Subterraneans*, although Kerouac strenuously objected. Inserting commas and full stops broke up the continuous flow of the text and ruined Kerouac's stated attempt to write a story as though it were being casually told by someone in a bar. He attacked the idea of publishers' revisions in themselves: "Well, look," he later explained to the interviewer for the *Paris Review*, "did you ever hear a guy telling a long wild tale to a bunch of men in a bar and all are listening and smiling, did you ever hear that guy stop to revise himself, go back to a previous sentence to defray its rhythmic thought impact?"[73] Kerouac's typewriter had somehow to reproduce the qualities of oral narrative and the intimacy of a vernacular monologue; with these aims in mind, punctuation had to be minimized. He had written *The Subterraneans* "like a long letter to a friend," and he had deliberately refrained from revising it himself.[74] When his publisher altered his punctuation and shortened his sentences, Kerouac denounced the revised text as "castrated writing." In Kerouac's version of the romantic typewriter, typing was a vital part of his own body and in particular of his masculinity. In the writing process, he frequently felt that something was being forcefully dragged out of himself. "Sometimes," he wrote, "my effort at writing becomes so fluid and smooth that too much is torn out of me at once, and it hurts."[75]

Memory Babe (1958) took scroll form, and the script of *The Dharma Bums* (1958) was also typewritten on to a scroll.[76] A further conflict with the publisher over *The Dharma Bums* ensued. Viking made 3,500 changes

to the text. Kerouac retaliated by restoring the original sentence structure in the galley proofs. Viking sent him a bill for the printer's time.[77]
The Vanity of Duluoz (1968) also took the form of a typed scroll, but
Kerouac retyped it on normal-sized pages.[78] By this time, a little more
than a year before his death, he was physically incapable of repeating
the exploit of *The Subterraneans* – a typing frenzy of such intensity that it
had, he claimed, left him fifteen pounds lighter and as pale as a sheet.[79]

In 1959, Truman Capote dismissed Kerouac's work as mere typing,
not writing, but it is not clear whether Capote was against typed first
drafts as such, or whether he had some deeper criticism to offer of
Kerouac's fast, raw, unrevisable drafts.[80] In Capote's own *Paris Review*
interview, he explained that he postponed using his typewriter until
he was ready to produce a third draft, so his own methods had little
affinity with those of Kerouac.[81] Kerouac perhaps realized better than
Capote the potential of the typewriter and the way it could assist his
unique style of unreflective composition.

The cases presented in this chapter are extremely varied. They have
ranged from fin-de-siècle fantasies and communications with the dead
to the Beat Generation of the mid-twentieth century, and from English
children's literature to a US dissident trying to write the great American
novel. In spite of their differences, they all shared some of the salient
characteristics of the romantic typewriter. Unlike the distancing effect
analysed in chapter 5, they did not feel detached or alienated from the
act of mechanical writing. Instead, they embraced it and envisaged the
typewriter itself as part of their living, breathing selves. They found it
marvellously well adapted to their project of composing a free flow of
prose, which they believed emerged instinctively and spontaneously
from their unconscious imaginations. Romantic typewriters sometimes believed that when they approached the keyboard, their unconscious ideas would naturally surface. Enid Blyton called this "opening
the sluice gates," whereas Kerouac achieved a similar result through
drug-supported nocturnal writing binges. For both, the speed of the
typewriter was critical for their writing practices. In this sense, the
typewriter signified for them a kind of creative liberation.

In this process, the typist's intellectual faculties were neutralized.
Like the automatic writing discussed in the first part of this chapter, the
best results depended on the virtual absence of the writer. His or her
conscious, critical, or analytical brain was not required – rather, it was
a potential handicap. Just like trainee typists, the writer, in his or her
account of their creative work, switched to automatic pilot. As a result,

a few problems could arise: this spontaneous style of composition was not compatible with scrupulous editing and revising; Blyton seems to have done very little of this, and Kerouac was regularly in conflict with publishers who demanded textual changes. Nor was such an approach conducive to detailed planning and premeditation. Writers who plotted their stories in advance in manuscript notes, and who revised their drafts meticulously in longhand, are discussed in the next chapter, which will consider the relationship between typing and handwriting.

7 Manuscript and Typescript

In Search of Lost Manuscripts

In July 2017, the world's media went on a feeding frenzy after J.K. Rowling, celebrated author of the Harry Potter series, revealed in an interview with the American news network CNN that she had an unpublished story hanging in her wardrobe.[1] The fairy tale in question was written all over a party dress she had worn at her fiftieth birthday. The theme of the costume party had been "come as your own private nightmare," and Rowling had gone as a lost manuscript. The news of the "hidden manuscript," or the "secret manuscript" by J.K. Rowling, scooped by CNN, rapidly did the rounds of the international press, from the *Daily Mirror* to the *Jakarta Post*, from the *Huffington Post* to *Vanity Fair*. The manuscript dress was of course neither lost nor hidden, as was dramatically alleged, and, if it had ever been a secret, its existence was now common global knowledge. What Rowling's party dress shows us is that the unpublished literary manuscript continues to carry a powerful mystique. The discovery of literary manuscripts has the power to tantalize fans, whet the appetite of bounty hunters, and make sensational news stories. But what is and what has been the role of handwriting in the work routine of authors during the typewriter century? Did they draft by hand and then edit on the machine, or did they write first on the machine and then revise by hand? Their choice of writing medium contributed significantly to the outcome they wished to achieve. This chapter addresses these questions by considering the relationship between typescript and manuscript in three phases of preparation: in preliminary notebooks, in drafting a text, and finally in the phase of revision. Just as in previous chapters, examples are drawn from both canonical writers and genre authors working in crime or espionage fiction. They show that, in spite of the mechanization of writing, writing in longhand was alive and well even if, like the young Harry Potter himself, it was sometimes shut up in a dark cupboard.

Elizabeth Eisenstein argued that the invention of printing brought about a revolutionary transformation of the world of scribal production, and yet handwritten texts showed a great resilience, which has sometimes been underestimated. Eisenstein claimed that the advent of the printing press in the mid-fifteenth century produced a significant communications shift; it made possible the production of a greater volume of books, it speeded up their circulation, and also contributed to the standardization and fixity of language in printed form.[2] Eisenstein was not the only scholar making huge claims for the revolutionary powers of printing. Marshall McLuhan also attributed changes in human thought processes and sense perceptions to the introduction of typography. As we saw in chapter 5, he argued that printing reinforced the Western tendency toward linear thinking, and privileged the sense of sight over smell, hearing, and touch.[3] Yet McLuhan, like Eisenstein, exaggerated the impact of printing; the developments to which he drew attention were the consequence of writing per se, and not exclusively attributable to the printing press.

Manuscript culture survived, and its survival was neither marginal nor residual. If an author wanted to reach a small circle of readers at little cost, and/or wanted to evade censorship, manuscript publication was preferable to print through much of the early modern period. It was especially suited to certain genres, like poetry and newsletters provided for a specific constituency of clients.[4] A new respect for scribal production in the past has been fundamental in rescuing women's writing in particular from complete oblivion and, through the Perdita Project, putting some of it online.[5] Print and manuscript coexisted for centuries, each medium fulfilling its particular purpose.

In some parts of Europe, manuscript culture played a very significant role right up to the twentieth century. During the long nineteenth century, the popular poets and "barefoot historians" of Iceland were assiduous collectors and copiers of epic poetry and played an unrivalled role in popular education.[6] There, scribes had for centuries copied out romances and sagas, to be recited by itinerant poets. Scorned by the church, such *rímur* (rhymes) were not considered worthy of publication and thus circulated only in manuscript and in oral form. Some scribes copied as many as fifty or a hundred sagas in their lifetime, including the humble priest Jón Oddsson Hjaltalín (d. 1835), who spoke Latin and read Voltaire, as well as copying and translating material in many genres, while trying at the same time to support his twenty-two children.[7] Meanwhile, needless to say, manuscript remained everywhere the primary form of communication between individuals in the form of correspondence.

This brief historical excursion serves to underline the enduring power of handwriting, as well as the continuing prestige that it enjoys. What else but this prestige can explain the passionate interest in J.K. Rowling's "hidden" manuscript, or the archival practices of popular romance novelist Jackie Collins? Collins wrote thirty-two best-selling novels, which sold over 500 million copies. Her Beverley Hills mansion contained a swimming pool, sauna, cinema, and a gym. There were five writing desks in various parts of the house, where Collins composed her novels in longhand using a felt-tip pen. Her computer, meanwhile, was reserved for research, emails, and browsing gossip sites. But the house also had an elegant library, where Collins shelved the manuscripts of all her own novels in leather bindings.[8] If she ever read John Donne's poetry, she might have sympathized with his sentiments, as translated from Latin by poet Edmund Blunden:

> What Printing-presses yield we think good store
> But what is writ by hand we reverence more:
> A book that with this printing-blood is dyed
> On shelves for dust and moths is set aside,
> But if't be penned it wins a sacred grace
> And with the Ancient Fathers takes its place.[9]

Alongside the "authority" of the printed text, we must also acknowledge the authority of the manuscript.

The rare books market reflects the power of the manuscript. Marcel Proust's manuscript of *Du côté de chez Swann* (*Swann's Way*), the first volume of his novel *À la recherche du temps perdu* (*In Search of Lost Time*), for example, was sold by Sotheby's in Paris in 2017 for €535,500.[10] There is a thriving market, too, in literary juvenilia, which also attracts scholarly interest, as literary historians search for traces of the youthful matrix from which mature works later grew. A manuscript poem by Charlotte Brontë, penned when she was only thirteen years old, was recently offered by Bonhams, London, for £45,000.[11]

Manuscript speculators hunt down their prey at the earliest opportunity, hoping to make an acquisition before a writer's stock rises and profit margins contract. In 1928, Ernest Hemingway reported a recent approach from an agent who offered him money for any of his unpublished manuscripts. At this point, Hemingway had published several short stories but only one major novel, *The Sun Also Rises*. He wrote humorously to Maxwell Perkins at Scribner's, his New York publisher:

> [A] gentleman named Burton Emmett sent me a check for $500 to buy some manuscripts of stories The Killers, Fifty G. [Fifty Grand] etc. Have

had various other offers. But have given most of these Mss. away during the great tissue towel famine. Don't however tell anyone this as if my eye started to go bad it might be a good provision against the future to start making manuscripts. At present there would seem to be more money in manuscripts than stories. I should think Scott's [i.e., F. Scott Fitzgerald's] original Mss. would bring thousands for the spelling alone. I wonder if Mr. Emmett prefers Mss. of mine before or after I put in the grammar? But I am afraid to joke with these Mss. buyers for fear they won't want them. Think I'll write back and say they are all in the British Museum except The Sun Also Rises which is in the Prado.[12]

Perhaps Emmett's timing was not ideal. In 1923, a suitcase of Hemingway's manuscripts, typescripts, and carbon copies was stolen from his wife Hadley Richardson in Paris, as she was preparing to board a train for Switzerland at the Gare de Lyon.[13] For a short time, Hemingway shared the misery of J.K. Rowling's private nightmare – losing one's manuscripts.

If anything, the increasing rarity of manuscripts in today's digital world has further inflated the market value of authors' private papers. The acquisition of Michel Foucault's personal archive between 2012 and 2014 cost the Bibliothèque nationale de France close to four million euros. At the same time, the Astrophil company offered shares in a business venture devoted to the purchase of rare manuscripts, ranging from Napoleon's letters to André Breton's handwritten surrealist manifesto. Sadly, 18,000 investors were hoodwinked by this Ponzi-style scheme, which sparked a judicial enquiry in 2014. Handwritten relics clearly have an enormous street value.[14]

One way or another, if the author's reputation is great enough, personal papers will rise to the surface after his or her death, if they have not already been dredged up from the bottom beforehand. The vast graveyard where unpublished material is quietly laid to rest is constantly being violated, either by admiring friends, well-meaning academics, or literary burglars.

Making Preparations: Agatha Christie's Red Herrings

There is a conventional expectation that behind every published book there must exist, or must have once existed, a "pre-book." Behind every printed text, in other words, there is imagined to be a body of manuscripts, notes, and rough drafts, used and discarded in the process of composition. English author Peter Parker called this the book's "hinterland," writing: "Behind every book that is published lies a hinterland its author knows only too well, though readers will never be aware of it.

This is a haunted landscape, populated by the ghosts of things written and excised, crisscrossed with paths that were thoroughly explored but came to a dead end, and alive with the faint echoes of stories that were eventually left untold."[15] The concept of the famous author's "literary estate," which took shape in the nineteenth century, endowed his or her surviving manuscripts with added value, the idea being that those manuscripts might contain insights not fully revealed in the printed oeuvre.[16] They tantalize the seeker after buried treasure, holding out the possibility of an unfinished and/or unpublished work. They may provide clues about the author's intentions that are not explicit in the published works, and those clues may also lead to new critical interpretations. Writers may leave traces of their modus operandi, indicating false starts and options that were never followed. The manuscript is secret, whereas print is public; print is definitive, but manuscripts sign-post many paths not taken, and they do not mimic the linear structure of the printed page.

Writers record ideas for stories, plots, and characters by hand in many different ways: on the backs of envelopes, in notebooks designated for the purpose, and sometimes in more unpredictable ways. Contemporary English novelist Will Self explodes the traditional writer's notebook into dozens of yellow Post-it notes, which cover one whole wall of his study.[17] The advantage of this method is that it makes all the notes visible at the same time. In the typewriter century, many authors relied on handwritten notes, sometimes accumulated over a long period of time. English humorous novelist P.G. Wodehouse, creator of Jeeves, would make hundreds of pages of notes for a new novel. "Most of them," he confessed to an interviewer when in his nineties, "are almost incoherent."[18] English children's writer Richmal Crompton, author of the William stories, was even more anarchic toward the end of her writing life. She made notes and recorded ideas and quotations on random scraps of paper. She wrote on the front and backs of envelopes, on the back of royalty statements from her publisher George Newnes, on invitation cards, on fan letters and pages torn from exercise books – no paper surface escaped her jottings, and the pile of fragments she produced creates a small nightmare for the archivist (figure 7.1).[19]

The use of manuscript notes and private jottings can be illustrated in more detail by examining the voluminous notebooks of Agatha Christie, painstakingly presented to the public by John Curran.[20] Christie's work covered a long time span. Her first novel, *The Mysterious Affair at Styles*, which first introduced her detective Hercule Poirot to the reading public, was published by Bodley Head in 1920; her last, *The Postern of Fate*, appeared in 1976, the year of her death, from Collins, to

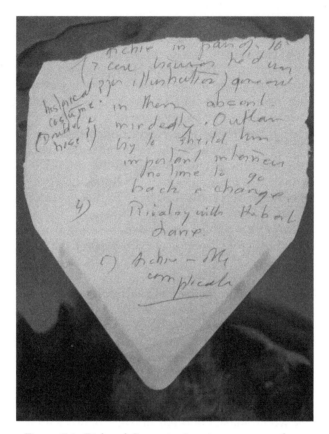

Figure 7.1. Richmal Crompton's notes on an envelope
(Source: Richmal Crompton Collection, University of Roehampton)

whom she had been contracted since 1924. Two posthumous novels followed, which she had probably written during the Second World War, although the dating of these titles is disputed.[21] Altogether, Christie published sixty-eight novels, over a hundred short stories, and seventeen plays. According to UNESCO, 400 million copies of her books had been sold worldwide by 1980, and sales reportedly reached at least two billion by 2018.[22] Since then, television series have continued to keep her name in the public eye. Her crime fiction became closely associated with two standard settings: first, the sleepy English village of St Mary Mead, where her spinsterish protagonist Jane Marple lived, and where dastardly murders had a habit of disturbing the general somnolence; and second, the closed world of a country-house party, a hotel, a ship, or a train, often populated with clergymen, retired army officers, and perhaps wealthy socialites among whom Hercule Poirot came into his element. Christie's stories reflected the cosy Edwardian world in which she had been brought up, revolving around regular church attendance, taking tea, and playing bridge, and weekends in large houses, always supported by an army of servants.[23] This world was cosy, of course, only until an ingenious murder violently interrupted its studied serenity.

In Christie's hands, the detective novel became characterized as an intellectual puzzle, in which individual characters were usually only superficially drawn and in which, in a dramatic dénouement, the detective outshone the police in revealing the identity of the criminal. Most of her notebook jottings thus concerned the construction of twisted plots rather than the task of lending substance to the *dramatis personae*. Commentators would probably agree that Christie was at the peak of her powers in the 1940s, and that the quality of her output declined thereafter.[24] Although, after 1950, she may have been marking time as a novelist, she still received a substantial income from dramatizations and films in the later years of her life.

Christie's writing maintained an intermittent rhythm as it found its place among an endless cycle of domestic obligations, and her notebooks revealed the constant pressures of daily life. She jotted down ideas for titles and plots in no particular order in seventy-three notebooks and exercise books, which have been carefully numbered by her daughter Rosalind Hicks.[25] Christie used almost anything that came to hand, including her daughter's school exercise books, account books, and out-of-date diaries. She wrote scraps of ideas for the same novel in different notebooks, making it very difficult to follow the development of her ideas. Very often, the notebooks had been first used for some other purpose, as recipe books or reminders of train times.[26] They were used at random, and they were unstructured and undated. Three notebooks contain nothing but chemical formulae, which Christie may have noted down during her nursing work in a dispensary during the First World War – work that later informed the use of poisons in her crime fiction. Sometimes the notebooks included reminders about a hairdressing appointment, while Notebook 71 contains her French homework.[27] Much of their contents, therefore, was anything but "literary." To complain, as reviewer John O'Connell did, that the notebooks were "chaotic" misses the point.[28] Such disorder is almost the defining feature of preparatory notebooks, exaggerated as it was in this case by Christie's use of them for multiple objectives.

Christie's handwritten notebooks reveal an author fully involved in domestic activities in a way that is not found in the notebooks of male authors. Whereas the very macho Erle Stanley Gardner scribbled down lists of guns, Christie recorded bridge scores, memos to herself about the dog, reminders of Christmas presents to buy and – in a very feminine touch – lists of tulips.[29] "The disappointing truth," Christie told the BBC in a radio interview in 1955, "is that I haven't much method," and this was true in the sense that preparations to write were always intertwined with and competing against domestic trivia.

The "literary" sections of her notebooks were used to try out various plot options. They show us an author finding her way, choosing between a myriad of possibilities, suggesting and discarding many plot lines. In some cases, she did not know at the outset who the detective was going to be. In preparing *The Sleeping Murder*, published posthumously in 1976, Christie wondered: "a T and T story? A Miss M story? An HP story?", unclear whether the chief protagonists would be Tommy and Tuppence, Miss Marple, or Hercule Poirot.[30] On occasions, she changed her mind more than once. *Death on the Nile* was originally intended as a Hercule Poirot story, but was first published in short story form with Parker Pyne as the detective. In Notebook 30, Miss Marple is listed as a possible character. Then when the story was published as a novel in 1937, it had once again become a Hercule Poirot mystery, this time definitively.[31] Christie certainly did not always know who the murderer was, either. The notes for *One, Two, Buckle My Shoe* (1940) begin: "Who? Why? When? How? Where? Which?", and there was further uncertainty in the formulation of the story that became the classic *Ten Little Niggers* (1939), also known, in the interests of greater sensitivity about racist language, as *And Then There Were None*. In Christie's notebooks for this story, there were never ten characters; at first there were eight, and later twelve.[32] Handwritten notebooks manage to suggest that some defining features of a published work were arrived at almost by accident.

Many more handwritten notes probably existed that have not survived in the numbered notebooks. Profuse notes covering seventy pages have survived, however, for *Mrs McGinty's Dead* (1952). Some preliminary notes for this novel date from 1947, five years before publication. Christie wrestled with several possible plot scenarios before settling on one of them.[33] In Notebook 43, she contemplated a long series of combinations, underlining the possible killer in each case:

Which?
1. A. False – elderly Cranes – with daughter (girl – Evelyn)
   B. Real – Robin – son with mother <u>son</u> [Upward]
2. A. False Invalid mother (or not invalid) and son
   B. Real – dull wife of snob A. P. (Carter) <u>Dau</u>[ghter]

3. A. False artistic woman with <u>son</u>
   B. Real middle-aged wife – dull couple – or flashy Carters (daughter invalid)
4. A. False widow – soon to marry rich man
5. False man with dogs – stepson – different name
   Real – invalid mother and daughter – <u>dau</u>[ghter] does it [Wetherby][34]

Every character runs the gauntlet here, as Christie considered various permutations to resolve the four past murders that form the backdrop of the story. Option 1B was the one she finally selected, but the choice concealed multiple alternatives that never surfaced in print.

In several novels, such as *Hallowe'en Party* (1969), Christie introduced the character of Mrs Ariadne Oliver, a friend of Hercule Poirot and a detective writer in her own right, who was a fictional version of Christie herself. Oliver is a successful, middle-aged writer struggling with publishers' deadlines, who, like Christie, invented a foreign sleuth, the Finnish detective Sven Hjerson. Like Christie, Oliver does not drink or smoke. The character has a habit of considering aloud all the possible interpretations of a murder, including some that sound outrageously far-fetched. She sounds amusingly like a talking version of Christie's own notebooks, rehearsing potential plots and their imagined resolutions, discarding many of them in frustration. The mythological Ariadne, it will be remembered, provided the thread that guided her lover Theseus out of the labyrinth of the Minotaur. Ariadne Oliver is less decisive than this, and Poirot (who is no Theseus) is the one who will find the exit from Christie's maze. Oliver's role is to list the false starts and wrong turnings that may distract the author searching for the most convincing way out. Through Ariadne Oliver, then, Agatha Christie effectively introduced the essence of her notebooks into her novels, giving a glimpse of all the paths not taken by the author of the mystery. In a remarkable exercise in self-reflection, Christie poked gentle fun at herself and her methods.

Drafting by Hand

During the typewriter century and indeed well beyond it, writers often made a first handwritten draft before committing their text to type. Claire Messud, a writer of Canadian and French-Algerian parentage, usually writes on Rhodia graph pads, appreciating the regularity of the squares and the sensuality of the smooth surface of the paper. She writes with a fine-pointed Pigna Micron .005.[35] These are quite deliberate choices of specific materials. Messud does not conform to the stereotype of the anguished writer screwing up page after page of useless drafts and discarding them in the waste-paper basket. In fact she wastes no paper at all. She prepares her draft without margins or paragraph breaks. Instead she begins a new paragraph with a bracket thus "[".

The Australian author Ion Idriess (d. 1979) was another who always wrote in longhand, usually in pencil. Sometimes he used the page landscape-style, leaving two or three blank lines between each line of writing for ease and clarity of editing.[36] When he was working on his biography of Sir Sidney Kidman, which became *The Cattle King* (1936), he made a long trip into southwest Queensland, where he filled four numbered notebooks with pencil-written notes, on birds, animals, terrain, and vegetation. He tagged sections with a paper clip to identify what he eventually used for the book. When he had incorporated the material, he drew a pencil line across the page of the notebook.[37] In 1936, he had a desk in the offices of Sydney publisher Angus and Robertson, where he went to work six mornings a week, including Saturday. He wrote in pencil on loose sheets of quarto paper, in writing that grew ever larger with his advancing age. When he was happy with his draft, he would give it to "the girls" (as he called them) to type.[38] Then he would go out and spend the afternoon drinking.

Romance writer Barbara Taylor Bradford composes partly by hand, sitting next to a typewriter and a computer. The typewriter is activated for a second draft and the computer used for preliminary research.[39] Writers like Bradford preferred to write by hand because it gave them more time to think as they worked. They could not think on the typewriter – or, at least, they had never learned to do so. American novelist Annie Proulx advised would-be authors to take their time, offering the following instructions:

1 Proceed slowly and take care.
2 To ensure that you proceed slowly, write by hand.[40]

American short story writer Andre Dubus (d. 1999) similarly found handwriting better synchronized with the pace of his thinking: "I write in longhand," he explained. "[I]t's more comfortable and it's slower. The next sentence starts shaping while I'm writing the one before it. Typing is too fast, and the rhythm becomes staccato. There are too many pauses between sentences, for the machine moves faster than my mind."[41] Andrew J. Offutt (d. 2013), an American science fiction writer, even had a neurological explanation for his preference for writing by hand: "I don't create at the typewriter. I get better copy by handwriting, and typing that next day. The *act* of typing and the *act* of creating-thinking use different sides of me and my brain."[42]

Thus, the principal quality that had first distinguished the typewriter – namely, its speed – was the precise reason why many writers by-passed it during the stage of early drafts. The speed of typing, when used for copying a text rather than for original composition, is estimated by psychologists as about one-third of the speed of speech. Normal handwriting speed – about twenty words per minute – is, in contrast, about one-tenth as fast as speaking.[43]

The problem of correcting typed text was another reason for resorting to handwriting for as long as possible. Dennis Wheatley (d. 1977), an English author of occult fiction, wrote with a pencil and an eraser and was convinced that the best authors, himself of course included, wrote by hand:

> The majority of authors use a typewriter, but I have always found that those who produce the best work always write in longhand. Some dictate but the mind goes too fast that way. One cannot build up suspense or get the best out of a scene, so later have to add in bits here and there. I write with pencil and rubber. One can always see what one has written so avoid using the same multi-syllable word in a paragraph. It is also easier and neater to simply rub out a sentence than make an untidy mess, scratching out ink work, then having to write the replacement in the margin.[44]

Manual corrections were always preferred by assiduous revisers such as John le Carré, who told an interviewer in 1997, "Well, I still don't type. I write by hand, and my wife types everything up, endlessly, repeatedly. I correct by hand too."[45] Le Carré's mania for handwritten revision (which imposed a considerable workload on his wife) will be discussed below.

Writers who composed in longhand wanted to retain control of their text for as long as possible, and they generally deferred sending their text to a typist until they were completely satisfied with it. Truman Capote, for example, made drafts in pencil and did not arrive at a typed version until the third draft.[46] Moving to a typed version was the first step in the long process, culminating in print publication, by which authors gradually surrendered oversight of their book. Retyping was the first degree of separation.

Serial Correction

After making preliminary notes, and then composing a first draft, came the phase of revision. This often took the form of making handwritten corrections to a typed text, on "hard copy" as the digital age would later call it. The continuing dialogue thus established between handwriting and type is demonstrated in the preparation of the spy novels of John le Carré.

Le Carré (real name, David Cornwell) began writing fiction in 1958; in 1963, his first great success, *The Spy Who Came In from the Cold*, enabled him to leave the British Foreign Office and become a full-time writer. Strictly speaking, his more recent novelistic output lies beyond the typewriter century, as I have defined it in this book. He nevertheless remains perversely a part of it in his resistance to the machine and his continuing preference for longhand composition and revision. By late 1996, le Carré had acquired a Macintosh computer, but his wife, Jane Eustace (herself a book editor), was the one who operated it. By this time, le Carré was resigned to his fate: "I am moving gradually towards it [using a computer]," he confessed. "I accept that it is quite impossible to stand aside from it. I happen to write by hand. I don't even type. I'll have to change my spots."[47] For le Carré, writing longhand signified a slow rate of composition and an extended period of manuscript revision.

"I am a slow writer," he told *Playboy* magazine in 1965, and he liked uninterrupted solitude while writing.[48] He found it when he wrote *A Small Town in Germany* (1968) in the seclusion of a hotel room overlooking the Rhine. At first, however, he rarely had the luxury of calm isolation. He wrote on the way to work, in cheap notebooks, on commuter trains, during his lunch breaks, and later, when posted to Germany, on the Rhine ferry.[49] From the first, he preferred longhand. "I never mastered the typewriter," he told another interviewer. "First draft in blue biro, revisions in red, final copy in green. In the afternoon, my secretary types out the sheets with green on [...] Then, in the afternoon, cutting, revision, selection."[50] He would temporarily abandon the process in order to conduct field research. For *The Little Drummer Girl* (1983), he went to the Middle East and interviewed Yasser Arafat before writing about Palestinian radicalism; he visited the Soviet Union for *The Russia House* (1989); and he talked to arms dealers in Panama before the plot of *The Night Manager* (1993) finally crystallized. He was, after all, Foreign Office–trained to observe and collect intelligence without becoming a participant. The writer, he would say, is a spy, and literature is simply espionage conducted by other means.[51]

Le Carré is a dedicated reviser. He might spend months on this task, possibly deleting extended sections of prose in the process. He was accustomed to writing perhaps 500,000 words before reducing this to a normal book-length of 90,000 through many stages of revision.[52] He learned this practice, as well as the practice of colour-coding drafts, from drafting Foreign Office memoranda, as he explained at length to an interviewer in 1966:

> One of the principles of Foreign Office drafting, whether you draft a tele-gram or whether you draft a despatch from your Ambassador, is that the smallest worm in the outfit tries to reflect what he hopes will be the Am-bassador's opinion on a given subject. This is done out on blue paper with triple or quadruple spacing. This piece of paper or this sheaf of paper then works its way up through all his colleagues until it reaches the highest authority – in this case the Ambassador – and each of these wretched people adds his comments, eliminates loose words, questions style, questions the line of thought, until finally when it reaches the Ambassador he makes his own alterations and then it comes all the way down again. So that if one had any thoughts about the glories of one's prose style or any thoughts about the lucidity of one's argument, one was soundly disillusioned by the time the piece of paper came back. This made one wary, economic; it is certainly the most rigid, the most astringent training that I have had. I suppose you can say I got my style from there.[53]

This humiliating experience taught him to hone and carefully consider every sentence. He preferred to do this by hand because it made all corrections and insertions visible alongside what had been corrected. "When one writes slowly," he told Pierre Assouline, "one self-censors, and with a glance one can see the archaeology of the manuscript."[54]

The archaeology of the manuscript is laid bare in the manuscripts and typescripts that le Carré left to the Bodleian Library in Oxford. For the sake of illustration, let me consider the process of writing *The Tailor of Panama*, which began with a handwritten version dated June 1995.[55] This was drafted on yellow paper in black ink, with changes stapled onto the original pages. Typed versions of different sections of the book appeared at intervals of a day or two throughout June 1995, always dated, and sometimes more than one each day. If we examine the opening chapters alone, we can count at least thirteen drafts over almost exactly a year from June 1995 to the end of May 1996.[56] At this point, the script was close to "final draft" stage, which le Carré reached in July 1996.[57] But this was not the end, because his scripts customar-ily went through no fewer than three proof stages, as he inserted even further corrections to the "final" typescript. Yet this scale of revision was comparatively moderate by le Carré's own standards. The archive of his earlier novel *The Night Manager*, for example, suggests a total of approximately twenty-three drafts between April 1991 and October 1992, not counting three sets of page proofs.[58]

The minutiae of le Carré's handwritten revisions, which all needed a typed text to work on, are apparent if the opening chapter of *The Tailor of Panama* is briefly considered. Le Carré started in June 1995 with the following:

> It was a sweltering day in Panama until Osnard rang up to make an appointment to be measured for a suit.
>
> "I'm sorry, sir," said Pendel, who took the call himself, though he was in the middle of cutting the back panel of a ceremonial naval uniform [...]
>
> Pendel spoke the Spanish of a gentleman, only in conversations with fellow Britons did he still occasionally feel branded on the tongue.[59]

Within a few days, le Carré's manuscript insertions into a typed version had altered this opening text as follows:

> It was an ordinary day in equatorial Panama till Osnard rang to make an appointment to be measured.
>
> Harry Pendel was in his work room, listening to Mozart and cutting patterns for a naval uniform [...]
>
> To Osnard, Pendel's accent was Whitechapel Jewish with aspirations.[60]

The text had become more succinct, but at the same time slightly richer; meanwhile the reference to Pendel's East End Jewish origins and aspirations would open up le Carré to charges of anti-Semitism, which surfaced later.

By 11 June, le Carré had added the detail that Pendel was listening to Mozart's 38th Symphony, and had changed "Whitechapel" to "East End." But this looks like compulsive tinkering at the edges. Nine months' work and possibly seven more drafts followed. If we rejoin le Carré at work in March 1996, we see that there had been a significant breakthrough. A new typed draft on white paper began: "It was a perfectly ordinary Friday afternoon in tropical Panama until Andrew Osnard barged into Harry Pendel's shop asking to be measured for a suit."[61] This became the final published version of the opening.[62] "Equatorial" has given way to "tropical," Osnard now barges in, and a lot of new material follows. The immediate sequel completely changed, and the scene of Pendel in his cutting room was pushed back to open chapter 2. He now preferred listening to Mahler rather than Mozart. Le Carré went on in this new version: "[B]oth men, as Englishmen, were branded on the tongue. To an Osnard Pendel's origins were as unmistakable as his aspirations to escape them. His voice with all its mellowness had never lost the stain of Leman Street, E.1." Pendel's

Jewishness was now implied rather than being spelled out. By now, ten months after beginning work, le Carré had an almost complete draft of the whole book.

A brief examination of the opening of *The Tailor of Panama* demonstrates the importance of the author's materials. Le Carré produced many versions on different coloured paper, and the colours were significant. Yellow paper was for early drafts, green signified an instruction to type, while thicker, cream-coloured paper was reserved for the final version to be sent to his agent. Le Carré was addicted to handwritten revisions and insertions, but he needed a constant supply of newly typed and retyped texts, usually provided by his wife, to work on. He would correct in black ink and sometimes stapled added sections onto the page, and further amendments would be stapled on top of already stapled additions. For le Carré, getting a version typed was like clicking "save" on a word processor. For him a typescript was never definitive, but merely a launching pad for further development and improvements, an invitation to apply another layer of doubt and inference. These improvements were usually added by hand. Unlike computer users, however, le Carré archived all his drafts, making it possible to discern the archaeology of their meticulous construction.

The Archaeology of the Text

The discussion that opened this chapter posed the question whether authors' notes and manuscripts could reveal hidden patterns not apparent in their published oeuvre, and whether they might conceal significant clues about the author's plans and intentions. In practice, however, an examination of Agatha Christie's notebooks suggested a state of confusion rather than a secret explanatory thread, as the author struggled to eliminate unworkable plot options and settle on a main character for the next story. In this case, the notebooks appear less like a parallel guide to the novels, and more like a random sounding-board, echoing a range of ideas, the majority of which would inevitably be discarded. A few might be resurrected in a later story, a process John le Carré called recycling his industrial waste, as he fleshed out characters he did not have time to develop in previous novels.

The examination of the relationship between handwriting and typed text has shown that they were intimately connected throughout every stage of composition in the typewriter century. Handwritten notes and notebooks rehearsed new ideas and prepared the ground for creative work. Handwritten drafts were the preferred next step of many authors cited in this chapter. Lastly, handwritten corrections on typed text were indispensable for inveterate revisers such as le Carré. Traditional writing practices survived, as the examples presented demonstrate the persistent imbrication of handwriting with typescript in the creative work of the genre writers considered here. For such writers, the word processor contributed far more than the typewriter did to the slow death of handwriting.

Writers preferred manuscript for several reasons. First, it forced them to write relatively slowly. They appreciated a creative method that reflected the pace of their own imagination. Handwriting encouraged what many considered to be a deeper consideration of the prose than that normally achievable on the machine. Second, like Claire Messud, they liked the sensuality of putting a pen or pencil to paper. Handling the paper and close physical contact with its smooth whiteness (or greenness in the case of le Carré) were tactile pleasures unavailable on the machine. Finally, there was the recurrent problem of making corrections to a typescript. Revising a script using handwritten insertions and deletions was far more convenient than trying to correct everything on the typewriter. Ideally, an author would correct by hand on a typed text, as le Carré likes to do, illustrating once again the close interdependency of manuscript and typescript forms. In addition, correcting by hand enabled every change to be archived – a practice that was very rarely carried over into word processing on screen. There, an old version disappears instantly and forever; the archaeology of the text is irretrievable. It is, of course, possible to archive electronic material, and to save every draft, but to my knowledge very few authors would consider this worthwhile.[63] With a combination of manuscript and the typewriter, however, it is still possible to make out modifications to the underlying contours of the text and to excavate its history.

8 Georges Simenon: The Man in the Glass Cage

Inside the Glass Cage

In 1927, Georges Simenon agreed with Eugène Merle, editor of the newspaper *Paris-Matin*, to perform an unprecedented publicity stunt. He volunteered to be shut in a glass cage at the Moulin Rouge nightclub with a desk and typewriter, and there he would write a novel within a week, in full public view. What is more, the readers of *Paris-Matin* would themselves vote on the title of the novel and choose the main characters. The contract was worth 300,000 francs.[1] Before the event could take place, however, the paper went bankrupt. The stunt never happened, but Simenon was forever remembered as the novelist in the glass cage, a writer who embraced making a public spectacle of himself as an effective promotional technique.[2] He could write anything on demand, and he wanted everyone to know it. Simenon was adept at managing his own reputation and controlling his own publicity. A legend grew up around Simenon, and he himself bears most of the responsibility for creating it. Other authors might have thought that the glass cage affair debased their profession, but Simenon fully accepted the project and had no regrets. The glass cage was significant in another sense: it was an appropriate symbol of the new "visibility" of the author as a public celebrity. In the twentieth century, literary authors stepped down from their pedestals. The author as creative genius was desacralized, and instead a star system developed, in which access to the media determined reputation and influenced sales. Georges Simenon was part of this process, a willing accomplice in its rising power.

Simenon wrote 192 novels in his own name, of which 75 featured the serene and compassionate Inspector Maigret, as well as another 190 under pseudonyms, mainly for the French popular fiction publishers of the interwar years – Ferenczi, Fayard, and Tallandier. No single title became an outright bestseller, but he wrote many of them. According to his publisher Gallimard, he sold an average of 8,000 copies per novel in the 1930s but, working at his extraordinary rhythm, he produced a dozen per year.[3] By the 1950s, the Presses de la Cité were producing his Maigret novels in print runs ranging from 39,000 to 92,000 copies each.[4] Simenon was obsessively concerned with the total number of novels he had written, in spite of his own nonchalant comments to the contrary. In 1961, he thought he might have produced 180, but, in any case, he said, his wife was keeping count.[5] In 1947, *Ici Paris* reported that Simenon was the writer whose books were most frequently stolen from Parisian municipal libraries, paying him a perverse compliment, but a compliment all the same. In 1955, UNESCO listed him as the third most translated author in the world, after Lenin and Stalin, but ahead of Shakespeare and Jules Verne.[6] He had become a global phenomenon.

His crime stories, many of them set in Paris, the north of France, or his native Belgium, were praised for their minimalist but evocative recreation of the atmosphere of the quays, the canals, the rivers, and the fogs of northern France. He wrote of a grey world of everyday realities and banal lives, in which ordinary individuals were pushed beyond the limits of endurance to commit extraordinary crimes. The first Simenon novel featuring his famous Inspector Maigret (*Pietr-le-Letton*) was conceived in 1929 in this very environment: it was written on a Royal typewriter with French keys on a folding table on his barge *Ostrogoth*, while cruising up the Meuse to Belgium and the Netherlands.[7] A contemporary cartoon by Soupault depicted Simenon with his typewriter and his pipe, producing a stream of text on the barge, which sailors relayed by hand to the printing shop. Soupault called him "the Citroën of literature."[8] As well as his evocations of the misty, cobbled North, Simenon's fiction presented a nostalgic portrait of Paris in the 1930s, with its cobblestones and its small local bars, its buses with rear platforms, and the nocturnal, working-class world of Les Halles market, emblematic of a Paris as yet unreconstructed by contemporary municipal planners.

This chapter considers the speed and high level of Simenon's productivity, which gave him an ambiguous status in the literary field, and examines the typewriter's place in his working methods. As I will show, he developed a unique combination of typescript and manuscript production. First, however, I will address the broad context and nature of his literary celebrity.

Literary Celebrity

Literary celebrity was not unique to the twentieth century. Antoine Lilti regarded the emergence of celebrity as synonymous with modern culture, placing it in the periods of the European Enlightenment and

Romanticism, the age of public figures such as Voltaire and Rousseau, Byron and Liszt.[9] Voltaire had corresponded with royalty; Jean-Jacques Rousseau's grave at Ermenonville became a pilgrimage site for his faithful admirers; thousands would later throng the streets of Paris for Victor Hugo's state funeral in 1885. Hugo's public reputation in the Third Republic rested to some extent on his political choices, especially his opposition to the Second Empire of Napoleon III, which had driven him into exile. In the twentieth century, in contrast, literary celebrity had little to do with political engagement. The popular writer enjoyed, if that is the right word, a new visibility. Readers and others could hear writers on the radio, and later see them on television. Their personal lives and working methods were laid bare and scrutinized in numerous magazine articles and press interviews (which was certainly the case for Simenon: *Paris-Match* alone ran eighteen articles on Simenon between 1952 and 2003).[10] Readers asked for photographs, autographs, and personal dedications in their books – behind the novel they could not avoid seeing the writer. The publicity media made authors well known to thousands of people who were not necessarily readers of their books.

In this new world where traditional literary values were being eroded by the imperatives of the market, the crime novel held pride of place. In France, Dominique Kalifa has noted how the *fait divers*, a brief newspaper report usually of a crime or an accident, took up more and more space in the popular press toward the end of the nineteenth century. Meanwhile, French crime fiction developed further after 1905 with the creation of Arsène Lupin, the gentleman burglar, and the serialization of the popular *Fantômas* from 1911. Crime fiction was acquiring a new legitimacy.[11] In the 1930s, Simenon wanted his books to have black-and-white images on their covers, reflecting the ambiance of the *roman noir*, but also echoing the actuality of newspaper photographs.[12] As a teenager, he himself had been a *faitsdiversier* on the *Gazette de Liège*, reporting crimes and accidents as well as frequenting brothels and writing a column on the Jewish threat. Simenon rubbed shoulders with a world very close to the criminal underworld of murderers and drug dealers.[13] In his novels, as in his early life, the boundary between transgression and a spotless life was easily crossed.

Literary celebrity thrived on the expanding market for cheap fiction and the popularity of crime stories in particular. Fame redefined authors' relationship with their readers. For the first time, authors like Simenon received a flood of fan mail. Readers had certainly written to authors in the past: scholars have examined readers' mail addressed to French writers such as Honoré de Balzac, Eugène Sue, and Émile Zola in order to study how their work was received and what aesthetic priorities organized their readers' preferences.[14] But twentieth-century literary fan mail was of an entirely different calibre and quantity. Simenon received at least 5,600 letters from readers between 1948 and 1989 – that is, slightly more than 130 per year; the true total is probably greater than this, because no one thought to preserve the letters systematically until 1953. Simenon replied to almost every letter, usually very briefly, except for about 300 lunatic letters consigned to his *bêtisier* (stupidity file). He responded by hand when especially touched. His second wife, Denyse, acted as secretary and often replied in his name as "Madame Georges Simenon."[15]

Why did so many readers write to Simenon, and what did they write about? Correspondents rarely discussed the contents of the books they read, except to correct technical details and inconsistencies. Instead they focused on the person of the author. They were "ordinary readers," quite different from literary scholars and professional reviewers, who, the fans sometimes thought, failed to appreciate the true warmth and humanity of Inspector Maigret. They thanked Simenon profusely for all the pleasure he had given them. They asked questions about his literary tastes, his personal habits, his political views. Above all, they identified the author with his fictional creation, Inspector Maigret. One Belgian reader wrote in 1953: "For me you were Maigret and Maigret was you."[16] They visited "Simenon territory" in Paris, looking for Maigret's favourite but fictional haunt, the *brasserie* Dauphine, and were surprised to find that it did not exist.[17] Readers assumed a personal rapport with the author, and they knew he had a life outside his books, because they had read in the press about his travels, his family life, and his multiple house moves. Yet there were still boundaries to be defended; if a reader wrote too intimately to Simenon, breaching the unwritten code of deference to the great man, or intruded too far into his problematic personal life, Simenon drew a line and replied curtly to put an end to the exchange.[18]

This was a new and more personal kind of adulation than that enjoyed by nineteenth-century novelists. Readers identified closely with both Maigret and Simenon, often writing as though they were the same person. When Maigret had a sleepless night, they recommended a reliable sleeping pill; they worried about the inspector's health and about his wife; one reader asked what brand of tobacco both Simenon and Maigret smoked.[19] They were passionately involved in his stories, and one woman spoke of being infected with "Simenonitis."[20] A few budding writers asked for advice on getting their own work published; Simenon wisely advised them to keep practising and to hang on to their day jobs.[21] In 1957, one fan, a would-be author, decided to imitate Simenon's work routine to the letter, sitting down to work at 6 a.m. and writing on a typewriter for the first time in his life, reporting: "I also experienced this rather fierce pleasure of typing on the keyboard, with the physical sensation of the words taking shape under my fingers, seeing phrases added to phrases, and pages to pages."[22] Simenon at his typewriter was a celebrity and a role model. A personal interest in his life and creativity was not even confined to his readers, but spread to others who never read him. This was a level of celebrity that required careful management.

Literary celebrities were known worldwide. Simenon left France after the Second World War, when his reputation was under a cloud. His bank accounts were frozen and he was temporarily subjected to *résidence surveillée* because during the war he had written for the German-controlled Continental film company, as well as contributing articles to collaborationist journals like *Je suis partout*.[23] From 1945 to 1955, he was based in America, settling for the last five years at Lakeville, Connecticut. The United States was perhaps more receptive to his work than France but disapproved of his unorthodox domestic arrangements. For a short time he lived under the same roof with his wife Tigy (Régine Renchon) and his mistress Denyse Ouimet.[24] The puritanical mores of America would not tolerate this *ménage à trois*, and Simenon divorced Tigy in 1949, although she continued to live nearby with their son Marc. He married Denyse in Reno in 1950. This incompatibility between French and American moral perspectives may have been one reason for his departure to Switzerland, together, of course, with the attraction of a lower tax rate and the view of Lake Geneva. For the man in the glass cage, however, complete withdrawal was out of the question. Simenon changed residence more than fifteen times during his lifetime, searching in vain for a solid home base, and perhaps haunted by the fear of becoming a *clochard* (tramp) like one of his uncles.[25] He signed some typescripts "Noland," suggesting that he had no address, but sooner or later the world's press caught up with him.[26] As far as producing novels was concerned, it apparently mattered little where Simenon was living: "I discovered countries that were entirely new to me [for example, Tahiti and Panama] [...] but I wrote not a word of my almost daily discoveries. No. Sitting at my machine, I wrote of the rue Lepic in Paris, of Bourges and of La Rochelle."[27] This is one of many cases where Simenon massaged the truth about himself. In fact, he never wrote any such novel while he was in Tahiti or Panama. But elsewhere, for example, in Arizona or Connecticut, Paris or Lausanne, he could evoke the sounds and smells of the distant Belgian canals he had once known well. When his fans wrote to him in English, he replied in English – he had become an international personality.

Simenon at Work

Georges Simenon, who wrote three autobiographies, remains the greatest source of information about himself. The first, *Pedigree*, was written in 1940–42 about his childhood and early life in Liège, but was published only later after the war, after André Gide advised him to switch to the third person and treat it like a novel.[28] A revised edition was issued in 1952, after Simenon had erased passages that had provoked some offended acquaintances into taking legal action for defamation. The second autobiography appeared in 1970,[29] and the third, his *Mémoires intimes*, in 1981.[30] The last of these was written as a tribute to his daughter, Marie-Jo, who committed suicide aged twenty-five in 1978: the book was perhaps a response to Simenon's unspoken sense of guilt. Although the book was addressed to all his children, it was a very self-centred and self-justificatory account of his own recent life.

As his biographers discovered, this large body of autobiographical knowledge was indispensable, but it was a minefield, booby-trapped with contradictory information by Simenon himself.[31] The role of alcohol in stimulating the writing process is one small example of Simenon's deception, or perhaps it was self-deception. In his early years, Simenon admitted, "When I got up at six in the morning and sat down at the typewriter, there would be a bottle of Bordeaux on the table and, in the course of the day, I might drink two or three bottles as I drafted my novel. I never got drunk, I felt fine."[32] But he insisted that, after he went to the United States, he often gave up alcohol for long periods, and usually drank nothing but Coke – at least that is what he told Brendan Gill in 1953 when interviewed for the *New Yorker*.[33] But these claims to relative abstinence were completely denied by his sons, Marc and John, who remembered their father as a heavy drinker.[34] Simenon was building an image, and he was writing himself as a fictional character in the novel of his own life.

Because of Simenon's vanity and tendency toward hyperbole, it was never entirely clear where fiction ended and autobiography began. He kept many things out of public view, like his casual but incriminating dealings with the Germans and with Vichy during the Second World War, and with his collaborationist brother Christian, whom Simenon had advised to join the Foreign Legion and who was subsequently killed in action in Indo-China. Nor, understandably, was he very forthcoming about his deteriorating relationship with his alcoholic and increasingly neurotic wife Denyse. Simenon's biographers were sceptical about many aspects of the autobiographies, but they rarely called into question Simenon's representations of his own working methods. In this area, they were surprisingly slow to dissect the many contradictions in his accounts. In spite of these problems, Simenon's reflections on his own creative processes, and his specific uses of manuscript and typed composition, make him an essential subject for a study of the uses of the typewriter.

He wrote at intense speed, even though press reports exaggerated his prowess. According to one journalist in 1945, Simenon was the champion of the typewriter and could write a chapter in two hours.[35] He boasted that he wrote his first novel in the course of a single sitting in a café. We do not need to believe this, but, by 1930, writing straight on to the machine, he could produce roughly a novel every month.[36] In fact Simenon at his peak was capable of finishing a novel in just a few days. Even when he was past his peak, he still produced six novels annually over the twenty years up to 1960.[37] There was often a gap of several months between novels, balanced by spurts of intense activity. In 1955, for example, he produced three novels within five months, and again, between April 1957 and February 1958, he wrote a novel every two months. When he wrote at this pace, he normally alternated a Maigret story with a non-Maigret novel. On average, both types of novels were written at a rate of sixteen to twenty-three printed pages per day.[38]

In the early 1950s, Simenon used airline calendars to block out the days devoted to writing and revision. For *Maigret voyage* (1958 – *Maigret and the Millionnaires*), a Pan-American calendar for August 1957 shows 10–17 August blocked out in red (eight days' writing), and then 27–30 August (four days) blocked out in blue and marked "Revision."[39] In the 1970s, he reflected on the time he took to finish a Maigret novel. At first twelve days was the norm, but as his writing became less flowery and more condensed, he gradually reduced the writing time to nine days. In one writing frenzy in 1960, he managed to complete a novel in seven days.[40] It was as if he was always challenging himself to break his own writing speed record, and he could do so only on the typewriter.

A few non-Maigret novels required more preparation. For *Les anneaux de Bicêtre* (1963) (*The Bells of Bicêtre*, or *The Patient*), for example, the usual single brown envelope on which he made notes proved inadequate to summarize his detailed research into anaesthetics, forceps delivery, and birth by Caesarean section.[41] He personally visited the Bicêtre hospital and studied the symptoms of hemiplegia, which doctors had explained for him. This was a research effort worthy of Émile Zola, and it required several large envelopes and a slower writing pace. But this was an exceptional case.

Simenon was a driven man, always feeling the need to assert his vigour and appetite for life. Perhaps this can be traced to 1940, when a local doctor erroneously told him he had a serious heart condition and had only two more years to live. Simenon believed this prediction all the more readily since his own father, whom he had idealized, died of a heart condition. His reaction was to demonstrate his stamina and lust for action. In 1977, he casually boasted to the Italian film director Federico Fellini that he had had 10,000 women since the age of thirteen and a half, a figure that his wife Tigy revised downwards to about 1,200.[42] Judging by his own account of his sexual relationship with his cook and housekeeper Henriette Liberge, these casual encounters were intense and abrupt. The vast majority of them were with prostitutes. It is not my intention to pass judgment on Simenon's sexual politics, but rather to suggest that these mathematical questions – "How many novels have I written?" and "How many women have I possessed?" – were perhaps symptomatic of the same anxiety. They had similar origins in an urge to life in a man very conscious that his health was vulnerable. The rate at which he was churning out novels and the rate at which he was visiting prostitutes were, for Simenon, both signs of vitality and important to his sense of identity. He needed to show himself that he could achieve an extraordinary level of activity. "I've already written three [novels] this year," he wrote in August 1961. "I was dreaming of writing five or six of them, like before, and, in my mind, it was sort of a way of proclaiming that I am not getting old, that I am still in good shape."[43]

My main concern does not lie either in Simenon's sexual life or in the temptation he offers for psychological speculation. I leave these matters to others, like Fenton Bresler, for example, whose book demonstrates a strong fascination both with the sex and amateur psychoanalysis.[44] Instead, what interests me is Simenon's working methods, and the complicated relationship between manuscript and typewriting in his creative processes. He provides a case study in the importance of the typewriter in the *habitus* of the pulp fiction writer; and he shows us, too, how the pace at which his stories emerged from the assembly line coloured the difficult relationship between popular writers and the literary elite, who were familiar with more traditional methods and valued different aesthetic priorities. Whatever the root psychological cause of Simenon's frenetic activities might have been, his speed was legendary. According to one story (which I cannot substantiate), the film director Alfred Hitchcock once telephoned Simenon, but was told that he could not come to the phone as he was busy writing a novel. "That's alright," Hitchcock replied, "I'll wait."[45]

Whether he was writing Maigret stories, his early potboilers (*romans alimentaires*), or the more serious fiction that he called his *romans durs* (hard novels), Simenon viewed hard work and disciplined application as essential foundations of the writing process. He compared himself to an artisan, like a plasterer or a stonemason: "I need the physical contact. I am an artisan. I have the feeling, in front of my machine, of painting or producing a sculpture. If I could engrave my novels in stone or steel, I would be even happier."[46] Earlier, Simenon had compared the novelist to a cobbler: "Before you start making luxury shoes," he insisted, "it is essential that you first get to know the different phases of manufacture."[47] Simenon referred often to this model of an apprentice learning a trade.

To some extent, this alleged affinity with skilled artisans, dedicated to hard physical work, was a way of distancing himself from effete literary authors and the Parisian intellectuals he despised. His wife Denyse emphasized his discipline and application in a letter of 1953: "My husband is a tremendous worker, and always has, and always will work very hard. He has a tremendous power of concentration and goes about his work with a very great self-discipline. He gets up early in the morning, goes downstairs to his office, and, come what may, turns out a chapter a day every day for as long as the novel is to be."[48] The metaphor of the author as artisan also underlined the craftsman's love of his own skilled handiwork. This applied even to apparent trivia: one reader offered Simenon an electric pencil sharpener, but Denyse declined the gift, saying that Simenon preferred to do the job by hand, and an electric sharpener would destroy the satisfaction of manual work.[49]

Simenon at the typewriter constantly strove to avoid being too "literary." He could achieve a more economical style on the typewriter than he could when writing longhand. When writing *Le chat* (1967), he preferred the typewriter because "[w]ith a pencil you feel yourself too much of an author. It calls for elegant turns of phrase, fine images." He preferred typing novels to writing them longhand because the typewriter put him "in direct contact without passing through the filter of writing in pencil which demands some conscious thought (*pondération*), which slows down the rhythm."[50] A typewriter enabled him more easily to eliminate traces of *littérature* from his work, suppressing all decorative tendencies and verbal artistry. He claimed he used a limited vocabulary of only 2,000 words.[51] For his more literary novels, however, which were not detective stories, beginning with *Le testament Donadieu* (*Donadieu's Will*) in 1937, he was prepared to take more time and produce a first draft in longhand.

Simenon was well aware that his fiction depended heavily on his use of the typewriter. He acknowledged the importance of the material object in his creative work in an interview with André Parinaud, broadcast on French radio in 1955. The interview contained the following exchange:

> GEORGES SIMENON (GS): I could manage to write novels entirely in longhand. But I couldn't revise them. I needed the machine to feel whether there was life in what I had written or not.
>
> ANDRÉ PARINAUD (AP): Is there a connection between your style and typewriting?
>
> GS: I think so. When I was writing by hand, in my early days, I always thought that, as Colette used to say, I made it "too literary." Because there was always the possibility of crossing things out, of having second thoughts, of going back over the previous sentence, or re-reading myself. You inevitably had a tendency to be literary and, because of paying too much attention to the form, you lost the rhythm. That's a serious matter, because I attach great importance to rhythm.
>
> When your machine is running it pulls you along. You have to follow. You cannot stop to re-read the last sentence, to cross something out, and you just press on, leaving the job of making some indispensable corrections until later.
>
> AP: So we wouldn't have the same Simenon without the typewriter!
>
> GS: Certainly not.[52]

Simenon's view of his own work had several dimensions, which were not always coherent or compatible. Although he valued hard work and compared himself to an artisan, his typewriting practices nevertheless echoed notions of inspiration and of the writer as a creative genius living on intuition. In admitting the power of intuition, he seemed to be contradicting the image of a hard-working skilled labourer. He was reluctant to recognize this. In May 1961, he wrote to himself: "Hope to write a novel in early June but don't have the slightest idea of a subject, or even the tone. But I really will have to write. I feel the need to. We will see if, between now and then, an inspiration comes to me. (The word is false, of course. But how else can I put it?)"[53]

How, then, did Simenon prepare to write a novel? As we shall see, he worked himself up into an almost trance-like state of tension and excitement before shutting himself away on a writing binge. In addition, the organization of emblematic material objects – typewriter, pencils, pipes – was an essential part of his theatre of writing.

First, we must deal with Simenon's denial that he even had a working method. In the radio interview with André Parinaud, he claimed that the creative process was completely unconscious: "At the moment when I am about to write a novel," he stated, "I don't know what it's going to be about (*j'ignore le thème*). All I know is that there's a certain climate, like a certain melodic line, like a musical motif."[54] He identified the characters in the story, but then "I know nothing whatever about the events that will occur later. Otherwise it would not be interesting to me."[55] He went further, elaborating new metaphors for the purely instinctive and sensual forces that allegedly guided him: "Often it starts with a smell. I am walking down a path, the day I have decided to write a novel I sense, let's say, a whiff of lilac. Well, the lilac reminds me of certain images from my youth, or of another time, another champagne, another place."[56] Marcel Proust had his madeleine; Georges Simenon had his lilacs. But in laying claim to a Proustian act of memory, was not Simenon suffering from delusions of literary grandeur? Although Simenon affirmed that when he began a Maigret mystery, he did not know where the story was heading, it is very probable that he *did* have some idea of the outcome, as Claudine Gothot-Mersch has argued.[57] There is always a small cast of characters in a Maigret mystery, so when it came to finding the culprit, options were limited. Simenon's real uncertainty lay not in finding the identity of the perpetrator, but rather in analysing the psychological motive for the crime.

Simenon began careful preparation of his material before launching into a novel. He made notes on the front and back of manila envelopes, many of which are still preserved in the Simenon archive in Liège. The envelopes were of different colours and different sizes, although after 1938 he frequently used A4. He wrote only on the outside of the envelopes, and they remained empty.[58] On these *enveloppes jaunes* were inscribed essential information: first, the title of the book, and then the main character's name, profession, address, and his connections and family relationships with other characters. Simenon gave the character a curriculum vitae and a family tree. The envelopes also carry addresses of hotels and cafés, hospitals and police stations situated near the action, as well as important telephone numbers. For *Maigret et le clochard* (1963 – *Maigret and the Dosser* or *Maigret and the Bum*) these notes include a list of the contents of the pockets of the dead tramp.[59] Simenon accumulated details on several characters on his envelopes, drew floor plans of apartments where they lived, found names for them in the telephone directory, and referred to the railway timetable to accurately chart their fictional movements. "I draw a little plan of the house," he explained, "because I also need to know, when he comes home, if he pushes the door to the left or the right."[60] His characters were therefore built on an accumulation of very concrete details. This is what historian Richard Cobb admired about Simenon, because he was working like a historian, constructing a picture around a bare inventory of possessions and embedding his fictional character in a specific time and place, perhaps a specific Parisian neighbourhood.[61] The manila envelopes acted as a memory aid, but they also succeeded in rooting characters and action in a specific location. They formed a database, occasionally carrying information on characters who never appeared in the novels; but they were held in reserve, ready to make an entry.[62]

When a group of Swiss psychiatrists interviewed Simenon in 1968 for the Geneva journal *Médecine et hygiène*, Doctor Rentchnick guessed that Simenon's meticulous preparations for work were symptoms of an obsessive-compulsive disorder.[63] Yet the visual appearance of the manila envelopes suggests a more chaotic style. They are inscribed in different media, either in ink or blue or red pencil, and additions were made at different times. Quite orderly lists are jumbled up with random notes, which are not aligned with each other but written at various angles.[64] The overall impression is one of disorder; as a result, it is difficult to imagine the envelopes being used systematically as reference tools.

Before starting to write, Simenon worked himself into a kind of trance. As he described it, "I can't see anything any more. The curtains are closed and I don't show myself. And when I return again to reality, I have the feeling that it's the world around me that's unreal. Whereas, my world is *the real one*."[65] He made sure he would not be interrupted for several days, and then "I try to put myself in a trance. What I call 'putting myself in a trance' really means creating a sort of emptiness inside myself, so that absolutely anything can find its way in."[66] Simenon was a disciplined writer, but he portrayed himself as an instinctive novelist, just as his sexuality was also instinctive and all consuming. He filled several of his famous pipes in advance, so that once he had triggered the writing process, nothing would interrupt it.[67] No one ever saw him writing; he retreated into monk-like seclusion with his typewriter until the work was complete. He typed with few deletions, except for eliminating redundant adverbs and adjectives, paring the text down to its essentials.[68]

Before launching into any novel, Simenon weighed himself, and he calculated that he might lose a kilogram and a half in the writing process.[69] He wrote of "[e]ight to ten days of preparation, as usual, the most disagreeable time, during which I am in a terrible mood (*de mauvais poil*)."[70] It was a physical ordeal that engaged his body as well as his imagination. Before writing, he cancelled all appointments for eleven days, and visited the doctor to check his blood pressure and get the all clear to proceed.[71] Once Simenon was *en roman* (in a novel), he could not be stopped. He became a prisoner of his own creative fever, declaring that the development of the novel was out of his conscious control.

He told one journalist that he stripped off his clothing as he grew hotter and hotter, so that when he later emerged from the room he might be completely naked.[72] His highly nervous state at the typewriter contradicted his assertions that he was simply a hard-working artisan.[73]

Whatever his writing plan for the day, Simenon surrounded himself with a well-organized set of props, which kept all his options open. He likened his ritual preparations to setting up a circus act.[74] To prepare the elaborate theatre of his writing, his wife first cleaned his typewriter and his various pipes. A bundle of five dozen or so pencils was assembled on his desk, together with his ever-ready sharpener, and a pot of hot tea or coffee warming on an electric ring nearby. Occasionally there was a glass of red wine at his side as well, although, as already noted, Simenon firmly denied that alcohol had anything significant to do with his creative processes (once again, we do not have to believe his denial).[75] A range of stationery was strategically placed to fulfill quite specific needs – the manila envelopes and the dressmaking paper that he used to cut out a plan of the apartment where the main action took place. He hung a "Do Not Disturb" sign on the door which he had "souvenired" from the Plaza Hotel in New York.[76] He would have a list of up to two hundred names, culled from the telephone directory, on which he would draw for his characters. These were important rituals, which Simenon admitted amounted almost to a superstition.[77] Simenon thus combined an ethos of hard work and concentration with traces of a more romantic view of the author as an inspired genius. He remained attached to the magic power of the rituals that surrounded the creative act.

Typescript and Manuscript

Simenon's personal writing scenario allowed for the dual roles of both typing and handwriting. He allocated specific tasks to each of them, depending on what genre of fiction he was writing. Occasionally, he would write a novel using manuscript and typescript simultaneously, as he did with *Les anneaux de Bicêtre*, but this was rare.[78] Normally he used different implements to compose in different genres.

Simenon became a professional writer as a teenage reporter on the *Gazette de Liège*, where he had begun by writing in pen and ink. He learned to take notes in a form of shorthand, and before long he became accustomed to typing everything he wrote. "What strikes me nowadays," he said in 1960, "is that I, who used so much to love beautiful papers, leather-bound notebooks, the pencil, the pen, I started, from the age of sixteen and a half, to write on the machine because it was the habit then at the paper where I was a reporter. I got so accustomed to it that for years, for decades even, I was almost incapable of writing by hand."[79] But he never learned to touch-type. At Mougins in 1955, he had three typewriters: he hit the keys so hard that one cylinder could not survive more than two novels.[80] Like many other writers, he was forced to relearn writing by hand while convalescing from an illness. In 1961, he wrote one novel, *Les autres* (1962 – *The Others*), entirely by hand, and his wife Denyse typed it for him.[81] For Simenon, however, writing by hand was not just a temporary necessity brought about by illness. His choice of handwriting was sometimes a deliberate ploy to escape his normal routine, and to enjoy breaking all the rules he had fixed for himself in his life.[82] There were many rules, for, as we have seen, Simenon was a man of habit and wedded to working rituals. He would write from 6:30 to 9:30 daily, then walk, lunch, take a siesta, read the papers and go to bed by 10 p.m. At least, that is what he told the world.

In contrast to fiction, personal writings always required manuscript composition. He originally wrote his autobiographical *Pedigree* in pen and ink, until Gide advised him to revise it and, at the same time, to compose it on the typewriter. For his second autobiography, *Quand j'étais vieux* (When I Was Old), he chose spiral-bound notebooks with quadrilled pages and a canvas cover.[83] Similarly, his *Mémoires intimes* were written in tiny script with a Parker pen in school exercise books.[84] Simenon's handwritten notebooks of 1959–63, which later became *Quand j'étais vieux*, contained random thoughts, reports of visiting the doctor for various tests and frustration with whatever the media was harassing him about at the time. He made notes on the Algerian crisis and his children. His manuscript notebooks were his anti-novel, containing all that was troubling him when he was not writing fiction.

His methods for a Maigret novel were quite the opposite. He knew the formula so well that he typed the text directly onto the page. Sitting down to write a story about a character as familiar as Maigret could even be comforting. As Simenon confessed, "It was relaxing for me to sit down at my typewriter; to rediscover my good old inspector, without knowing anything more than he did about the conclusion of his investigations until the final chapter."[85] These novels, never more than about two hundred pages long, could be read at one sitting and were always the fastest to produce.

For his other novels, however, he employed a mixture of techniques. He sketched notes on a yellow pad first, and perhaps roughed out a whole chapter by hand in the evening, ready to be taken up again the next day. In the morning, however, his "revision" of the manuscript version might be drafted without any reference to the text he had previously prepared. "So the chapter," he explained, "was written by hand in the afternoon or the evening and, at six o'clock in the morning, I typed it, often without looking at the 'rough copy,' because the machine gives me a different rhythm."[86] Manuscript composition helped him get his ideas in order, but the typewriter liberated him from merely copying a previous draft, and it gave him greater fluency.[87]

Simenon claimed that, although he had a previously handwritten draft of a chapter at his side, when he came to type the chapter he did not pay much attention to his draft. Once again, he is probably overstating the freedom and fluency that he claimed the typewriter gave him. According to the researches of Claudine Gothot-Mersch, there are very few typed versions of Simenon novels that could *not* have been based on an earlier manuscript version.[88] Naturally, some details and nuances were changed from one version to another, as Simenon edited rather than copied his previous script. He might change the order or pace of a sentence, or expand a section, but, in spite of his assertions, there was nevertheless a great deal of fidelity between handwritten and typed versions.[89] Typing was an essential stage of Simenon's creative process, but it was not always as independent of manuscript drafts as he wanted everyone to imagine.

Between Literature and Pulp Fiction

Simenon's writing desk, his dozens of pencils, typewriter, and numerous tobacco pipes became very familiar to the general public and were frequently photographed by the press as the writer's legend grew. Yet his status as a writer remained ambiguous. He wrote crime fiction, but he also wrote more "literary" novels, and it was not easy to classify him. In this section, I sketch his precarious standing as a popular fiction writer in the literary field.

Simenon was no modernist, and it would be difficult to associate him with any literary or avant-garde movement. Nevertheless, his editors in Gallimard's prestigious Pléiade series tried valiantly to situate Simenon within the intellectual currents of his time. They claimed that he was close to the *Front populaire* populism of the 1930s, and subsequently the existentialism of the 1950s.[90] This labelling of Simenon was a way of claiming that he was not a solitary eccentric figure, and that he was not engaged solely in producing "industrial literature" in great quantities and at great speed. Simenon might be best seen as an element in rising middlebrow culture (*le roman moyen*), but even this assessment is based only on his non-Maigret novels. He can be considered as an author who revived the traditions of naturalist fiction as pioneered by Zola, Maupassant, and others, which by the 1930s had been discarded by the literary avant-garde.

He exemplified what Véronique Rohrbach calls "the aesthetics of mediocrity," writing about very ordinary lives under stress.[91] The lower-middle-class settings of his stories appealed to his readers, whose fan letters testified that they recognized themselves in his portrayals of *les petits gens* (humble people). Within this framework of his writing, however, there was a hierarchy of popular genres, and Simenon had set out to climb it. At the bottom of the heap were the sentimental romances with which he began as a young man, above them were adventure stories, and at the summit of the pulp fiction hierarchy stood the crime novel. The same holds true today: the weekly or monthly press sometimes reviews the latest crime fiction but would never give the same attention to Harlequin romances. As a crime fiction writer, Simenon stood at the top of a hierarchy, somewhere between trashy pulp fiction and legitimate literature.

Simenon, however, aspired to even greater things. He had ambitions: "I will turn out Fords," he once said, "for one part of my life and I will make a lot of money. After that, I will make Rolls-Royces for my own pleasure!"[92] His switch to Gallimard as his main publisher in 1935 committed him to producing six novels per year but also signalled an aspiration for greater literary legitimacy. The posthumous publication of some of his novels in Gallimard's classic Pléiade series indicated he had indeed achieved some literary recognition, but this did not happen until 2003. Even then, the Pléiade preferred to publish the *romans durs*; out of twenty-one novels selected for the series, only two were Maigrets.[93]

In fact, Simenon detested the French literary establishment, and the feeling was mutual. The man in the glass cage was considered unashamedly self-promoting in the most vulgar way possible, he typed his work absurdly fast, and his talent was questionable. Publisher Gaston Gallimard had admitted Simenon into his stable of authors, but Jean Paulhan, as editor of Gallimard's *Nouvelle revue française* (*Nrf*), found it hard to tolerate his work. Paulhan wrote to Gaston Gallimard in 1935: "Would it annoy you if the *Nrf* spoke harshly about Simenon? (I can hardly see how it could talk of him tenderly; but of course it could just shut up)."[94] As long as Gallimard welcomed Simenon as a member of "la maison," Paulhan had to accept this situation even if he did so under protest. Above all, Simenon's speed of production and the inferior genre in which he wrote disqualified him as a literary author. Paulhan was supremely condescending toward Simenon's career ambitions when he wrote:

What is Simenon whingeing about? There are something like a hundred million novels circulating throughout the world in his name. Add fifty million that he has written under other names. All that is fine: these are the kind of myths and stories that people need. As far as literature is concerned, there is very little of it. And yet Simenon will not rest until his stories have passed into "great literature," the literature of tragedy, just as he has already passed brilliantly from the anonymous (and sometimes erotic) novel to the detective novel then from the detective novel to the populist novel. It is touching to find such a need for progress in an author. Even more so, if that author is able – as we have been informed – to write a novel in nine days.[95]

This text was part of a 1963 review of Simenon's *Les anneaux de Bicêtre* – a review that Gallimard rejected for publication. The review appeared later as part of Paulhan's works. In a marked tone of superiority, Paulhan here accurately outlined the fiction genre hierarchy as well as Simenon's inability to transcend it.

There was one exception to this exclusion of Simenon from literary circles: his friendship with eminent novelist André Gide. He met Gide in 1935, and they corresponded until 1950. They were unlikely correspondents. Gide was the bourgeois, while Simenon was the chronicler of the *petits gens*; Gide was homosexual, Simenon a rabid heterosexual. Gide was twice Simenon's age. Yet they established a rapport, at least temporarily. Simenon addressed Gide as "Mon cher maître" and Gide always replied to "Mon cher Simenon," as an elderly professor might address a promising student. Gide was interested in crime fiction and liked Simenon's work. Simenon saw Gide as a mentor, and he had indeed asked for and followed his advice to rewrite *Pedigree* on the typewriter. This implied, however, that theirs was never a relationship between equals. Richard Cobb, an admirer of Simenon as an acute micro-sociological observer, suggested that the rapport between the two men survived only as long as the narcissistic Gide felt flattered. The older man liked the idea that he was helping an aspiring novelist who had a lot to learn from the master: "Gide was flattered by his interest, but the correspondence between the two is revealing only of the fatuity of the *pontife*, purring as he was stroked, and the anxiety of the pupil to do well at such a prize-giving."[96] Gide's responses to *Pedigree* seem to bear this out: "In general, very good work," he wrote on 21 August 1942, "keep going without fail" – all of which sounded like a teacher's comments on a student essay.[97]

Gide paid Simenon a great compliment when he wrote "I consider Simenon a great novelist: perhaps the greatest and most genuine novelist that we have in France today."[98] In the notes Gide compiled for a study of Simenon, which he never published, he elaborated on his judgment. Simenon, thought Gide, was the victim of a "misunder-standing," although Simenon himself was largely responsible for it. The public had stereotyped him as no more than an entertainer, a writer of potboilers and detective stories. But, according to Gide, he was capable of much better than this, if only the public would follow him. As this implied, Simenon's poor literary reputation derived from the discred-ited genre in which he wrote, which confined him to "the suburbs of literature." In addition to this handicap, Gide realized, what ruined his standing was his prolific production.[99] Simenon thus inhabited a limbo between popular success and literary acceptance. He could not have both because the two were almost incompatible: the literary elite would welcome Simenon only if he ceased to be a crime writer. Such rejection was the fate of pulp fiction authors who wrote fast and in abundance, no matter what their aspirations may have been.

Simenon still hoped to be accepted as a legitimate writer, aspiring to the consecration that a Prix Goncourt or a Nobel Prize would give him, but neither of them eventuated. Simenon had probably damaged his case for acceptance by leaving France for America after the war. In 1947, he switched publishers again, leaving Gallimard for Sven Nielsen at Presses de la Cité. This was a new turning point, at which Sime-non turned his back definitively on the French literary establishment and the patronage of André Gide. He had been unable to throw off the stigma of the glass cage, and he now chose media celebrity rather than seeking a literary reputation.

Simenon learned to adapt successfully to typewritten composition, turning from the machine to the pencil and back again according to the genre in which he was working. Nevertheless, as a speed typist and media junkie, he remained on the margins of literary legitimacy. He was hard to place in any corner of the literary field. He perhaps fared better in America, because it was less tolerant of the literary snobbery that he encountered in Paris. As late as 1964, Hubert Damisch, a French philosopher and art historian, launched a violent polemic against Ha-chette's series of *livres de poche*, arguing that cheap paperbacks gave the masses merely the illusion that high literary culture was now available to them. Damisch deplored the fact that books had been reduced to consumer objects and were now being sold "under the same conditions and in the same way as any packet of detergent."[100] But this was Sime-non's world. In a few decades, widespread Internet usage would make Damisch's lament about mass access to traditional cultural products utterly futile.

9 Erle Stanley Gardner: The Fiction Factory

The Stigma of the Typewriter

Whenever an innovation in writing technology is introduced, the new technique always has its detractors as well as its partisans. In the field of art and literature, a few practitioners obstinately refuse to legitimize new methods. Mohandas Gandhi, for example, feared the typewriter would destroy the ancient art of calligraphy,[1] and English novelist Evelyn Waugh insisted on using a dip-pen and prided himself on being two hundred years behind the times.[2] Old and obsolete objects become fetishized, in spite of the practical advantages clearly offered by new technology in terms of speed and convenience.

When the genesis of the typewriter opened up new possibilities, many authors nevertheless persisted with past writing technologies. They denigrated the machine as the instrument of hack writers, who, like Robert V. Carr, used it to grind out "literary sausage" ever more rapidly.[3] The typewriter was sometimes viewed as appropriate equipment for inferior writers who churned out fiction for purely mercenary motives and at an obscene speed. It could never, in this view, be the tool of creators of true literature. This chapter considers a twentieth-century example of an author who defiantly extracted the maximum from new technology: the American crime and adventure writer Erle Stanley Gardner, who was happy to label himself "the Fiction Factory."

Erle Stanley Gardner became one of the world's best-selling crime authors of the twentieth century. Born in Massachusetts in 1889 he moved with his parents to California, which was thereafter his base and the preferred locale for his fiction. He spent a turbulent youth, being expelled from high school, working for a time as a pugilist, and being involved in an unsuccessful business venture. He studied law in his spare time and was admitted to the California bar in 1911. Bored with the routine life of the law office, he began to write short stories, which he sold to pulp magazines. For the best part of a decade, Gardner invented many different characters, and wrote under many pseudonyms (A.A. Fair, Kyle Corning, Charles M. Green, Carleton Kendrake, etc.) while continuing to work full time in his legal practice. True success only came in the 1930s with stories featuring his best-known character, Perry Mason, a smart and unorthodox California defence attorney, aided and abetted by his loyal secretary, Della Street. The Perry Mason mysteries, which always came to a climax in Gardner's trademark courtroom dramas, made his fortune and were reproduced in comic strips and radio shows, before becoming the subject of a very successful television series of the 1960s starring Raymond Burr and Barbara Hale. Gardner travelled often, especially to the desert and to Baja California; as we shall see, he loved the outdoor life and the ranch he built at Temecula for himself and his extensive entourage, where he died in 1970.

By the time of Gardner's death, his New York publisher William Morrow had published 141 of his books, of which 80 were Perry Mason stories. By 1979, he had sold almost 311 million copies of his work, 170 million of those in the United States alone.[4] Morrow's strategy was to produce the first hardback edition of a Perry Mason mystery at two dollars; two years later, a paperback was issued by the reprint company Grosset and Dunlap, priced at seventy-five cents. About five years after initial publication, Pocket Books would produce a cheaper twenty-five-cent edition – the price increased to thirty-five cents in 1957 – and this was the format that proved most profitable. Thayer Hobson, Gardner's trusted agent, estimated that, over a decade, a Mason title could earn its author between $16,000 and $20,000. That does not seem a huge sum over ten years, but Gardner produced four new books per year for more than a decade. In addition, he would earn income from comic strips, radio shows, and the CBS television series based on Perry Mason stories.

Still, it took many years for him to earn enough from writing to be able to abandon his legal practice. In 1931, in the depths of the Depression, his income exceeded $20,000 for the first time. As a journalist commented later in the decade, "It had taken something over a million words to earn that much; but the electric typewriter made it possible."[5] By 1938, Gardner was so successful that Morrow invited him virtually to write his own contract.[6] By the 1950s, he was earning about $90,000 per year from Pocket Books royalties alone, an estimated sum based on an annual sale of three million copies.[7]

Gardner wrote fast and prolifically, and never aspired to produce great literature. "I'm in the game for MONEY," he brazenly told Harry North, assistant editor of *Black Mask* magazine, "and if I have any talent

I haven't prostituted, and find it out, I'll start her out on the streets to-night."[8] The typewriter was a key element in Gardner's self-proclaimed pimping of his own abilities. The typewriter assured his continuous and gigantic output and, as this chapter will describe, the assembly line of production that he eventually established was built around it.

Gardner categorized himself as an unashamedly professional writer, but this attitude obscured important contradictions. He started as a pulp fiction writer and, essentially, although he also wrote travel books as well as radio and television scripts, he always remained one. At the same time, an inner urge aspired to something better. While never pretending to be a literary author, he nevertheless craved recognition by a more respectable and discerning readership. His love-hate relationship with fashionable magazines like the *Saturday Evening Post* betrayed the ambiguity that lay within his self-portrayal as the Fiction Factory.

The Pulp Fiction World in the 1920s and 1930s

Gardner's apprenticeship and emergence as a professional writer were framed by the pulp fiction magazines of the 1920s and 1930s. *Black Mask*, *Top Notch*, *Dime Detective*, and their like appeared either weekly or monthly, costing only ten or twenty cents, and publishing short stories or slightly longer "novelettes." They dealt in a variety of genres, including adventure stories, westerns, mysteries, and fantasy fiction. They were produced on cheap, unglazed paper so coarse that readers could sometimes see pieces of wood chips embedded in it. Hence they were known as "the pulps," a rare example of a literary genre defined by the rough material of which it was made. The "pulps" were usually in seven-by-ten-inch format, each issue offering 130 pages of densely packed print between lurid covers. They paid authors by volume: the going rate for *Black Mask* was three cents per word. At one stage in his career, Gardner had a word-counter attached to his typewriter, which registered every time he hit the spacebar.[9] The pulps followed a dated business model that relied on news-stand sales and cheap production costs rather than advertising revenue.[10] There were about 200 pulp magazines in circulation in the 1930s.

The pulps catered to a mainly masculine, working-class readership. Their stories glorified an independent, smart-talking, and fundamentally honest hero struggling against an impersonal and highly regulated world. According to Erin Smith, this formula appealed to working men who felt threatened by Italian immigration, deskilling, and the rise of a female labour force.[11] The genre had patent tendencies towards machismo. In 1927, *Black Mask* called itself "The He-Man's Magazine," and it carried advertisements for guns and male body-building.[12] The stories it published were tough, violent, and fast moving. Their celebration of a certain conception of manliness was sometimes expressed in homophobic attitudes and anxieties about women, who were often cast as predators or deceitful manipulators. Gardner's own daughter Grace was forbidden to read them.[13]

Gardner established his reputation in this "hard-boiled" genre of popular fiction. Little sophistication was required from pulp magazine authors, just hard work and consistency – assets of which Gardner possessed an infinite supply. Apart from Gardner himself, the major exponents included the now forgotten Frederick Nebel and John Carroll Daly, as well as the more highly regarded Dashiell Hammett and Raymond Chandler. Chandler led the masculinist charge against the fashionable but "insipid" English country-house detective fiction of Dorothy Sayers and Agatha Christie. The more realistic American brand of fiction, he argued, was sweeping away Christie's stuffy spinsters and mincing dandies and instead featured proletarian heroes who defended their honour with their fists and commanded a sharp-witted rhetorical repertoire.[14]

Gardner created many characters under various pseudonyms for this market: Speed Dash, the Human Fly, who climbed up skyscrapers and crushed raw potatoes in his bare hand to improve muscle tone; Ed Jenkins, the Phantom Crook, who infiltrated Chinatown disguised as Doctor Chew, a Chinese herb merchant; Lester Leith, the gentleman thief; and the mismatched pair of detectives Donald Lam and Bertha Cool, created under the pseudonym A.A. Fair. These were just a few of the recurrent characters in Gardner's fictional imaginary. It is impossible to say in this period that he was developing his authorial voice – he spoke in several voices at once, depending on which pseudonym he was using at the time and which magazine editor was commissioning his work.

When Gardner first entered the circle of writers around *Black Mask*, he saw it as a fraternal partnership, which he compared to a baseball team, with the editor (then Phil Cody) as its coach. Before very long, however, Gardner was fuming at his pulp fiction rivals, and he felt slighted whenever one of them was singled out for public praise. He attacked what he called the "Hammett-Hemingway" school of fiction, which was distinguished by its "crisp photographic" style, and he was jealous and nauseated when *Black Mask* touted Hammett as its "fair-haired boy child."[15] But he recognized the popularity of their style, and to some extent he tried to incorporate it in his own work.[16] While acknowledging the dominant fashion, he was determined to protect his own individuality as an author. His growing frustration with "Captain" Joseph Shaw, editor of *Black Mask* from 1926 to 1936, derived from his conviction that Shaw was forcing all his authors to imitate Dashiell Hammett, which was producing a very monotonous magazine. According to Gardner, Chandler was imitating Nebel who was imitating Hammett. He, Gardner, aimed to be different.[17]

Gardner began as an author by publishing short stories in different genres in pulp magazines. He embraced the unpretentious world of hard-boiled fiction, and it gave him his basic income as an author. But he wanted to break into the more up-market magazines, the so-called "slicks," such as *Liberty*, *Collier's*, and the *Saturday Evening Post*. The "slicks," unlike the "pulps," were produced on glossy paper and aimed at a more genteel, middle-class readership. In 1930, the *Saturday Evening Post* had a circulation of just under three million, and an actual readership that may have numbered ten million.[18] The slicks survived on income from advertising, and they paid authors more generously. Whereas pulp magazines targeted working-class men, the slicks wanted also to appeal to middle-class women. In fact, the pulps and slicks had more in common than they admitted: some companies owned both pulp and slick magazines at the same time but, to Gardner, they seemed opposites. To break into this market, Gardner knew he would have to write differently. For the respectable magazines, he needed to tone down the melodrama and develop well-rounded characters instead of emphasizing only the plot and the action. He could not write for the *Saturday Evening Post* about characters with names like Speed Dash or Sidney Zoom. A certain amount of self-censorship was called for. In spite of his warm espousal of his role as a trashy fiction writer, which this chapter will fully demonstrate, Gardner nevertheless had aspirations to something more. He wanted to conform to pulp fiction formulas and yet make his own individual mark. He wanted to be accepted by respectable magazines, suggesting his implicit acceptance of the cultural hierarchy that marginalized *Black Mask* and its ilk.[19]

Gardner broke through this barrier with great difficulty. "I want to be particularly careful to keep from getting into the category of a pulp fiction writer that tried to crash the slicks, but couldn't make it stick," he told his second agent, Jane Hardy, in 1934, after *Liberty* magazine had rejected one of his stories.[20] The smooth-paper magazines gave him stage fright, he confessed.[21] The *Saturday Evening Post* pressed him to introduce a love interest into the Perry Mason stories, but Gardner resisted. "There isn't any love interest in a football game," he argued, "but it brings thousands of spectators to their feet, screaming with excitement."[22] He succeeded in his ambitions only when the Perry Mason stories were serialized. In 1937, the *Saturday Evening Post* accepted *The Case of the Lame Canary* for $15,000, and gave Gardner an escalating contract for future serials.[23] Even then there were problems. For example, the magazine turned down *The Case of the Counterfeit Eye* on the grounds that a story about a false eye was too gruesome. He was not complimentary about the magazine's taste in crime fiction. "They do not want corpses," he ranted, "their murders must de dehydrated affairs with no blood flowing from the victims. Their murders must be unreal, lady-like affairs."[24]

Gardner had bridged a cultural gap, reaching a new audience and commanding greater financial rewards, but without ever completely severing his roots in sensational adventure fiction. "I am very much interested," he said, "in reaching the more cultured type of reader."[25] The context of this remark was his discontent with cheap-format Spanish and French editions of his books, but it revealed his inner desire for acceptance. He was a self-made man who both resented the snobbery of the "slicks" and, at the same time, wanted them to recognize him. Selling stories to them was harder but much more lucrative than selling to the wood-pulp magazines. It also rewarded the author with a new source of cultural capital.

One reason why Gardner was successfully able to navigate the treacherous passage between pulps and slicks was his deep-seated sense of morality. Whereas some writers and editors tried to rescue the pulp magazines from insolvency by piling on sex and violence, Gardner refused to take this route. Indeed, his regular discussions with Thayer Hobson over cover illustrations revealed a certain prudery in his outlook. He did not want his books sold with a "sex jacket."[26] In fact, most of the Pocket Books editions of his books *did* feature an alluring woman on the cover, and the cover of his *The Case of the Half-Awakened Wife* (1945) depicted a woman actually getting out of bed in revealing nightwear. His protests about some cover illustrations thus appear slightly disingenuous. His covers, however, were relatively discreet compared to the blood-spattered sadism and sex in Mickey Spillane, who appeared on the scene with *I, the Jury* in 1947, and whom Gardner deplored.[27] Gardner always wanted to keep Perry Mason stories free of explicit sex. His fiction had to be suitable for female and adolescent readers if it was ever going to appear in the *Saturday Evening Post*.

Eventually, the pulp magazines died; the paper shortages of the Second World War hurt all magazines, and they found it hard to compete with radio and television. As he broke free of their grip, Gardner understood that crime fiction was evolving, and he seized his opportunity. After the end of Prohibition, the removal from the streets of the worst manifestations of gangster violence, and the emergence of a stronger federal police force, the public started to have more confidence in the police and the law, instead of regarding them as ineffectual as well as corrupt. This new respect for law enforcement meant that the days were numbered for stories about Raffles-type gentleman criminals, Robin Hood–style crooks, or the private eye as hero (like Hammett's Sam Spade). Instead there was a growing space for stories about police detectives and lawyers. Gardner first cashed in on this with his Doug Selby series (*The D.A. Lights a Candle*, etc.), and then with Perry Mason, the fighting lawyer who won his victories in courtroom dramas and, in so doing, gave the reading public an education in US court procedure and the rules of evidence. "We are moving into new territory," he told *Country Gentleman Magazine* in 1937, where "the hero is not a superman, but an intelligent chap and the story is about real detective work."[28]

The Self-taught Writer

Gardner had various jobs as a young man, and they all provided fuel for his fiction. He had trained as a pugilist, and came to see Perry Mason in a prize-fighting role. In the prize-fighting story formula, the gladiator is always reluctant to fight but is drawn into action to defend the weak and to secure justice by fair means or foul.[29] Gardner succinctly characterized Mason's role as "ingenuity in support of righteousness."[30] After the First World War, Gardner went into a business venture selling car parts and accessories. The enterprise went bankrupt in 1921 and left Gardner broke. In spite of this failure, he always claimed later that he knew a bit about salesmanship, and he freely lectured publishers on how to sell his books. He studied law in his own time to pass the California bar examination. He established a reputation in the town of Oxnard defending the local Chinese community – a connection that later gave him material for his Ed Jenkins stories. He always remained a lawyer. His personal library of over two thousand titles was dominated by books on court procedure, trial cases, the sciences of fingerprint identification and lie detection (the Polygraph), and forensic medicine and toxicology. He subscribed for years to the annual reports of the Los Angeles Police Department.[31] In later life, he created a television series called *The Court of Last Resort*, in which old cases were re-examined to avoid or expose the execution of innocent people. His later Perry Mason stories were dedicated to members of the legal profession – forensic medical practitioners or judges who had made a difference – and he valued the endorsement of his stories by prominent lawyers for the air of authenticity this lent them.

Gardner was a self-taught writer, and he thought he had learned a few things from life experience: "I have no natural aptitude as a writer," he insisted. "Everything that I have found out about writing I have learned from long hours of study and bitter experience which has included the making of virtually every mistake every writer has ever made."[32] He repeatedly declared that he had no talent as a writer but that he was a good plotter. He systematically broke down plots into their component parts, talking of his "gambits," "clue sequences," and finding the "common denominator" of reader interest. Sometimes writing was a chess game; sometimes it was a case of hypnotizing the reader; sometimes he applied the "iceberg theory," which in a crime story meant showing the readers only a hint of what lay below the surface. If the author showed readers too little and they were literally clueless, they lost interest, and if he showed them too much, then there was no mystery and they could too easily predict the outcome.

These chess and iceberg metaphors recur in Gardner's numerous plot notebooks, in which he conducted a dialogue with himself about plotting and the priorities that he needed to keep in mind.[33] In order to teach himself how to write, he consulted William Wallace Cook, the inventor of Plotto, a mechanical plotting device, which Gardner bought, used, and improved on. He created his own cardboard plotting wheels. These systems provided random permutations of different plot components – the setting, the main character, the victim, motives, complicating themes, and so on. It was no doubt from Wallace that Gardner first took the title of "the Fiction Factory."

As well as plotting, he learned the art of composing titles. Gardner's philosophy of titles was not that they should always be alliterative, as many of them were (*The Terrified Typist*, *The Loquacious Liar*, etc.), but that they should be rhythmical, with the last word being of just one or two syllables (as with *The Case of the Velvet Claws* or *The Case of the Counterfeit Eye*).[34] His notebooks are scattered with title possibilities. The title of a detective mystery was so important in arousing the reader's curiosity that at one point (*The Case of the Stuttering Bishop*, 1936) Gardner seemed to be starting with a good-sounding title and then building a plot around it – but he learned that this approach could be too restrictive.[35]

Gardner was a "quadernophiliac" – a notebook freak. He kept notebooks for many different purposes. Some were simple organizers, like diaries, address books, or accumulated golf tips and lists of guns. Others were commonplace books, in which Gardner recorded jokes or snappy phrases that he wanted to use in the future, like "with all the cruelty of a barbed fish hook" or "kicking up as much rumpus as a cat in a bath tub."[36] His archive includes nine boxes containing approximately 150 notebooks of different formats, from large ledgers to spiral-bound stenographers' pads, covering several decades. He wrote in these notebooks everywhere – in airports, at his ranch, at sea, in hotels. Above all, he used his notebooks to list plot ideas and possible characters, always in alphabetical order, and to suggest stories to himself, without at first knowing whether they would turn out to be a Perry Mason case, an A.A. Fair story, or something else entirely. He copied and pasted extracts from *Writer's Digest*, searching for the hidden secret to structuring a successful detective story.[37] From *Writer's Digest*, for example, he copied advice never to criticize marriage, motherhood, or capitalism and never to insult anybody's religion.[38] He clearly referred to these extracts regularly, underlining salient points in red, and drawing manicules pointing to key statements. He would ruthlessly castigate himself in his notebooks for his lack of progress. About *The Case of the Stuttering Bishop*, he wrote, "Scrap the whole damn 112 pages and go back to first principles."[39] "Be interesting," he commanded himself, "and be damned quick about it."[40] He often returned to favourite scraps of Chinese wisdom: "The journey of a thousand miles begins with but a single step [...] Let all thinking be on that next day's step."[41] Gardner emerges from his notebooks as a man who did not for one moment believe in concepts like talent or inspiration. He accepted his own lack of ability, and even thrust it in the face of agents and magazine publishers: "I'm more or less green at the game," he said. "Dog-goned if I know much about my own story analysis."[42]

He was confident, however, that he could learn the trade. In the early days, he was very receptive to criticism. He appreciated rejection letters, most famously from *Black Mask*. His first rejection letter told him that his characters "talked like dictionaries and the so-called plot had whiskers on it like unto Spanish moss hanging from a live oak in a Louisiana bayou." This made him chuckle, and he wrote back to thank the magazine and promised to revise the story.[43] "I like to get letters like yours," he told Harry North at *Black Mask*, "in which you tell me my stuff is rotten. How can a fellow ever learn what you like and what you don't like unless you spit it out."[44] He frankly outlined his ideal relationship with editors in his opening letter to Bob Hardy in 1925, inviting him to act as his agent: "I want some one to weed out the bum ones in advance, and to get rough with me and tell me when my work is sloppy and careless [...] I want an agent who has more education than I have. (I know law pretty well, but I'm careless in English, and I forgot all the grammar I ever knew)."[45] In fact there was nothing wrong with Gardner's English, except for his tendency to spell villain as "villian." But like many self-taught intellectuals, he was extremely conscious of his own lack of formal education. He told Thayer Hobson to give him absolutely honest critiques of his books, assuring him that he could take anything on the chin. He valued Hobson as a mentor and as a guinea pig for testing his story ideas.

Once Gardner had gained some recognition, however, his attitude changed and he became increasingly sensitive and egotistical. He responded to criticism by claiming he knew his readers' tastes. "Five million book customers every year take my side of the argument," he claimed in the 1940s.[46] He relied for marketing information on his "listening posts." His secretaries were his first readers, and he listened to their reactions. Whenever he travelled by plane, he examined airport bookstalls and what they were displaying, and he read voluminous fan mail and replied to some of it – but all that he knew about his readers was based on anecdotal information. From time to time he thought the readers must be getting tired of Perry Mason mysteries, but the sales figures showed otherwise, as Hobson told him.

Constructing the Fiction Factory

Having carefully studied plots, Gardner had to learn how to type. The history of the Fiction Factory really began with the rejection of his story "The Shrieking Skeleton" (1923). He revised this story after a day's work at his law office, typing with two fingers until they bled:

> I became enthused as I revised that story. I was up just about all night for three nights hammering away at the thing. My typewriter didn't have rubber keys. The technique that I had was a two-fingered technique which caused the pounding on the hard typewriter keys to pull the flesh at the end of my fingers away from the fingernails. I got to spattering blood on the typewriter keys so I covered the ends of my business fingers with adhesive tape and kept right on hammering away.[47]

By the end of 1925, he was employing a part-time typist, and, as he began to earn enough from writing to gradually disengage from his legal practice, he could afford to hire a secretary for the first time in 1927.[48]

His own typing struggled to keep up with his thoughts. As he worked on "The Serpent's Coils" (1924), he reported that "I can actually feel the emotions of my characters, and I tear along on the typewriter oblivious of time, grammar and punctuation, trying to keep pace with the action."[49] He needed to find ways to accelerate production. By 1932, he was employing two typists, and he owned an electric typewriter for his first drafts. He described the process: "I started out writing in longhand and copying my stories on a typewriter. I graduated to direct composition on a typewriter, then to an electric typewriter, and finally to dictating machines." In April and May 1931, he wrote 348,500 words on his electric typewriter.[50] Each step enabled him to compose faster. An important breakthrough came when he stopped simply copying on the machine and began to "think on the typewriter": "My goal in those days was to learn to think on a typewriter. I tried time after time, but I could never do it. Always the mechanical aspect of the typewriter, the collection of characters leering up at me from the keyboard interfered with my constructive thinking. I stayed with it, however, and gradually got so that I could think on the typewriter."[51] Here Gardner clearly experienced the distancing effect caused by the machine, discussed in chapter 5. He made an exceptional effort to overcome this experience of dislocation and achieve greater fluency.

Gradually the elements of the Fiction Factory took shape. He fitted out a campwagon (a mobile home), which enabled him to escape from interruptions from litigants and law clients. It was fitted with a bath and hot water, a typewriter desk, and a dictation machine that ran off the vehicle's battery.[52] In 1933, he went one step further, taking portable transcribing machines in the wagon, and he was accompanied by three women, the Walter sisters, who were now working for him. "Here's the Gardner Fiction Factory all on wheels," he announced to Hobson.[53] After 1938, he established headquarters at the El Paisano ranch he bought at Temecula, six miles northeast of San Diego, the chosen location for the Fiction Factory.

What did Gardner mean when he called himself the Fiction Factory? He presumably did not mean that his system churned out products that were always identical; although he was a formula writer, his stories and his heroes were never exact replicas of each other. He no doubt implied that the system he had created involved a string of workers engaged in performing largely mechanical tasks (taking shorthand, typing, transcribing dictated texts), in a largely repetitive sequence. Dictation, typing, revision, and retyping followed each other in a steady, uninterrupted rhythm until a finished novel rolled off the assembly line. And by the time it was completed, others were already being processed. As in a factory, production was never interrupted. The typists at his command did not "clock in" for work at a regular time, because most of them lived at the ranch itself. But Gardner involved them in a continuous factory-like process of fiction production, and the background clacking of several typewriters at Temecula resembled the monotonous hum of factory machines in operation.

It is conventional to separate literary production on the typewriter from the new office routines of the early twentieth century discussed in chapter 3, because the latter seem far removed from the world of literary inspiration and creative imagination; but these two worlds fed and nurtured each other. In this case, Gardner, who had personal experience of how a legal practice functioned, imported his own private typing pool into his ranch at Temecula and adopted the bureaucratic practices of any small or medium-sized business. No doubt this attention to bureaucratic efficiency explains why his papers and correspondence now seem so meticulously and professionally preserved, organized, and classified in the archives of the Harry Ransom Center in Texas.

The Walter sisters – Jean (Gardner's future wife), Peggy, and Honey – were all typists essential to the functioning of the Fiction Factory, and later Gardner would reward them with a share of royalties.[54] He jokingly called them his "harem."[55] Jean was a loyal devotee and a permanent fixture, managing Gardner's travel and his staff. She was perhaps the model for Della Street, although she graciously declined this compliment on the grounds that the collective effort of the whole team was what really counted.[56] They took shorthand, transcribed recordings, and typed drafts. When Gardner was on the move, he express-mailed his recording cylinders (later discs) to Honey Moore in Temecula or Los Angeles.

At first, Temecula was an unprepossessing collection of cabins, but Gardner soon enlarged its facilities to accommodate his production line, until it consisted of more than twenty buildings, including Gardner's study, office buildings, and guest cottages. "Like Topsy," Jean Walter (then Bethell) commented, "it just growed."[57] He had a cook, a ranch manager, and several temporary secretaries, many of whom did not stay long because of the demands of the job: they were isolated on the ranch, and they had to be prepared to travel and accommodate Gardner's high-powered work schedule. There were usually between five and seven secretaries at Temecula at any one time working on Gardner's texts. "My fiction business," Gardner wrote in 1945, "has suddenly grown from a relatively small business into something that is quite large and which has a great many ramifications."[58] By 1955, Gardner had a staff of fifteen employees. In *The Case of the Terrified Typist* (1956), Gardner described a miniature model of the Fiction Factory itself, with Perry Mason and his law library; Della Street, the personal assistant and office manager; Paul Drake, the private detective; Jackson, the law clerk; two permanent secretaries; a receptionist and switchboard operator; and temporary agency typists. These all paralleled the real-life team of Gardner himself: Jean Bethell, his first secretary; the ranch manager Sam Hicks, and various secretaries. Just like Perry Mason, Gardner also had his personal law library.

Gardner had indeed become a small business operation. He dictated his stories onto cylinders or records, to be transcribed by several secretaries at once, receiving from them in exchange a typed version, which he revised either by hand or perhaps by more dictation. Then a final version would be typed.[59] "Things are exceedingly hectic here," he told Jane Hardy in 1935. "Right at present, we have five girls banging out typewriters far into the night and the place sounds like a boiler factory."[60] At the core of this workforce were the Walter sisters, all separated or divorced, and especially Jean Bethell. They dealt not only with his fiction but also with a huge business correspondence, managing copyright matters, Gardner's income tax, and the portrayal of his creations in the press and on the radio, not to mention an avalanche of fan mail. According to Bethell, they sent out 20,000 words of correspondence daily on top of their fiction work.[61]

The Fiction Factory was periodically mobile, and operations had to continue while Gardner was travelling, in North America or overseas. He normally took secretaries, typewriters, and transcribing and dictating machines with him wherever he went. He would book a hotel suite ahead of his arrival, taking along two or three secretaries with their transcribing equipment and typewriters. When he went on a Pacific cruise in 1934, he had the shipping company fit out an office for him in a stateroom on board.[62] When Jean Bethell was rushed to hospital for kidney surgery in 1941, he rented an office nearby in Riverside to keep working while visiting her.[63] The only exception was his visit to China in 1931. On that occasion, he had to improvise. Stranded for three days by a typhoon in Macao, where the power supply was temporarily cut, he wrote a novelette sitting on the toilet in his hotel bathroom, which was the only place with enough natural light to work by.[64] The pace was relentless, no matter what the location.

Typewriters were an integral part of this frenetic activity. An equipment inventory in Gardner's archive shows that, between 1939/40 and 1965, he bought at least forty-five typewriters, favouring IBM electrics, for their proportional spacing, and Smith-Corona portables, not to mention numerous Dictaphones and transcribing machines.[65] This does not include what he may have bought before 1939. The Fiction Factory consumed typewriters in such bulk that suppliers were keen to send a personal sales representative to the ranch to demonstrate new models. There was a constant turnover of machines; used models were traded in to their original dealers, sold to the secretaries, or ended up in storage.

Was the Fiction Factory the product of Gardner's success, or the means by which he achieved it? Daniel Karlin preferred the first formulation, but it seems more appropriate to conclude that it was both the product of his rising income and also the means to even greater celebrity.[66] The Fiction Factory took shape very gradually, and, until Gardner was earning a respectable income, he could not hope to maintain such a complicated and well-staffed establishment. Yet neither could he have sustained his extraordinary pace of production through the 1950s and 1960s without his own private typing pool and the secretarial infrastructure he had created.

Quantity and Speed

Gardner adopted the model of factory-style mass production, based on the typewriter. He called himself a "quantity writer" and closely monitored his own output. For the month of September 1932, he calculated his output at 235,000 words. He dictated *The Case of the Velvet Claws* in three and a half days, besides writing twelve novelettes, all between 10,000 and 27,000 words long.[67] It was as if he had imbibed the imperatives of scientific management theory and was conducting continual time-and-motion studies on himself. Already by the mid-1930s, he was producing fiction on an industrial scale, and he embraced the achievement: "I am the manufacturer, you are the wholesaler," he told his agent Bob Hardy, and he repeated it almost verbatim to Thayer Hobson, which suggests he was fond of the phrase.[68] He counted how many words he wrote each day and each month, and from the mid-1930s to the mid-1940s, he maintained a consistent quota of 100,000 words per month.[69] In the 1950s, he was producing four Perry Mason books a year for his publisher Ed Morrow, not counting an A.A. Fair novel almost annually, as well as shorter stories. He was simultaneously revising television scripts for the CBS Perry Mason series, and for *The Court of Last Resort*. When observers speculated in disbelief that some of this output must have been written by others, he reacted strongly. One reviewer in the *Atlanta Journal* rashly suggested that Gardner must have relied on ghostwriters to produce as much as he did: Morrow immediately offered $100,000 to anybody who could find one of them.[70] The money was safe. Gardner had turned age-old prejudices against "industrial literature" on their head: he could think of writing *only* as a manufacturing business.

As well as a self-styled quantity producer, he also produced at speed. He often related how his first published book (*The Case of the Velvet Claws*, 1933) was dictated in only three and a half days. He told Thayer Hobson at Morrow that he could start a novel on a Saturday or Sunday, dictate it on the Monday and finish it within a week, typed and ready to send.[71] In practice, it usually took slightly longer than this to complete a full-length book. Once he had conceived and planned a plot, which could take between half an hour and half a day, he could produce the draft of a novel within two weeks, and, when it was fully functional and fine-tuned, the Fiction Factory could revise and produce a final version with a month from inception. His notebooks for 1952 and 1953 chart the progress of two novels in detail. For *The Case of the Grinning Gorilla* (1952), he started plot work on 20 July 1952, and Hobson read the complete draft at Paradise Camp on 19 August – almost exactly a month's work of plotting, dictating, and revising. Similarly, and at the same pace, he began dictating *The Case of the Green-Eyed Sister* (1953) on 20 May 1953, and even though he decided at a late stage to "revise the guts" out of it, he had finished it by 14 June – again in less than a month, about half of which was taken up with dictation and the other half dedicated to revision.[72]

Some considered such speed unseemly for a creative novelist. His agent Jane Hardy advised him not to advertise the fact that he worked so fast, because it might not go down well with New York editors. But Gardner had no intention of keeping his methods secret. He replied that he was a pulp magazine writer, and in that environment speed was an asset. He remarked to Jane Hardy, "Granted that it would be better to be known as a slow, methodical worker who turned out perfect stuff. But if I tried that while I am in the wood-pulps, the editors would brand me as a hypocrite and a liar."[73] Thayer Hobson could not understand how he managed it. "At this rate," he told Gardner, "we'll make Edgar Wallace look like a kangaroo with one leg."[74] Gardner was a high-pressure, high-speed creator who was not greatly interested in carefully manicured outcomes. This inevitably took a toll on his health. "For sixty-two years," he said in 1951, "I have driven myself at a mad pace. My mind has rolled up a lot of mileage. There are evidences that I am going to crack up unless I take things easier. My mind is a high-speed motor and a high-speed motor has a tendency to get loose piston rings."[75] But there is no sign that he ever slowed down.

"Give Me Cayenne Pepper"

Gardner loved the outdoor life. In fact, one reason he started a career as a writer was not because the Muse was calling, but precisely in order to escape routine office work and enjoy the freedom and independence of travelling around rural California, especially in the desert of his beloved Baja California, where his ashes were later scattered. He had a hideout in the Sierra Nevada foothills (Paradise) and another in the San Jacinto hills (Idyllwild), and later he stayed on a houseboat on the Sacramento delta. He loved campfire camaraderie, barbecuing steak at sunset, hunting, and fishing. He played archery golf, bow-shooting his way around the equivalent of eighteen "holes." With his bow and arrows, he shot bullfrogs, skunks, and rabbits. He hunted moose in Canada (without success), he sought out head-hunters at Bontoc (Philippines), and then came home to his dogs and his pet coyote Bravo. "If variety is the spice of life," he wrote in his unpublished autobiography, "give me cayenne pepper."[76]

According to Jean Bethell, family and domestic problems were an unwanted distraction for Gardner. For him, she said, "marriage was a nuisance [...] as Erle would write to fans, Perry and Della were too busy working on cases to think of marriage."[77] His relationships with women could be flirtatious in a patronizing way. He called his agent Jane Hardy his "little fish" and told her she should be spanked; of course, he adopted a totally different tone with men.[78] Possibly his controversial break with Jane Hardy in 1937 can be ascribed to an inability to deal with a woman as a business equal who would trade verbal blows with him, as did Bob Hardy and Thayer Hobson. His first wife, Natalie Talbert, accompanied him on cruises and to China, but most of the time allowed him to live a quasi-bachelor lifestyle. He provided for her after their separation in 1935, and never divorced her, marrying Bethell only after Talbert died.

Gardner was proud of being a straight-talking westerner, who lived far away both physically and in spirit from the urbane New Yorkers who were at the centre of his publishing universe. But he was born in Massachusetts, and perhaps a streak of New England Puritanism fuelled his over-developed work ethic. He felt a sense of inferiority as a writer, publicly confessing his own lack of natural expertise but, at the same time, stridently defending his achievements. He wrote prolifically and at high speed. If a title was selling slowly, his response was simply to write more books, faster. He had no time for aesthetic niceties and, rather than accepting the potential stigma attached to his style of mass production, he defied it. Indeed, he gloried in the assembly-line production he installed in his Fiction Factory.

Some writers identify their trade as craftsmanship, valuing the slow, thoughtful pace at which a text develops and matures, improving at every stage of revision. Their advice sometimes seems to mirror the ideals of the Italian slow food movement. Gardner represented the antithesis of this method in which the writing slowly evolves and a typewriter is an unwelcome intrusion. "Frankly, Hammett is an artist. I am a hack writer," he disarmingly told Joe Shaw in 1930.[79] A few years later, he proudly told his agent he was producing not fiction but merchandise.[80] By the 1950s, Gardner had left the time far behind when he revised rejected stories until his fingers bled. Typewriters remained essential to his factory production, even though he had by then delegated the typing to others. The kind of formula fiction that Gardner wrote had to be produced at great speed and quantity to keep his faithful readers constantly supplied. The weekly magazines needed a regular supply of stories, while Gardner had created, and now needed to satisfy, a boundless demand for Perry Mason mysteries. He also needed to provide a constant output to keep his name in the public eye. Only mechanical production on an industrial scale made possible the Erle Stanley Gardner phenomenon. The Gardner Fiction Factory was a direct product of the typewriter century.

10 Domesticating the Typewriter

Anxieties of Authorship

Historically speaking, women authors have hesitated to take up the pen. Critics writing about nineteenth-century English literature have pointed to the feelings of fear and guilt that deterred a woman from assuming a public role as an author – fear of male hostility or condescension, guilt and fear about trespassing into male territory and defying society's expectations of a "proper lady."[1] This chapter must consider how far such inhibitions dissipated in the twentieth century and how far, as Mary Poovey pessimistically put it, ideological constraints on female autonomy remain "sedimented deep in the layers of our culture and our consciousness."[2] I take Agatha Christie, along with writers of romance and children's fiction, to examine what, if anything, was different or characteristic about women's writing practices, as opposed to men's, in the typewriter century.

This chapter will examine two distinct aspects of this issue. First, I will explore the extent to which women writers were compelled to integrate their writing and their typewriters into a domestic context. Women were obliged to find a space and time for writing, while at the same time fulfilling all their domestic obligations. Men expected women to juggle both roles at once. Second, I examine the notion that "typewriter women" tended to accept the status of a professional writer with a certain reluctance. This is not to imply that they lacked determination to succeed: the case of Catherine Cookson offers spectacular proof, if need be, of the naivety of that suggestion. Throughout her life, Cookson fought powerful inner demons and the stigma of her illegitimate birth, as well as multiple miscarriages and a debilitating blood disorder, to become a best-selling author. Women writers nevertheless tended to resist the notion that fiction writing, which they had seen as a part-time amusement, had become an activity that defined them as a person.

The reluctance of twentieth-century women writers to accept professional status had deep historical roots. The bourgeois domestic ideology of Victorian Britain valued women primarily as mothers and housekeepers, gendering the private sphere as feminine and the public sphere as masculine. This made the notion of professional authorship especially problematic for nineteenth-century women, who were encouraged to play a domestic role and protect the moral high ground, leaving men to battle with their greedy, competitive fellows in the marketplace, including the literary marketplace. In a feminist perspective, the model of separate spheres perpetuated gender inequality and reinforced the subordination of women to a male ideal. The domestic ideology cast women as selfless, submissive "angels of the house." This model was part of the middle-class social imaginary, but, by the twentieth century, it fitted increasingly uneasily with social realities, if indeed it had ever adequately described them. It underestimated women's unpaid activities outside the home, as well as fathers' engagement with their children. The private/public dichotomy obscured the grey areas in between, like the local or community sphere in which many women were active. Whatever force the model once exerted, it was growing weaker in the twentieth century, as women (usually unmarried) entered the workforce not just in traditional employment as domestic servants, but in new roles as shop workers, typists, and professionals. Nevertheless, many women internalized social norms that discouraged them from speaking out, or writing, in a male-dominated public arena. They were compelled either to defy or somehow accommodate the lingering effects of social disapproval.

As feminist scholars have shown, women writers were accustomed to avoiding high visibility for themselves. Speaking out might induce a sense of guilt at having transgressed a boundary. To overcome the anxieties of authorship, they adopted a variety of strategies either to subvert or accommodate dominant gender expectations.[3] They impersonated men, or declared their complete indifference to making any profit from their work, or perhaps vicariously enjoyed a freedom denied them in real life through the struggles of their fictional protagonists. George Eliot (otherwise known as Mary Ann Evans) adopted a male persona, although this device became transparent after 1859. Refusing to write "like a man," she rejected literary transvestism. Unlike many amateur women writers, she never considered literature merely as a charming sideline. Instead she became a true professional, responding and adapting to the demands of writing for periodicals. Writing gave her the financial independence she needed to escape a provincial life of domestic labour. But she had a serious purpose: a sense of moral duty justified her writing life and overcame any residual reluctance

to publish. Historical inhibitions, however, persisted into the twentieth century. Eliot was a distant, mid-nineteenth-century precedent, but
Agatha Christie, writing seventy years later, also contemplated a male
pseudonym. By this time, expectations had evolved: her publisher John
Lane talked her out of it.[4]

By the mid-twentieth century, the female writer was a common
phenomenon. The frontier she had to cross had shifted: it lay not in
the act of writing itself, but in embracing it and the income it earned
as a professional career. Catherine Cookson, for example, would not
plunge as deep as this into the literary marketplace, and seemed to be
accepting patriarchal constraints when she denied that she wrote for
any mercenary motives. Making money from novels, Cookson insisted,
was never her prime consideration, although this nonchalance could
frustrate an agent or a publisher. "I've never written for money," she
insisted. "I once astonished my agent, in fact he nearly fell on the floor,
when I asked him not to press my publisher for a rise on my next book,
that I was quite satisfied with what I was getting [...] He thought I was
clean barmy; no author talked like that."[5]

Women writers were more likely to see the benefits of their work in
terms of emotional satisfaction rather than monetary gain. As for enjoying a vicarious freedom through their fictional creations, Enid Blyton's
invention of the "tomboy" George/Georgina in her Famous Five series
is open to interpretation as an expression of the author's own suppressed rebellion against gender conventions. As for Barbara Taylor
Bradford, discussed below, there was nothing coded or disguised about
the bold power-drive of her heroines. The tenacity and social ambition
of Emma Harte in *A Woman of Substance* were unmistakeable. By the
1980s, the reading public was ready for a fictional heroine who was a
determined business tycoon in her own right.

Women writers frequently drew inspiration from female literary
ancestors. "A woman writing," noted Virginia Woolf, "thinks back
through her mothers."[6] Enid Blyton explicitly recognized Louisa May
Alcott's *Little Women* as a forebear.[7] Barbara Taylor Bradford situated
herself in a line descending from the Brontë sisters to Colette, although
she paid due homage to Dickens and Hemingway as well.[8] Agatha
Christie, on the other hand, acknowledged no specific female predeces-
sor; her real model lay in the Sherlock Holmes stories. Nonetheless, for
many authors, affiliations with an established tradition of female writing provided sustenance and laid claims to legitimacy. In what follows,
then, we must attend to the problems that women writers faced as
women, traditionally educated to play a self-effacing and subordinate
role, which constrained their personal autonomy. At the same time, we

must identify the defence strategies they deployed to deflect any anticipated disapproval of their outspoken independence.

Even when women writers did assert themselves, they ran into further problems. The woman writer who, however apologetically, com-
peted with men in the literary world risked criticism that she was
neglecting her domestic or maternal duties. Women's energies were
seen as a zero-sum game, in which time devoted to professional writing
inevitably diminished the quality of attention that they could invest in
the family. When Agatha Christie accompanied her husband on trips to
the Middle East (where she set many of her stories and where she had
originally met him), she was successfully combining her wifely duties
with her authorship and her own interest in Sumerian archaeology. As
for Enid Blyton, tensions between herself and her daughters were concealed until long after her death, when one of them accused Blyton of
neglect.[9] Perhaps she had not always successfully juggled the author's
work with maternal imperatives. Social pressure insisted that domestic
duty was paramount. As a result, the women authors considered here
found their time hedged in by domestic minutiae; and, if their role as
mothers and housekeepers suffered, they also felt hesitant, doubtful,
and even guilty as writers. The typewriter crystallized the dilemma:
where could it fit within the domestic sphere, without undermining the
woman's family obligations?

The typewriter was an essential signifier of the female professional
writer. Agatha Christie began on a borrowed machine, but that did not
last long. Barbara Taylor Bradford's father bought her a typewriter as
soon as she sold her first short story.[10] By 1927, Enid Blyton, too, was
gradually giving up longhand for typing.[11] The typewriter defined the
professional writer, but, in the cases reviewed below, it had to be integrated into the woman's domestic role.

Women's use of the keyboard itself was not intrinsically different
from that of men, except that women tended to be more competent on
the machine, having often done a Pitman course on shorthand and/or
typing in their youth. No doubt this partly encouraged male expectations that women would do their typing for them. A typical illustration
of this production model is the photograph taken of Leo Tolstoy at his
home in Yasnaya Polyana during the last years of his life (figure 10.1).
The stern, venerable, bearded figure of the male writer stands upright
in the background, holding a text, while two seated women await his
instructions. His favourite daughter, Sacha, sits poised at their Russian
Remington No. 10, while his wife, Sophia Andreyevna, is opposite her.
There is a superficial harmony in this image, but it is based on obedi-
ence to the master. In fact, even the superficial impression of harmony

Figure 10.1. Leo Tolstoy dictating at Yasnaya Polyana
(Source: SPUTNIK/Alamy)

is probably illusory. At his advanced age, Tolstoy and his family knew that anything the great man wrote would be seized on as something of interest and value to posterity. Even before Tolstoy's death, both his wife and daughter were intriguing to wrest control of his literary estate both from each other and from Tolstoy's friend and secretary Vladimir Chertkov.[12] For the time being, however, the two women acquiesced in their role in this model of the patriarchal typewriter.

In earlier chapters, the typewriter was considered as an item of office equipment, bringing about the modernization of bureaucratic and business work practices in the early twentieth century. Several male writers perpetuated this scenario, by importing the typewriter into their own office or study, which was conventionally a private space where they worked isolated from everyday domestic activity. The contribution of the typewriting women considered in this chapter is that they brought the typewriter into the home. By immersing it in domestic life, they represented a new way of using the machine.

Case studies in preceding chapters have concerned male writers with an exaggeratedly masculine presence. Simenon's rampant sexual behaviour, Gardner's enthusiastic hunting, and Hemingway's shooting, fishing, and drinking all fall into this category. Hemingway, in particular, is closely identified with a masculine image of the typist, hunched over his machine as he hammered out his newspaper copy, in a haze of cigarette smoke and with an indispensable glass of liquor within easy reach. "Write drunk, edit sober," was Hemingway's advice, but it was flawed since, as poet and novelist Blake Morrison suggests, "the rat-arsed aren't capable of writing."[13] I do not exempt all women from the category of hard-drinking writers either, but, on the whole, women writers did not drink (Patricia Highsmith being one exception). In general, alcoholic support was a man's need, or a man's problem.

In this chapter, the perspective on typewriter usage is widened to embrace the broader context in which women writers worked. I concentrate on a handful of female British writers, consisting of Agatha Christie, romance novelist Barbara Taylor Bradford, and children's authors Richmal Crompton and Enid Blyton, with occasional reference to romance novelist Catherine Cookson. Once again, these examples select themselves for three reasons: either these writers reflected on their career and writing methods in autobiographical works (Christie and Cookson); or they were celebrities who made relevant information public in press interviews (especially Bradford); or they have left or donated papers to an archive where they are accessible for study, leaving clues about their creative processes (Crompton, Blyton, Bradford).

What distinguished these women from their male counterparts was their attitude to writing itself and its place in their lives. The role of writing and typing depended, in a way that was rarely the case for male writers, on their marital status and whether or not they had children. Blyton had two daughters, who sometimes had to take a back seat to her typing, and they expressed divergent views about this later. Christie had two marriages and one daughter; Bradford is and Cookson was married, but neither had children; Crompton never married. For the last three, household duties were accordingly different and perhaps lighter. It also mattered whether or not the writers concerned were tied down in an enclosed domestic sphere, or whether they forged a life outside the home. Blyton was relatively immobile, whereas Christie travelled far and wide, sometimes accompanying her second husband on their archaeological digs in the Middle East. Crompton, too, was largely home-bound, but this was not by choice but because polio had restricted her mobility. Finding a place for the typewriter within the home depended on who and how many people inhabited it, and on how tightly the writer herself was bound to its domestic rhythms.

It depended, too, on income levels. Virginia Woolf famously declared that a women writer needed money and a room of her own.[14] The money could buy time by paying for domestic servants, but only successful women writers, or those married to wealthy husbands, could afford this luxury. Enid Blyton, for instance, employed a series of nannies to look after her daughters. Agatha Christie, too, could afford a large house but deliberately chose not to work in a private study. For many others, a house large enough to provide a separate study was often out of reach. The typewriter did not necessarily have a permanent place in the home. It had to fit in wherever and whenever it could.

Enid Blyton and the Domestication of Typing

Domestic and maternal obligations had an inevitable impact on women writers' work and their use of the typewriter. Australian playwright and screenwriter Betty Roland, for example, had a relationship with a Marxist colleague, Guido Baracchi, with whom she had a daughter. She and Guido parted company in 1942. She told an interviewer in the late 1980s: "When Guido did leave me, Gilda was four. I had to make her feel doubly secure. I used to work when she was at school. When she'd come home at four o'clock, the typewriter was put away. She was never put aside for anything."[15] When a child's needs pushed the typewriter aside, it could be very frustrating. Nancy Cato described her situation as a writing mother: "I did have help with the house and the children. This was what enabled me to go on writing [...] Some days when I had lots of children and lots of housework to do, and it would get nearer and nearer to night-time, I would have almost a physical craving to get to the type-writer, but it couldn't be done."[16] Another Australian writer, Charmian Clift, believed the typewriter craving had a hidden benefit, in that it com-pelled better time management. "All my writing life," she confessed,

> I have been chained to a domestic situation that made me in a sense be a very disciplined person about writing. I write at certain set hours, I've always had to. When I was very young and had babies it was at night, but it couldn't be all night because I had to get up very early in the mornings. I've always had to allow myself so many hours a day when I was at my typewriter and I would like to say that that has always been sacrosanct – I mean, that was the general idea of it but it can't be, of course, with the demands of a family.[17]

For women writers, the typewriter beckoned, but it occupied a low rung on the ladder of urgent tasks to be completed.

Enid Blyton found her own solution to this dilemma. She not only typed in a domestic setting, but she also made her domestic surround-ings the subject of her writing. For women writers, the places of typing were usually quite different from men's places. Consider Erle Stanley Gardner, who had a huge personal study at his Temecula ranch, deco-rated with Mesoamerican artefacts, rifles, bows, spears, and knives.[18] He typed or dictated surrounded by his personal collection of weap-ons. Enid Blyton, on the other hand, sat in her suburban garden with a portable on her knee, or typed sitting on her veranda. In adverse weather, she would set up her typewriter on a board and ensconce her-self in a comfortable fireside armchair. The setting was informal and domestic. In a photograph taken in 1949 and frequently reproduced in the press, she is typing on the veranda of her home at Green Hedges in Beaconsfield, with her two young daughters looking eagerly over her shoulder.[19] These two contrasting cases of the warrior's retreat and the playful family highlight the gendered nature of spaces for typing.

An almost contemporaneous photograph (from 1952) of Agatha Christie typing at home in Devon further demonstrates the domestic setting in which women writers used the typewriter (figure 10.2). In this posed image, Christie shows a degree of stiffness, but, although there are books nearby, she is not working in a study or a "home office." Although she could afford Virginia Woolf's "room of one's own," she preferred not to use a writing study. Most probably, this photograph depicts her at work at one end of her drawing room, an impression reinforced by the hint of a coal scuttle at the left-hand margin. The pol-ished table with turned legs and folded-down flap does not resemble

Figure 10.2. Agatha Christie typing at home, 1952
(Source: akg images/ Picture Alliance)

a desk. Apart from a writing pad and pen, no desk paraphernalia are present. Compared to Georges Simenon, surrounded by his pencils, pipes, envelopes, and reference books, Christie's immediate surroundings are very bare. She is not using a dedicated work space.

Like that of the other women writers cited above, Enid Blyton's writing was interspersed with domestic tasks. As she very typically recorded in her diary in the winter of 1926: "Wrote Nature Lesson all a.m. and till 3.30. The Electrolux man came at five and I told him I'd have one." Or, in the same vein, "Wrote etc in a.m. Polished bannisters in afternoon."[20] In addition to the Electrolux man, she had to deal with a stream of unsatisfactory nannies, many of whom were summarily dismissed as "bad girls." When the children were unwell, domestic tension mounted, especially when Blyton's husband, Hugh, was sick at the same time, as was the case in October 1938. This situation stretched her to the limit: "Did a little writing but it is very difficult." A few days later, in desperation, she confessed: "I feel as if it would be nice to run away and leave everybody!"[21]

Blyton, faced with the challenge of writing professionally in a male-dominated environment, chose to specialize in genres (children's fiction, nature writing) where she would not compete with male rivals. Her way of accommodating prevailing gender expectations was to work in safe territory where she did not trespass on any male preserve and did not subvert the dominant gender hierarchy. Her model was *Little Women*, which fictionalized a female and matriarchal group that mirrored her own with her two daughters. Such female communities, real or fictional, belonged to a "magical sisterhood" that helped to sustain women writers in their professional endeavours.[22]

The banal stresses and strains of parenthood reminded women of their domestic obligations and constantly interfered with writing. Blyton reacted by turning her domestic situation into literary content. In her magazine newsletters, she wrote about her house, her garden, and her pets. Her own family life, or a censored version of it, became the subject of her regular contribution to *Teachers' World*. When she wrote a gardening book in 1934, it was a book about her own garden at Green Hedges, where she also had her own vivarium, with frogs and toads she could observe for the purpose of writing her gardening book. In her autobiography, which was addressed to her child readers, she devoted the first five chapters to her pets and her garden. There were books, too, focused on her pet dog Bobs. Bobs died in 1935, but the books continued to appear as if he were immortal. In these ways, Blyton integrated her home life into her writing, fictional and otherwise. Mundane events that happened around her became points of interest in new stories, newsletters, and nature reports.

Blyton thus succeeded in domesticating the typewriter. What is remarkable is that the deeper problems of her own family situation, which was less than idyllic, were never made public. As a teenage girl, she had been emotionally disorientated when her father left home. To avoid social disgrace, the family pretended he was absent on a visit. She blamed her mother, avoiding contact with her, and refusing to attend her father's funeral.[23] In 1942, she faced the stigma of her own separation and divorce from her first husband, Hugh Pollock. Following the legal requirements of the time, Pollock agreed to manufacture fictitious evidence of his own adultery in order to keep Blyton's name out of public view. She never allowed him to see their children again.[24] Not until Barbara Stoney's biography appeared in 1974 did Blyton's fans realize that her second husband, Darren Waters, was not in fact the biological father of her two children. The immaturity of Blyton's behaviour in these matters has been the subject of adverse comment.[25]

The integration of the fictional and the domestic therefore came at a price, and the price paid was to avoid the public exposure of Blyton's divorce and remarriage. Her younger daughter, Imogen, resented her mother's attitude and accused her of neglect. In her view, Blyton was an "emotional cripple," a distant parent uninterested in childcare. The elder daughter, Gillian Baverstock, however, did not have the same experience and became the champion and guardian of her mother's reputation and archive.[26]

Reluctant Professionalism: Richmal Crompton and Agatha Christie

For much of the typewriter century, married women were not expected to work for a living, even if they were working at home. As a result, writing professionally was not easily compatible with social expectations. "Writing professionally" is used here to mean a for-profit occupation that was the writer's principal means of livelihood. It signifies writing for money as a more or less full-time career. This did not come easily for the women writers under review, and first efforts were frequently disappointing, even when they found a publisher. The first fee received in payment for a story might barely pay the wages of the typist who produced the text. Catherine Cookson, who employed a part-time typist, described this experience by offering a detailed budget:

> I started my serious writing in 1947. My first effort was accepted in 1949, and I was paid a hundred pounds, out of which I paid ten pounds to the agent, together with £1.11s.6d. to prepare an agreement with Macdonald's

[her London publisher], not forgetting the six pence for stamping it, total £11.12s.0d. And then, of course, there was £10 to the typist. Of course this doesn't take in the cost of the reams of paper I used in writing my story in longhand. So what was left of that hundred pounds? Only enough to pay for mending nine of the twenty-six leaks in the roof.[27]

But Cookson had found a typist, an agent, and a publisher: whether she realized it or not, she was well on the way to a professional career. For Richmal Crompton, on the other hand, this was a frustrating process.

Richmal Crompton became famous for her thirty-eight books of stories in the William series, featuring the eponymous William, an opinionated eleven-year-old schoolboy to whom the adult world seemed incomprehensible, his gang the Outlaws, and his girlfriend and nemesis, Violet Elizabeth Bott.[28] Richmal, a family name, confused many about her gender. She produced thirty-eight William books, which had sold over 90 million copies by 1987. The first William story appeared in 1919 in *Home Magazine*, a women's monthly, and the early stories were thus destined for an adult readership. Crompton wrote for multiple audiences. Unlike Enid Blyton, she was not afraid to use long words for younger readers – "why not enlarge their vocabulary?" she asked.[29] The stories also enjoyed great success as radio dramas and television series.

Crompton, however, did not rate her William stories very highly. She saw them as "pot-boilers," and her true desire was to write novels. After five books of William stories, she wanted to abandon him, but he became her "Frankenstein," a creation out of the author's control. He started as a hobby, but the monster took over.[30] Crompton wrote forty adult novels, in parallel with the William books, but she abandoned them in 1960 and they are now almost entirely forgotten. Unlike Blyton, she had not been content to work in "lesser genres" – she aspired to something more. William, however, had trapped her, and she could not emerge from the "safe" but marginalized field of children's fiction. On one fragment in her archived papers, Crompton scribbled, "All promise – no fruition?", a question that might be seen as an epitaph for her own literary ambitions.[31] In another fragment, she wrote what was probably a plot summary: "Couple perpetual friction clash of wills – one deliberately surrenders independence for sake of peace – question – is it worth it – decides it is."[32] Perhaps this too echoed Crompton's own resignation, and the eventual acceptance by a woman writer of the impossibility of escaping from what were traditionally women's genres.

Crompton was reluctant to accept her status as a professional writer, especially as it was identified with William, about whom she had mixed feelings. She sometimes expressed some irritation that he had taken over her writing life, because this signified her failure as a serious novelist. "I used to have a William book and a novel going at the same time," she said, "and it could be quite a relief to get away from him to something more serious."[33] Crompton was a classics teacher, but in 1923 the onset of poliomyelitis forced her to drop her teaching career. This gave her more time for writing, and she increasingly depended on it for her livelihood. Her status as a professional writer was thus forced upon her by the disease that handicapped her mobility.

Crompton's portable Underwood is on display at the University of Roehampton, London, but she first wrote her books by hand, then corrected them and typed the revised draft.[34] She wrote notes and ideas on any paper surface that came to hand. Her papers include scraps with jottings of quotations from authors ranging from Freud, Proust, and Pirandello to Teilhard de Chardin and Dostoevsky. This collection was like a commonplace book illustrating her impressively wide reading in European literature, except that there was no book – simply loose pieces of paper of all shapes and sizes.[35] Crompton was an extraordinary paper recycler. Drafts of William stories were composed on all sorts of paper – pages torn from ledgers, the backs of previous drafts, the backs of invitation cards, the backs of royalty statements, on fan letters, and literally on the backs and insides of envelopes. This confusion and profusion disguised her disappointment at the collapse of her private literary ambitions. When she could no longer teach, however, she had to earn a living by writing what would sell.

Most of the writers considered in this chapter specialized in romance and children's fiction – conventional feminine genres. Agatha Christie is the odd one out. Today, readers of detective fiction can enjoy the way that a new generation of women writers have revived and enriched what was once a traditionally masculine genre, but Christie had been there long before them. Jane Marple was already pruning the roses in St Mary Mead in the 1930s.

Agatha Christie was slow to accept recognition as a professional author and for many years was in denial about her true position. As we saw in chapter 7, her notebooks interleaved domestic concerns with her fiction, recording flowers to buy and hairdressing appointments along with plot options. Here I focus on her changing status as a writer during the 1920s, and her own reflections thereon.

Christie wrote her first novel (*The Mysterious Affair at Styles*, 1920) in response to a challenge set by her sister Madge. She composed it in longhand, and then typed it on Madge's Empire typewriter before sending it to a professional typist.[36] In fact, Christie had trained as a shorthand typist in a secretarial college, but, after she married, it was out of the question that she should use these skills in gainful employment.[37] For a short time in the 1920s, she dictated to her secretary-*cum*-governess, Charlotte ("Carlo") Fisher, but she found this slowed her down and made her feel self-conscious.[38] When she later broke her wrist, she resorted to a Dictaphone, but she soon found this method made her too verbose and repetitive. Economy of style, she wrote in her autobiography, is essential for detective fiction; ideally, crime novels should not exceed 50,000 words in length.[39] As a rule, Christie preferred in her early years to write in longhand and then type up her draft.

Domestic duties inevitably intruded. "If you lead a busy life, which I do," she explained, "it's very hard to find a couple of weeks without interruptions."[40] In her autobiography, Christie turned this problem into a positive asset. Cooking, she admitted, was creative and therefore demanded constant attention or else the result would be soggy Brussels sprouts. But other domestic chores allowed her to "switch off" and enjoy some mental relaxation. She approved of Robert Graves, who was her near-neighbour in Devon, when he told her that "washing up was one of the best aids to creative thought."[41]

Christie only gradually accepted her status as a professional writer. For years, she considered herself primarily as a married woman and a mother with merely a sideline in fiction writing. In her hesitancy, she followed a nineteenth-century precedent in contemplating adopting a male pseudonym, but John Lane at Bodley Head persuaded her that this was unnecessary.[42] In her reluctance to explicitly embrace full-time professional status, she reflected the contemporary expectations of working women, as in the case of typists who were expected to leave employment after marriage. Meanwhile she wrestled with problems common to all women writers saddled with domestic duties. For some years she wrote in the interstices of domestic life, "in spells and bursts," as she herself put it.[43] When she and her second husband, Max Mallowan, travelled to their archaeological digs in the Middle East, she bought a portable Royal in Baghdad and improvised space and time to type whenever she could.[44] Her typewriter usage had become quite promiscuous, and she wrote anywhere: if necessary on a bedroom washstand, or at the dining table in the intervals between meals. In the mid-1930s, she did have a personal workroom, but the house was bombed during the war and she never subsequently took the opportunity to establish a room of her own.[45] Still, somewhere between gardening, cooking, travelling, and excavating in Iraq, she managed to produce two or three books per year in the 1940s.

Like other female authors, Christie risked poor treatment from male publishers and the hostility of male critics. Looking back, she judged herself naive in so easily accepting the first contract she ever signed, with Bodley Head in 1920. She was persuaded to forgo any royalties until 2,000 copies of *The Mysterious Affair at Styles* had been sold, as well as pledging her next five novels to Bodley Head. In the end, she received only £25 from serial rights to the book.[46] The fact that two publishers had already rejected the book no doubt played a part in her eagerness to accept unfavourable conditions from Bodley Head. In addition, Christie would run the gauntlet of male critics. When Raymond Chandler attacked English country-house mysteries as stuffy and insipid, there were several dimensions to his hostility.[47] One was jealousy of her commercial success. Another was Chandler's anti-British prejudice. A third was no doubt a hyper-masculine antipathy toward heroes he considered effeminate.

Ultimately, Christie learned to avoid exploitative situations and defy sexist critiques, but the process of professionalization was slow, and the "anxieties of authorship" persistent. In 1923, after the appearance of her *Murder on the Links*, she reflected on her position: "It was by now just beginning to dawn on me that perhaps I *might* be a writer by profession. I was not sure of it yet. I still had an idea that writing books was only the natural successor to embroidering sofa-cushions."[48] A turning point came with the composition of *The Mystery of the Blue Train*, started in 1926 and published in 1928. This coincided with the aftermath of a cataclysmic moment in Christie's life. In 1926, her mother died and then her first husband left her, inducing a traumatic psychological shock. In a state of severe distress, she fled from home and could not be found. After a police hunt that made headline news on both sides of the Atlantic, she was "discovered" ten days later in a Harrogate hotel, where she had registered under the name of her husband's lover. Many have speculated on Christie's state of mind, suggesting she was suffering from amnesia, or perhaps that she hoped to shock her husband into returning to her.[49] Why she chose to identify with her husband's lover remains obscure. Perhaps she was fleeing from a public role, but, if so, the public sphere refused to allow her the emotional privacy she required. What is important here is that she now had to face divorce and establish her financial independence, and she needed an income. Writing was no longer a sideline; it had to become her main source of support.

She was proud of completing *The Mystery of the Blue Train* because she had disliked writing it. For Christie, being a professional meant writing material even when it gave her no pleasure but continuing because financial pressures demanded it.[50] Becoming a professional writer was truly inaugurated by her new contract with Collins in 1928, which tripled her advances to £750 per novel and promised her a handsome

20 per cent royalty. An American contract with Dodd, Mead gave her a further lucrative income stream (and later, income tax problems to go with it). Identifying herself as a professional writer went hand-in-hand with greater familiarity with the typewriter. In 1929, she began to write directly onto her Corona, except for opening chapters and difficult passages, which would first be drafted in longhand.[51] Even then, she later recalled, "I don't think that I considered myself a *bona fide* author," and she preferred to describe herself formally as a married woman.[52] For many women writers, self-identification as a professional author was achieved only after much hesitation and phases of denial.

I earlier canvassed the possibility that women writers created fictional surrogates to express the independence that the authors, as women, were usually denied. Christie's Jane Marple is such a case. Marple frequently encountered male condescension, in the form of patronizing male policemen who marginalized her as far as possible. Marple defeated them, either by calling on her allies in high places – that is, at Scotland Yard – or, more importantly, by beating them at their own game. She demonstrated her talent for acute empirical observation and logical deduction based on the evidence. These qualities of rationality, usually coded masculine, enabled Marple to outshine any male detective.

Newspapermen Don't Cry: Barbara Taylor Bradford

Barbara Taylor Bradford never liked being called a "romance novelist." Unlike Enid Blyton, happily camped within a traditionally feminine field, she refused to be stereotyped as a female sentimental novelist. She preferred to think of herself as a writer of family sagas, producing books about the problems of growing up in the world.[53] Her fiction was not "romantic" in the sense that it narrated love affairs that encountered setbacks before being resolved in sugary happy endings. She wrote of power and ambition on a dynastic scale, of seduction, rape, and unwanted pregnancies resulting therefrom. She had the advantage of writing at a later date than Blyton, Crompton, or Christie, when expectations about women's roles had changed. Taylor's fictional protagonists are women who fight hard for themselves and enjoy exercising power. By 1985, her first novel *A Woman of Substance* (1979) had sold eleven million copies worldwide and made her a millionaire. By 2011, her novels had sold eight-six million copies. She understood the professional obligations of being a fiction writer more clearly than did several of the other typewriter women quoted above.

Bradford was born in Leeds. Ignoring her parents' wishes that she should aim for a university education, she took a shorthand typing course and entered the typing pool at the *Yorkshire Evening Post* before her sixteenth birthday. By the age of eighteen, she was the editor of the paper's women's pages, and at twenty she was working in Fleet Street as fashion editor of *Woman's Own*. Her apprenticeship as a typist and reporter taught her discipline and a resilient working routine on which she later drew as a fiction writer. The newspaper world was a masculine one. As a young teenage reporter on the *Yorkshire Evening Post*, she occasionally broke down in tears. Her friend and colleague Keith Waterhouse (*Billy Liar*, 1959) told her, "If you want to be a newspaperman, luv, you can't cry in the newsroom, you're going to have to cry in the ladies' room."[54] Since becoming a newspaper*woman* was apparently not an option, the ladies' room was an essential hiding place. She made so many typing mistakes that, to avoid detection, she sometimes took refuge there to burn her copy in the toilet.[55] "The writing and the typing," she later recalled, "was like being in the salt mines – hard graft."[56]

Nevertheless this unfriendly atmosphere taught her her trade: "Newspaper work made me a pro," she said. "It gave me a great sense of story, drama, detail and setting. It pointed out the overriding human factor – People. They must come alive for a novel to truly work. I learned how to research and organize material and how to work with a deadline."[57] When drafting fiction, she worked regular hours from about 6 a.m. until the afternoon, with short breaks. "A lot of men," she admitted, "wouldn't put up with the life I lead when I'm writing."[58] When she gave advice to young writers, she emphasized desire, dedication, discipline, determination, and drive – the "five D's." They needed "to get into that room and work every day," and they needed to stay at the typewriter whatever the distractions. "A novelist," she warned, "cannot be a social butterfly."[59]

Bradford liked the solid bulk of her IBM Selectric. In a photograph taken in 1984 in her Manhattan penthouse apartment, it sat in her study on a tidy U-shaped desk, with plenty of space at the sides for editing and an exercise bike in the corner of the room. There was no computer in sight.[60] If she used one at all in later years, it was solely for research. Longhand first drafts served her well when she was writing *A Woman of Substance*, with subsequent retyping and revision. As she became more practised, she still preferred longhand for chapter openings, descriptions of landscape, and for the "deep psychological stuff," but she switched to the keyboard for fast dialogue.[61]

Bradford told reporters that she wrote for her own sanity and wellbeing, and clearly it was a compulsion. At the same time, she never lost sight of the hard grind of being a writer. "It's the salt mines, sheer drudgery most of the time," she confessed.[62] After her unsatisfactory early attempts, writer Richard Condon (*The Manchurian Candidate*,

1959) had advised her not to try to publish until she had first practised novel writing by writing a thousand words per day, and she com-
plied.[63] She was a dedicated rewriter of her own work, claiming to have
written every page four or five times before reaching a version of which
she approved.[64] For some of her more recent novels in the Cavendon
series, she produced her own typescript and sent it to a professional
for a word-processed version. Then she would again correct by hand or
perhaps add a typed section, so that the surviving typescript consists of
a mixture of typed, word-processed, and handwritten text, sometimes
combining a century of different writing technologies on the same page.
In 2012, she was still using correcting fluid to make amendments.[65] To
the five D's she recommended to aspiring writers, she might well have
added a sixth: D for drudgery, because Bradford knew that this, too,
was an inherent part of the career to which she had committed herself.

The rewards were clear and worth advertising. The press never tired
of visiting her penthouse, mesmerized by the show of wealth it exuded,
by her antique furnishings and Impressionist paintings. She was interviewed as much about her interior decoration as her writing techniques.[66] Here, at least, Bradford took a conventional view of female
priorities: she was responsible for the home and she made it a beautiful
one. It was tempting to classify her writing career as a rags-to-riches
story, from Upper Armley to Manhattan, that paralleled that of Emma
Harte, her socially ascendant protagonist in *A Woman of Substance*. Bradford corrected this impression: she was already well off and married
to a very wealthy film producer *before* she started writing fiction. But
she could not avoid being cast as the "Dallas of the Dales."[67] Richmal
Crompton shunned the media, Agatha Christie tried in vain to escape its
clutches when she left home *incognita* in 1926. Barbara Taylor Bradford,
former typist, journalist, and magazine editor, understood the game. She
welcomed press attention and exploited it with aplomb. She played the
Yorkshire card to good effect, instructing her word-processing assistant
to retain traces of local dialect in her text even if they were confusing,[68]
and she expected American readers to know what Eccles cakes were.
This, too, was part and parcel of being a professional writer in the late
twentieth century; becoming a "newspaperman" had been her first step.

Surviving the Salt Mines

In keeping with the overall tendency of this book, I have concentrated
in this chapter on non-canonical authors. The volume of their production and the longevity of their writing careers attracted unusual public attention, and this celebrity provides the historian of writing with
sources offering clues about their working methods and objectives. In

contrast to male writers of the mid-twentieth century, they tended to excel in specific genres like children's literature and romance fiction. The contrasts go further: women writers thought of writing differently, and they typed in very different sites of writing.

All the typewriter women considered in this chapter were governed and constrained by prevailing social conventions about marriage and the role of women. Most risked the general disapproval attached to marital separations and divorces. The stigma of illegitimate birth today seems irrational, but it induced such a weight of guilt in Catherine Cookson that in the end it overpowered her and brought about a psychological collapse.[69] Perhaps there was something especially British about the stifling fear of social disgrace, and a broader spectrum of examples from elsewhere might reveal a less consistent pattern. It was important, however, for all typewriter women to negotiate dominant expectations about working women. Married women were not expected to work – or at least, if they did, they were expected not to usurp their male partner's role as principal, if not sole, breadwinner. Here lay one root of the reluctance we have detected in their acceptance of the status of a professional writer. Writing professionally was thrust upon Crompton, but she was never married. Cookson starting writing primarily for psychological remediation. Christie slowly accepted her professional status. Blyton and Bradford learned to embrace it fully. These women writers overcame their inhibitions and defied gender expectations, and their earning power eventually far surpassed that of their husbands.

Typewriter women had to find a place at home for their machine. Their site of writing was often not a stable one – Blyton carried the machine indoors and outside, depending on the weather, while other mothers pushed the typewriter aside when children called. Typewriter women always had to deal, like Blyton, with the intrusions of the Electrolux man or the need to polish bannisters. What made them different from male writers was the domestic context of their writing, and the informal and familial sites of writing where they composed.

Bradford advised young writers not to embark on writing for a living unless it was utterly necessary for their well-being and sanity. She herself had negotiated all the hazards and hardships, she had survived what she called the salt mines, to constitute herself as an irresistible role model in mink coats and expensive jewellery, with her penthouse in Manhattan, her *pied-à-terre* in London, and her house in Connecticut. Although she may still make egregious spelling mistakes on her IBM Selectric,[70] there now exists an editorial army to correct every blemish.

11 The End of the Typewriter Century and Post-Digital Nostalgia

"Old Media Never Die"

The first chapter of this book signalled two events that marked the beginning and the end of the typewriter century: the period opened in the 1880s with Mark Twain's claim to be the first novelist to use a typewriter, and Len Deighton's adoption of an early IBM word processor in 1968 foreshadowed the typewriter's impending demise. It is now time to revisit the typewriter's decline and the shrinking of the typosphere brought about by the triumphant spread of computerized word processing. The word processor has had many shortcomings, especially in its earliest manifestations, but it promised to satisfy writers of all kinds who had always struggled with the difficulty of correcting text on the typewriter. The word processor opened up a new world of instant editing.

By the 1990s, the media had doomed the typewriter to obsolescence. Newspaper articles entitled "Requiem for the Typewriter" or, in a more flippant register, "What's a Typewriter, Mommy?" were the funereal music that supposedly ushered it to its grave.[1] Obituaries for the typewriter, however, were premature. As this chapter will show, typewriters have survived, even if their uses have become limited and specialized. Some institutions still prefer them as a means of avoiding electronic surveillance. In addition, along with other "old technologies" like vinyl records, the typewriter has inspired a new generation of enthusiasts. Their post-digital nostalgia for the machine has been described as a retrograde or romantic form of Luddism. Strictly speaking, this is inappropriate. Unlike the machine breakers of the early nineteenth century (the anonymous followers of an imaginary "Captain Ludd"), contemporary typewriter lovers and collectors have no wish to destroy any computers. Their hobbies remain perfectly compatible with the word processor.

Their efforts have given the typewriter an unexpected afterlife, proving that, as media scholar Henry Jenkins asserted, "Old media never die."[2]

The Typewriter's Electric Swansong

The electric typewriter was a comparatively late development of the typewriter century. Until the 1950s, the typewriter had been a very stable technology, but electrification changed it and, at the same time, ushered in its departure. Electric typewriters had been introduced by Remington in 1927, and then after the Second World War by several other companies, but they had difficulty in overcoming consumer resistance. The most commercially successful electric typewriter was produced by IBM in 1935, and, by 1958, the company had manufactured one million of them.[3] In fact, IBM never made a standard manual or even a portable typewriter – electric machines were their speciality. In 1958, 8 per cent of IBM's entire income came from electric typewriters. In 1961, the company incorporated proportional spacing into its popular Selectric model, the "golf ball" typewriter. It offered two different pitches: the typist could easily switch from pica (ten characters per inch) to elite (twelve characters per inch). With this machine, jammed typebars became a thing of the past, and, since the ball was replaceable, different fonts could be incorporated into the same document. Most writers appreciated the lighter touch of the electric typewriter, and a finished product that resembled print even more closely than before, in exchange for the disadvantage of having to connect the machine to an electricity supply. A few, however, like Judith Krantz and Paul Auster, hated its persistent hum and vibration.[4]

Some electric typewriters came with a correcting facility and a small memory, and they could produce a neater page than before. But the most capable models cost over $US1,000, and they were heavy. The IBM Selectric III weighed thirty-six pounds (over sixteen kilograms). There were still advantages for the manual typist, according to Ronald Donovan in *Writer's Digest*: "You burn substantially more calories typing on a manual so you help keep your weight down, and you will be able to cover the Apocalypse, since electricity will be the first thing to go."[5]

In the 1970s, the electronic typewriter went further, but in hindsight it merely occupied a brief interlude before the word processor superseded it, taking over and expanding its innovative functions. Before the advent of word processors, the typewriter could already paginate, set margins, produce right-justified text, and work in more than one typeface. Electronic typewriters could remember up to 10,000 words, allowing the typist to make some revisions without retyping the whole text. It could reproduce stock phrases (macros) in its memory, such as "Yours sincerely" or "The cheque is in the mail."[6] These innovations, however, locate the electronic typewriter in the prehistory of the word processor rather than the declining years of the typewriter. Higher speeds, machine memory, automatic spelling, the incorporation of images and diagrams, data sharing across a network, the ability to instantly correct and manipulate texts, all increased exponentially to make the typewriter redundant. The electronic typewriter had brought us to the furthest edge of the typosphere, where cyberspace beckoned.

Major manufacturers were compelled to adapt or die. Hence Olivetti and Brother turned to producing personal computers, while still trying to breathe new life into portable typewriters. In the 1960s, the Olivetti Valentine, with its distinctive red casing, was marketed as a typewriter that could be used in a café or on the beach. Its name suggested its availability for writing love letters. It was anything but a work apparatus. Its designer, Ettore Sottsass, compared the Valentine to "a girl wearing a very short skirt and too much make-up."[7] The Valentine targeted a young international market, and it was itself designed to be a work of art. But the excellence of contemporary Italian design could not postpone the approaching reality: the days of the typewriter were numbered. Many of the old pioneering companies had vanished by the 1970s. Blickensderfer had closed down in 1919 and was later taken over by Remington. The last Oliver typewriter was made in England in 1959. Underwood had been swallowed up by Olivetti in the same year. Imperial was defeated by competition from computers in 1974. The main focus of typewriter manufacture shifted for a time to the Third World, especially to factories in India and Brazil, and during the Cold War to Communist Bloc countries starved of word processors. The typewriter century was drawing to a close.

The Computer's Dry Embrace

The typewriter's gradual progress toward the scrap yard seemed to accelerate in 1992, when Smith-Corona decided to close its last North American factory in Cortland, New York, and move its operations to Mexico. Smith-Corona had been a pioneer in portable typewriters since the late 1950s, and in the United States its popular models had been ritual graduation gifts to successful sons and daughters.[8] It had already stopped producing manual typewriters in 1983. Within ten years, it had been defeated by cheaper imports from Asia.

This decline was a global phenomenon. Indian company Godrej was still selling 50,000 typewriters annually in 1991–2. In India, the machine was then essential equipment for government offices, banks, and court-rooms, while in large cities like Mumbai – as in others all over the Third World – typewriter scribes installed themselves outside official build-ings, ready to produce formal correspondence on request for their cli-ents.[9] Until 2009, Godrej was the last major manufacturer of typewriters in the world, but it had ceased production by 2011. In Africa, the story was the same. In Kigali, Rwanda, a handful of housewives set up their stalls as nomadic typists in Nyabugogo Taxi Park, catering to all sorts of administrative and legal correspondence, but unable to afford office rent. They were the last of their kind, and they feared police raids: reg-ulations have already made them illegal.[10]

The word processor's advance was inexorable, in spite of early diffi-culties. It did not necessarily prove to be a labour-saving device; in fact it created more tasks for the writers, who learned that they could no longer simply hand a draft to a professional typist: they were obliged to edit it themselves, since this was now so easy to do. It also created new tasks for secretaries, who now had to supervise the maintenance and replacement not just of one machine, but a complex of different devices, including keyboards, monitors, printers, and mice. There was always a risk that the machine would "crash" or that a novice operator might accidentally delete valuable data in a rash key-stroke. In the beginning, there was no possibility of "automatic save," and writers had to create their own back-up files. Of course, there was a certain degree of par-anoia in the common fear of accidental erasure; the risk of losing ma-terial was hardly new, as the theft of Ernest Hemingway's suitcase of manuscripts in Paris in 1923 reminds us. Early word processors offered no choice of font and, on a dot-matrix printer, printing quality was exe-crable. A tractor-feed slowly drew a pile of pages into the printer, a little like Kerouac's scroll, producing paper copy with rows of holes in the left and right margins. The resulting paper output was a cumbersome con-certina, and torn edges revealed its origins as a continuous document.

The word-processed text could be moved and more text freely inserted, while the document as a whole flowed into a new shape of its own accord. There was no need to push back the carriage return at the end of the line, because the word processor miraculously "wrapped" the text around. Most importantly, the word processor allowed immediate editing on-screen. There would be no future need for erasing fluid, no overtyping X's to obliterate mistakes, no obligation to retype a whole page containing one or two errors. The typewriter's most enduring problem had been eliminated.

Throughout this book, I have argued, wherever appropriate, for the unseen connections between creative writing on the typewriter and the bureaucratic writing of the modern office. The word processor extends this connection into the digital age. I write this text using Microsoft Word, but one glance at my toolbar reminds me that I am working within a suite of applications called Microsoft Office. Whether I am drafting a book review or a household budget on my screen, I am creating "files," "folders," and "documents," using a vocabulary borrowed from the paper-based office of the early twentieth century. Such continuities as this link the modernization of the twentieth-century office with typewriting and word processing in other, non-bureaucratic settings.

The implications of the change to word processing were multiple and perhaps they are still in the process of being absorbed. Matthew Kirschenbaum has drawn his expert attention to some of them.[11] A vision of the immaculate text came into focus for writers. They could now realistically aspire to produce a perfect text. The distancing effect that arose at the moment when writers first viewed their own compositions in the cold light of print was dramatically enhanced because their word-processed version now approached publishing quality even more closely than before. Those writers who had felt uneasy because the typed text depersonalized their work were likely to become even more anxious in front of a screen.

In addition, the days of handwritten drafts were numbered. Just as writers had learned to think on the typewriter, so now they learned to think on the computer. They enjoyed the luxury of the delete key, and, with its every use, a previous draft disappeared from view and from the record. The study of any work's textual genesis became impossible, since earlier versions had been edited into oblivion. Admittedly, it is technically possible for a writer to save every draft, or to track the changes made to earlier versions. But it seems highly unlikely that any writer would make the effort to do this, unless he or she had an unusually high valuation of their own importance, and an unusual premonition of the needs of posterity. The word processor wipes out the history of any composition and makes it impossible to discern what John le Carré called the "architecture of the text." A manuscript by Proust, say, with all its insertions and deletions in plain view, bears witness to its first iteration, just as the grain in a polished pine table "remembers" its origins as a tree. But a word-processed text has no history. It exists only in the present, in which it is marooned.

There was always some resistance to the advent of word processors, and there still is. Some resistance has been obtuse, some sentimental. American writer and environmental activist Wendell Berry combined a bit of both when he refused to accept the computer on the grounds that he did not want to owe money to energy corporations and he preferred to work in a sustainable environment. In practice, this meant having his wife continue to do the typing on her trusted Royal. Gordon Inkeles responded with a sarcastic letter making explicit Berry's recommended alternative to the computer: namely, the Wife as a low-tech energy-saving device that was perfectly eco-friendly. Today this reader's response (suggesting a mild form of gendered labour exploitation) seems more pertinent than the article to which it reacted.[12] Both writers, however, had underlined one advantage the typewriter retained over the computer: the manual version, at least, never needed to be plugged in to an electricity supply. Moreover, it did not suffer from built-in obsolescence and it did not require an annual update.

Some creative writers were repelled by the notion that their noble art could be defined as "processing words." This sounded too mechanical, too factory-like, to describe the individual creative mind at work. As we have seen, pen users had once felt exactly the same way about the typewriter. The early Amstrad, introduced into the market by Alan Sugar in 1984, was an integrated system, incorporating keyboard, monitor, and printer, but it did not look appealing. Poet Hugo Williams called it a "grisly gulag of beige plastic" and went back to his Adler. English novelist Iris Murdoch was another rebel. "Why not," she asked, "use one's mind in the old way, instead of dazzling one's eyes staring at a glass square which separates one from one's thoughts and gives them a premature air of completeness?"[13] Just as some authors at the beginning of the twentieth century had felt intimidated by the mechanical typewriter, so Murdoch reiterated the same sense of detachment before the Amstrad's flickering green cursor. Barbara Taylor Bradford, to take another example, owns a computer, but for a long time still preferred to prepare her romance novels in handwritten notes on postcards, and in longhand drafts, which she retyped. She uses her computer exclusively for research and email, not for creative writing.[14] Larry McMurtry, accepting his Golden Globe in 2006, concludes this short list of refractory writers who rejected the computer: "Most heartfelt," he told his audience, "I thank my typewriter. My typewriter is a Hermes 3000, surely one of the noblest instruments of European genius. It has kept me for 30 years out of the dry embrace of the computer."[15]

As we have seen throughout this book, writers humanized their typewriters, treating them as old companions, or tempting sirens calling them to work, or therapists waiting to receive a personal confidence. This kind of attachment was hard to break; the computer very rarely engendered an equivalent level of affection. Its embrace remained, for some, sterile and unwelcoming. It was the solution to a problem they denied they ever had.

Post-Digital Nostalgia

Today, the typewriter attracts a new fascination for the retro, in parallel with a revived interest in vinyl records and Super 8 cameras. Hence in 2009 Cormac McCarthy sold his portable Olivetti Lettera, which he had used since 1963, at auction for $254,000 and donated the proceeds to the Santa Fe Institute in New Mexico, where he lives. When the dealer who sold it took stock of all the work that had been produced on McCarthy's manual machine, he compared it to "Mount Rushmore carved out with a Swiss Army knife."[16] Presumably McCarthy would not have agreed with the auctioneer that his typewriter was to this degree unfit for its purpose. He did not abandon typing; he bought another Olivetti for $11.

Typewriter museums and collectors proliferate. Actor Tom Hanks is a particularly high-profile typewriter enthusiast, who relishes the sound of the machine in action and designed a computer application (Hanx Writer) that reproduces both the sound and the distinctive typeface of traditional typewriters.[17] Perhaps, as Siobhan Lyons suggests, there is a degree of inverted snobbery attached to this ostentatious preference for the obsolete.[18] Enthusiasts have nevertheless gone some way toward substantiating the claim that typewriters are crawling back from their near-death experience.[19] Fans gather for "type-ins" and swear to observe periods of "digital detox" in collective protest against the all-pervasive power of the information society.[20] At the Regional Assembly of Text in Victoria, British Columbia, anyone can visit the premises to rent time on a manual typewriter to produce correspondence on real paper and in real envelopes.[21] Richard Polt elevates this counter-cultural movement to the status of a "typewriter insurgency," which embraces old technology and rejects the contemporary trend to slice all information up into pre-digested thirty-second sound bites.[22] *Harlequin Creature* (no relation to the romance series) is a journal established in New York in 2011 in the same spirit, appearing in small editions of 100 copies, of which 50 are typewritten in typing bees and the rest issued in carbon copies. But it does have an on-line presence as well.[23]

The return to snail mail and to slow writing (echoing the slow food movement) appeals to a number of younger people; it is not solely the prerogative of veteran typists like Cormac McCarthy, aged seventy-six at the time of the auction of his famous Olivetti. These younger enthusiasts are members of what Ashlea Halpern calls "the analog underground," indulging "an idiosyncratic desire to unplug from our overly digitized existence."[24] Visitors to type-ins in major American cities, and fans who scour flea markets for vintage typewriters, are not old enough to be resurrecting a distant memory. The low-tech bubble attracts people who are experiencing the typewriter for the first time in a spirit of discovery rather than reliving their own past. They are, for the most part, too young to have a typewriter past of their own; they are finding the typewriter anew, and it remains to be seen how long the novelty will endure.

There are logical reasons behind some of this post-digital revivalism. The typewriter offers a way of evading the electronic surveillance of sensitive institutional communications. Edward Snowden has warned us all: "Any unencrypted message sent over the internet is being delivered to every intelligence service in the world."[25] Hence the New York Police Department uses typewriters to avoid the hacking of confidential information.[26] Similar precautions are reportedly taken by the Kremlin, Britain's MI6, and the Indian High Commission in London.[27] The revelations that emerged in 2014 that the US National Security Agency had bugged German chancellor Angela Merkel's telephone provoked an unexpected surge in typewriter sales for Olympia.[28]

Some regimes have tried to exert surveillance over typewriter usage itself, as former residents of communist Rumania are aware. In 1983, the Rumanian government ordered all citizens to register their typewriters with the police, in an attempt to stifle the production of home-made anti-communist propaganda leaflets.[29] This is the context of Carmen Bugan's memoir of her childhood in Rumania before her family was able to leave that country in 1989. Bugan's parents evaded surveillance by owning two typewriters. One, which was lawfully registered with the authorities, acted as a kind of smokescreen for their work on the second (illegal) typewriter, an East German Erika 115, which was secretly buried in the family garden. Bugan's parents dug it up and worked on it at night, blacking out their living room by covering the windows with towels. The Securitate (secret police) found the machine and imprisoned Carmen's father, Ion, for sedition.[30]

Besides the desire to avoid surveillance, there are other reasons for turning again to the typewriter. Some contemporary authors, such as British novelist Zadie Smith, recommend the typewriter because it removes the temptation of the Internet and enables them to write without distractions.[31] Smith, born in 1975, is too young to have experienced creative writing before computers, so here she is "reverting" to a technology she never knew. In this case, the typewriter's limitations are transformed into a virtue: unlike a laptop, the typewriter is made *only* for writing. It is discrete, self-contained, and single minded. It requires an occasional clean but needs no battery or accessories beyond a renewable supply of inked ribbons. Writing was what it was built for. Thus when Baroness Amos recently urged the reform of the United

Nations, because the institution had become "a Remington typewriter in a Smartphone world," she created a misleading analogy: it would be an extraordinary feat to write a full-length novel on a Smartphone.[32] Admittedly, Iranian-Kurdish refugee Behrouz Boochani did – out of necessity, not choice – compose his prize-winning autobiographical work on a phone, as a series of thousands of WhatsApp messages smuggled out of Manus Island, where he was incarcerated.[33] They then had to be converted into PDF files. This was perhaps a unique exception.

The History of Things

This has been the study of a material object in time. It takes its place among the "history of things," like the sewing machine, the bicycle, or the water closet. Like any history of technologies, it makes sense only when seen through the eyes of its users. Only then does it cease to be a dry scientific description of techniques and begin to acquire cultural and historical significance. The everyday technologies, including the typewriter, studied by David Arnold were meaningful only in their context as agents of modernization in Indian society.[34] The great historian Fernand Braudel studied pepper and coffee, but only in the framework of the development of global capitalism in the early modern period.[35] The impact of the typewriter, too, has been approached here from the users' perspective, examining the ways in which they responded to, fantasized about, and represented the typewriter. It was imagined as a jazz piano and a stuttering machine-gun. It helped to define the "New Woman" of the 1890s, just as later it became associated with the "Typewriter Girl." The typewriter helped to shape the social imaginary of the twentieth century.

The history of the book is another "history of things," and one I have frequently turned to for inspiration. The story of the manufacture of the book, and of its sale and distribution, can never be complete, however, without a history of its readers. Instead of taking a book's readership and reception for granted, we should, as one historian urged, "interrogate the audience" to discover how readers invested meanings in any given book in their multiple acts of reading.[36] The history of the typewriter, too, will never be fully understood without similarly "interrogating the typists."

I have interrogated them quite indiscriminately, including in the conversation office typists, literary writers, and contributors to pulp fiction magazines. A good literary reputation has been an insufficient qualification for inclusion. I have consulted a range of writers, the main criterion for introducing them being their capacity for reflection on their own methods and instruments. They reflected in public, in interviews and autobiographical writing, and sometimes in private, in correspondence with agents and publishers. A few of them, mostly writers of popular fiction, have briefly taken centre stage as case studies because of their conscious awareness of their own creative process and of the importance of the typewriter within it. The typewriter symbolized modernity and was embraced for this reason by the futurists and early twentieth-century avant-gardes. We have seen how they and the modernist poets adapted the new technology to their work, using typewritten text to undermine conventional poetic form, and to turn the typewritten poem into a visual as well as a verbal performance.

For almost all of the pulp fiction writers reviewed, the speed of the typewriter was all-important, enabling them to achieve greater output and potentially facilitating a more fluent style of composition. They wrote for different motives – for wealth and fame certainly, but also seeking some level of peer recognition. Erle Stanley Gardner wanted a profession that allowed him time to enjoy an outdoor life; Catherine Cookson wrote as personal therapy. There is no single answer to the question, what was the impact of the typewriter? Each individual appropriated the machine differently.

Nevertheless, two common typologies have emerged. In the first of these, coming face-to-face with mechanical writing proved initially intimidating. The typewriter exteriorized and standardized a draft, which had hitherto seemed very personal and handmade. In so doing, it provoked anxiety, and the newly typed impersonal text generated a critical and detached view, which I have designated as "the distancing effect." In the second group, the typewriter was seen not as an alien object, but a functioning part of the writer's own body. It opened up the possibility of a faster and more natural style of writing, which I have described as the instinctive, spontaneous, or automatic writing of "the romantic typewriter."

This study has also examined the role of other technologies that supported or supplemented the typewriter. Marshall McLuhan noted the role of the voice in the process of dictation, and it had a close relationship with the typewriter in our period; similarly, the role of manuscript has been evaluated in preliminary notes, handwritten drafts, and manual corrections to a typescript. The typewriter did not eliminate handwriting but simply allotted different roles to it. Its usage developed within a network of different media in which the typewriter interacted with both handwriting and voice recordings.

At various stages in the story, it has become very apparent that the transformation of the modern office that opened the typewriter century was in some senses the crucible of all that followed. The creative fiction writers discussed in this book inherited some of its essential characteristics. Erle Stanley Gardner bought the latest dictation and transcription machines, and office equipment manufacturers sent representatives to his ranch to pitch their wares in person since his contract was substantial. Agatha Christie and many others delegated typing to a secretarial agency, like the one she fictionalized in her novel *The Clocks*. Without such an agency, Henry James would never have encountered his favourite assistant, Theodora Bosanquet. Barbara Taylor Bradford began work as a teenager in a typing pool, realizing there that she could write her own news stories if she dared. The parallels go further, because they touch the very heart of twentieth-century office culture. The instinctive speed writing of the romantic typewriter, for example, echoed instructions to office typists to silence conscious thought in the act of copying. Furthermore, the new gendered division of office labour inaugurated by the "white-blouse revolution" became the norm and was reproduced in the working lives of many male authors.

If there is after all an underlying unity and coherence in the typewriter century, it is a unity that relies on the material objects themselves. It derives from all those Remingtons and Royals, those Underwoods and Smith-Coronas that are now eagerly sought after in flea markets, and that collectors proudly show off to each other like vintage cars. The typewriter is an antique and a museum piece, but it profoundly transformed the history of writing practices in the century of the typosphere.

Notes

1. Introduction

1 Matthew Solan, "Tracking Down Typewriters," *Poets and Writers*, September–October 2009, 33; Robert Messenger, "Typing Writers: An Endangered Species (But Not Yet Extinct)," *Canberra Times*, 14 February 2009, 16. The IBM Selectric survived this attack.

2 Messenger, "Typing Writers," 16.

3 Paul Auster and Sam Messer, *The Story of My Typewriter* (New York: Distributed Art, 2002), 22–3. This book, combining Auster's text with Messer's artwork, is in itself a tribute to Auster's Olympia. See also Evija Trofimova, *Paul Auster's Writing Machine: A Thing to Write With* (London: Bloomsbury, 2014).

4 Billie Figg, "The White Rose Booms Again," *Guardian*, 18 March 1983, 12.

5 Fergus Fleming, ed., *The Man with the Golden Typewriter: Ian Fleming's James Bond Letters* (London: Bloomsbury, 2015), 13.

6 "Me and My Typewriter," *Writer's Digest* 61 (January 1981): 28.

7 Robert DeMott, *Steinbeck's Typewriter: Essays on His Art* (Troy, NY: Whitston, 1996), 312–13.

8 Ernest Hemingway, *Selected Letters, 1917–1961*, ed. Carlos Baker (New York: Granada, 1981), 45, letter to Grace Hall Hemingway (the author's mother), 21 January 1921.

9 Miles Franklin, *My Congenials: Miles Franklin and Friends in Letters*, vol. 1, *1879–1938*, ed. Jill Roe, Sydney (Sydney: Angus & Robertson, 1993), 277, letter to Margery Currey, 4 January 1933.

10 Patrick White, *Flaws in the Glass* (London: Vintage, 1981), 133 and 158–9.

11 Marshall McLuhan, *Understanding Media: The Extensions of Man* (London: Abacus, 1974).

12 Jacques Derrida, "Le papier ou moi, vous savez ... (Nouvelles spéculations sur un luxe des pauvres)," in his *Papier machine: Le ruban de*

machine à écrire et autres réponses (Paris: Galilée, 2001), 246–58. In this 1997 interview with *Les cahiers de médiologie,* Derrida was actually discussing the decline of paper. All translations are my own unless otherwise indicated.

13 Walter Benjamin, "The Work of Art in the Age of Mechanical Reproduction" (1936), in *Illuminations,* ed. Hannah Arendt, trans. Harry Zohn (New York: Shocken, 1985), 222 and 231.

14 Jacques Derrida, "Le livre à venir," in Derrida, *Papier machine,* 29.

15 Charles-Augustin Sainte-Beuve, "De la littérature industrielle" (1839), in his *Portraits contemporains* vol. 2 (Paris: Calmann-Lévy, 1888–9), 444–71.

16 François Bon, "Plume d'oie, plume de fer," in *Le tiers livre* (n.d.), at www .tierslivre.net, read 22 July 2016.

17 Flaubert to Louise Colet, 1 February 1852, cited in ibid.

18 Jules Janin, "Les influences de la plume de fer en littérature" (1831) *Revue de Paris* 93 (December 1836): 292–302.

19 Gerald Nicosia, *Memory Babe: A Critical Biography of Jack Kerouac* (Berkeley: University of California Press, 1994), 588.

20 David Arnold, *Everyday Technology: Machines in the Making of India's Modernity* (Chicago: University of Chicago Press, 2013), 11.

21 Catherine Viollet, "Écriture méchanique, espaces de frappe: Quelques préalables à une sémiologie du dactylogramme," *Genesis* 10 (1996): 193–208.

22 Matthew G. Kirschenbaum, *Track Changes A Literary History of Word Processing* (Cambridge, MA: Belknap, 2016).

23 Elizabeth L. Eisenstein, *The Printing Press as an Agent of Change: Communications and Global Transformations in Early Modern Europe* (Cambridge: Cambridge University Press, 1979).

24 Kirschenbaum, *Track Changes,* 7.

25 "Me and My Typewriter," 31.

26 Nettie Palmer, *Nettie Palmer: Her Private Journal "Fourteen Years," Poems, Reviews and Literary Essays* (St Lucia: University of Queensland Press, 1988), 57–9.

27 Friedrich A. Kittler, *Gramophone, Film, Typewriter,* trans. Geoffrey Winthrop Young and Michael Wutz (Stanford, CA: Stanford University Press, 1999).

28 *The Letters of T.S. Eliot,* volume 1, *1898–1922,* rev. ed., ed. Valerie Eliot and Hugh Haughton (London: Faber & Faber, 2009), 158, letter to Conrad Aiken, London, 21 August 1916.

29 André Parinaud, *Connaissance de Georges Simenon,* tome 1, *Le secret du romancier suivi des entretiens avec Simenon* (Paris: Presses de la Cité, 1957), 403.

30 Roger E. Stoddard, "Morphology and the Book from an American Perspective," *Printing History* 17 (1987): 2–14.

31 Francis Joannès, "The Babylonian Scribes and Their Libraries," in *Approaches to the History of Written Culture: A World Inscribed*, ed. Martyn Lyons and Rita Marquilhas (Cham, CH: Palgrave, 2017), 21–38.

32 Kittler, *Gramophone*, 214.

33 *Aufschreibesysteme 1800/1900* was translated as *Discourse Networks, 1800/1900* by Michael Meteer and Chris Cullens (Stanford, CA: Stanford University Press, 1990); *Grammophon, Film, Typewriter*, translated as *Gramophone, Film, Typewriter*, by Young and Wutz.

34 Geoffrey Winthrop Young and Michael Wutz, translators' introduction to Kittler, *Gramophone, Film, Typewriter*, xxxix.

35 Jonathan Rose, "Rereading the *English Common Reader*: A Preface to a History of Audiences," *Journal of the History of Ideas* 53, no. 1 (1992): 47–70.

36 Jussi Parikka and Paul Feigelfeld, "Friedrich Kittler: E-Special Introduction," *Theory, Culture and Society* 32, nos 7–8 (2015): 349–58.

37 Alex Magoun, review of *Gramophone, Film, Typewriter*, in *Technology and Culture* 42, no. 1 (2001): 175.

38 Kittler, *Gramophone*, 198–200, citing Heidegger's *Parmenides*.

39 Arthur Conan Doyle, "A Case of Identity," in his *The Adventures of Sherlock Holmes* (London: George Newnes, 1892).

40 Kirschenbaum, *Track Changes*, xiv.

41 Mark Twain, "The First Writing-Machines," in *The Complete Essays of Mark Twain Now Collected for the First Time*, ed. Charles Neider (Garden City, NY: Doubleday, 1963), 326.

42 Matthew Kirschenbaum, "The Book-Writing Machine," *Slate*, 1 March 2013, at http://www.slate.com/articles/arts/books/2013/03/len_deighton _s_bomber_the_first_book_ever_written_on_a_word_processor.single.html, read 25 February 2018.

43 Kirschenbaum, *Track Changes*, 166–71.

44 Gideon Reuveni, *Reading Germany: Literature and Consumer Culture in Germany before 1933* (New York: Berghahn, 2006), 2.

45 Ibid., 208.

46 Joseph McAleer, *Popular Reading and Publishing in Britain, 1914–1950* (Oxford: Clarendon, 1992), 84.

47 Seven Stories (National Centre for Children's Books), Newcastle-upon-Tyne, Enid Blyton Archive, EB/02/01/01/04, 1927 diary, entries for October, November, December.

48 Robert Druce, *This Day Our Daily Fictions: An Enquiry into the Multi-Million Bestseller Status of Enid Blyton and Ian Fleming* (Amsterdam: Rodopi, 1992), 31.

49 Ibid., 310.

50 National Library of Australia, ms 9149, Gordon Clive Bleeck papers.

51 Jean Devanny, *The Point of Departure: The Autobiography of Jean Devanny*, ed. Carole Ferrier (St Lucia: University of Queensland Press, 1986), 83.

52 William Burroughs, "The Technology of Writing," in his *The Adding Machine: Collected Essays* (London: Calder, 1985), 37.

53 Jane Yolen, "I Am a Typewriter," *Writer* 94 (January 1981): 9.

54 Agatha Christie, *An Autobiography* (New York: Dodd, Mead, 1977), 284.

55 Laura Thompson, *Agatha Christie: An English Mystery* (London: Headline Review, 2007), 425–34.

56 Véronique Rohrbach, "L'ordinaire en partage: Le courier des lecteurs à Georges Simenon" (doctoral diss., Université de Lausanne, 2015), 324.

57 Outside the Western world, it should be noted, the division of labour could be very different, following racial rather than gender lines. In colonial India, for example, most typists were Indian men. See Arnold, *Everyday Technology*, 86–94.

2. The Birth of the Typosphere

1 Trevor J. Pinch and Wiebe E. Bijker, "The Social Construction of Facts and Artefacts: Or How the Sociology of Science and the Sociology of Technology Might Benefit Each Other," *Social Studies of Science* 14, no. 3 (August 1984): 411.

2 *Typewriter Topics: The International Office Equipment Magazine* 48, no. 2 (June 1921): 115, for a Noiseless Typewriter advertisement.

3 Darren Wershler-Henry, *The Iron Whim: A Fragmented History of Typewriting* (Ithaca, NY: Cornell University Press, 2007), 45–6. For the prehistory of the machine, see also Richard N. Current, *The Typewriter and the Men Who Made It* (Urbana: University of Illinois Press, 1954); Michael H. Adler, *The Writing Machine* (London: George Allen & Unwin, 1973); Wilfred A. Beeching, *Century of the Typewriter* (London: Heinemann, 1974); and Arthur Toye Foulke, *Mr Typewriter: A Biography of Christopher Latham Sholes* (Boston: Christopher, 1961).

4 Wershler-Henry, *The Iron Whim*, 47.

5 Jan Eric Olsén, "Vicariates of the Eye: Blindness, Sense Substitution, and Writing Devices in the Nineteenth Century," *Mosaic: A Journal for the Interdisciplinary Study of Literature* 46, no. 3 (2013): 83.

6 Wershler-Henry, *The Iron Whim*, 40.

7 Adler, *The Writing Machine*, 125–9.

8 A surviving example may be seen in action in the video "Nietzsche's Writing Ball," www.vimeo.com/43124993, viewed 24 September 2019.

9 Adler, *The Writing Machine*, 174; Wershler-Henry, *The Iron Whim*, 48–9.

10 Friedrich A. Kittler, *Gramophone, Film, Typewriter*, trans. Geoffrey Winthrop Young and Michael Wutz (Stanford, CA: Stanford University Press, 1999), 207.

11 Ibid., 200–7.

12 Adler, *The Writing Machine*, 94.

13 Beeching, *Century of the Typewriter*, 19–20.

14 Ibid., 28.

15 Current, *The Typewriter*, 125.

16 Foulke, *Mr Typewriter*, 62–5.

17 Current, *The Typewriter*, 4.

18 Foulke, *Mr Typewriter*, 68–9.

19 Current, *The Typewriter*, 32–5.

20 Ibid., 90.

21 Ibid., 49.

22 William Shakespeare, *Julius Caesar*, 4.2.268–9; Current, *The Typewriter*, 16.

23 Current, *The Typewriter*, 60; Bruce Bliven Jr., *The Wonderful Writing Machine* (New York: Random House, 1954), 51. Bliven's work is often invoked in the scholarship of typewriter history, although he provided few references and was fond of hyperbole. Bliven was a journalist for the *New Yorker,* and his book was commissioned by the Royal typewriter company, although this did not deter him from writing plenty about Remington. See Douglas Martin, "Bruce Bliven Jr., 85, Author Who Brought Verve to an Assortment of Subjects," *New York Times,* 14 January 2002, at http://www.nytimes.com.2002/01/14/arts/bruce-bliven-jr-85-author-who-brought-verve-to-an-assortment-of-subjects.html, read 20 July 2012.

24 The first line of the oft-recited ballad "Casabianca" by Felicia Dorothea Hemans.

25 Scott Bukatman, "Gibson's Typewriter," in "Flame Wars: The Discourse of Cyberculture," special issue of *South Atlantic Quarterly* 92, no. 4 (Fall 1993): 637.

26 Mark Twain, "The First Writing-Machines," in *The Complete Essays of Mark Twain Now Collected for the First Time,* ed. Charles Neider (Garden City, NY: Doubleday, 1963), 324–6.

27 Ibid., 324–5.

28 Current, *The Typewriter*, 11.

29 Ibid., 36–7.

30 *Nation* (New York), December 1875, cited in Current, *The Typewriter*, 86.

31 *Typewriter Topics* 48, no. 2 (June 1921): 98–9, editorial comment.

32 *Typewriter Topics* 28, no. 1 (September 1914): 32.

33 Current, *The Typewriter*, 87.

34 Cynthia Monaco, "The Difficult Birth of the Typewriter," *Harvard Business Review* 67, no. 2 (March 1989): 214.

35 Current, *The Typewriter*, 133.

36 Ibid., 128.

37 Beeching, *Century of the Typewriter*, 167.

38 Diane Gilbert Madsen, "'To Pound a Vicious Typewriter': Hemingway's Corona #3," *Hemingway Review* 32, no. 2 (Spring 2013): 111.

39 *The Crisis: A Record of the Darker Races* 5, no. 3 (1913), Emancipation issue, 148 and 153 for these regular advertisers in a journal published by the National Association for the Advancement of Colored People.

40 *Typewriter Topics* 48, no. 2 (June 1921): 125, advertisement for Corona. A 1924 folding portable Corona No. 3 may be viewed at www.youtube.com /watch?v=3JPeozDv_ME, read 25 September 2019.

41 *Typewriter Topics* 28, no. 1 (September 1914): 12.

42 *Typewriter Topics* 48, no. 2 (June 1921): 104–5, and 48, no. 4 (August 1921): 322.

43 Geo. Carl Mares, *The History of the Typewriter: Being an Illustrated Account of the Origin, Rise and Development of the Writing Machine* (London: Guilbert Pitman, 1909), 1–2.

44 Beeching, *Century of the Typewriter*, for a near-exhaustive alphabetical list.

45 Marco Maffioletti, *L'Impresa ideale tra fabbrica e comunità: Una biografia intellettuale di Adriano Olivetti* (Rome: Collana Intangibili-Fondazione Adriano Olivetti, 2016), 185–6.

46 Ibid., 350, 444.

47 Lothar Müller, *White Magic: The Age of Paper*, trans. Jessica Spengler (Cambridge: Polity, 2014), 230.

48 Adler, *The Writing Machine*, 42–3.

49 *Typewriter Topics* 28, no. 1 (September 1914): 41, advertisement for Underwood.

50 Bliven, *Wonderful Writing Machine*, 112.

51 Ibid.; Wershler-Henry, *The Iron Whim*, 232. Beeching, *Century of the Typewriter*, dates this article to 1877, which may be an error; normally Beeching follows Bliven's account, which gives 1887.

52 Wershler-Henry, *The Iron Whim*, 234; Bliven, *Wonderful Writing Machine*, 114–15.

53 Bliven, *Wonderful Writing Machine*, 116–30. After the introduction of Linotype, compositors also raced each other competitively. I am grateful to Michael Winship for this information.

54 *Typewriter Topics* 28, no. 2 (October 1914): 102–3.

55 Arthur M. Baker, *How to Succeed as a Stenographer or Typewriter* (New York: Fowler and Wells, 1888), 10–11 and 34.

56 Charles Dickens, *David Copperfield* (Ware, UK: Wordsworth Classics, 2000), 465–6; Hugo Bowles, *Dickens and the Stenographic Mind* (Oxford: Oxford University Press, 2019).

57 Delphine Gardey, *Écrire, calculer, classer: Comment une révolution de papier a transformé les sociétés contemporaines* (Paris: La Découverte, 2008), 61–2.

58 Monique Peyrière, "La fabrique de l'objet," in *Machines à écrire: Des claviers et des puces: La traversée du siècle* (Paris: Autrement, 1994), 21–2.

59 Adler, *The Writing Machine*, 205–7.
60 "The Case of QWERTY vs Maltron," *Time* 117, no. 3 (26 January 1981): 57.
61 Thomas S. Mullaney, *The Chinese Typewriter: A History* (Cambridge, MA: MIT Press, 2017). In a five-minute video, Mullaney assembles a Double Pigeon typewriter as if it were an IKEA furniture kit. See https://vimeo.com/204102277, viewed 3 April 2019.
62 Sheila Melvin, "How Chinese Typewriters Led Way to Predictive Text on Smartphones," *Caixin Online Society and Culture*, 26 March 2016, http://english.caixin.com/2016-03-26/100924780.html, read 18 August 2016.
63 R. John Williams, "The *Technê* Whim: Lin Yutang and the Invention of the Chinese Typewriter," *American Literature* 82, no. 2 (2010): 389–419.
64 Darryl C. Rehr, "QWERTY-DVORAK: 'The Keyboard Wars'," *Office* 111, no. 4 (April 1990): 12–19.
65 Dwight D.W. Davis, "An Analysis of Student Errors on the Universal and Dvorak-Dealey Simplified Keyboard" (MA thesis, University of Washington, 1935), 27 and 51; Viola Elsie Goehring, "Comparison of the Typewriting Achievements of Students Trained on the 'Universal' and the 'Dvorak-Dealey Simplified' Typewriter Keyboards" (MA thesis, University of Washington, 1933; Ann Arbor, MI: University Microfilms, 1961), for conclusions based on a very small cohort.
66 Stan Liebowitz and Stephen E. Margolis, "Typing Errors," *Reason* 28, no. 2 (June 1996): 28–35.
67 Paul A. David, "Clio and the Economics of QWERTY," *American Economic Review* 75, no. 2 (1985): 332–7.
68 Beeching, *Century of the Typewriter*, 42.
69 Jared Diamond, "The Case of QWERTY," *Discover* 18, no. 4 (April 1997): 34–42.

3. Modernity and the "Typewriter Girl"

1 *Forum* 44, no. 6 (December 1910).
2 Elsewhere, the arrival of the typewriter had to be accommodated by different scribal cultures. In India, where there was a shortage of white women workers, most typists were upper-caste men. See David Arnold, *Everyday Technology: Machines and the Making of India's Modernity* (Chicago: University of Chicago Press, 2013), 86–94.
3 Margery W. Davies, *Woman's Place Is at the Typewriter: Office Work and Office Workers, 1870-1930* (Philadelphia: Temple University Press, 1982), 5.
4 Joli Jensen, "Using the Typewriter: Secretaries, Reporters and Authors, 1880–1930," *Technology in Society* 10 (1988): 255–66.
5 Delphine Gardey, *Écrire, calculer, classer: Comment une révolution de papier a transformé les sociétés contemporaines* (Paris: La Découverte, 2008), 15–16.

6 Davies, *Woman's Place Is at the Typewriter*, 37.
7 Elyce J. Rotella, *From Home to Office: U.S. Women at Work, 1870–1930* (Ann Arbor, MI: UMI Research Press, 1981), fig. 5.1.
8 Davies, *Woman's Place Is at the Typewriter*, 52.
9 Delphine Gardey, *La dactylographe et l'expéditionnaire: Histoire des employés de bureau, 1890–1939* (Paris: Belin, 2001), 65.
10 Leah Price and Pamela Thurschwell, "Invisible Hands," in *Literary Secretaries / Secretarial Culture*, ed. Price and Thurschwell (Aldershot, UK: Ashgate, 2005), 4–5; Gregory Anderson, "The White-Blouse Revolution," in *The White-Blouse Revolution: Female Office-workers since 1870*, ed. G. Anderson (Manchester: Manchester University Press, 1988), 7.
11 Rotella, *From Home to Office*, 68.
12 Ibid., 68–9.
13 Gardey, *Écrire, calculer, classer*, 61–2.
14 Leah Price, "Stenographic Masculinity," in Price and Thurschwell, *Literary Secretaries*, 36–41.
15 Gladys Carnaffan, "Commercial Education and the Female Office Worker," in Anderson, *White-Blouse Revolution*, 82.
16 Davies, *Woman's Place Is at the Typewriter*, 6; Lisa M. Fine, *The Souls of the Skyscraper: Female Clerical Workers in Chicago, 1870–1930* (Philadelphia: Temple University Press, 1990), 78.
17 Georges Simenon (Jean du Perry, pseud.), *Le Roman d'une dactylo* (Paris: Ferenczi, 1924). A photocopied version exists at the Simenon archive in Liège, but there is no reason to rescue this work from the oblivion it deserves.
18 Dashiell Hammett, *The Maltese Falcon* (New York: Knopf, 1930), ch. 1.
19 Erle Stanley Gardner, *The Case of the Terrified Typist* (1956; London: Pan, 1964).
20 Agatha Christie, *The Clocks* (1964; New York: HarperCollins, 2011, 180–1.
21 Price and Thurschwell, "Invisible Hands," 4.
22 Fine, *Souls of the Skyscraper*, 51.
23 Ibid., 37.
24 Teresa Davy, "'A Cissy Job for Men: A Nice Job for Girls': Women Shorthand Typists in London, 1900–1939," in *Our Work, Our Lives, Our Words: Women's History and Women's Work*, ed. Lenore Davidoff and Belinda Westover (Basingstoke, UK: Macmillan, 1986), 127–32.
25 Rotella, *From Home to Office*, 156.
26 George Gissing, *The Odd Women* (1893; Oxford: Oxford University Press, 2008), 31 and 41.
27 Rotella, *From Home to Office*, 159; Davies, *Woman's Place Is at the Typewriter*, 68.
28 Gardey, *La dactylographe*, 120.

29 Grant Allen (Olive Pratt Rayner, pseud.), *The Type-Writer Girl* (London: C.A. Pearson, 1897).

30 S. Brooke Cameron, "Sister of the Type: The Feminist Collective in Grant Allen's *The Type-Writer Girl*," *Victorian Literature and Culture* 40 (2012): 235.

31 Jessica Gray, "Typewriter Girls in Turn-of-the-Century Fiction," *English Literature in Transition* 58, no. 4 (2015): 486–502.

32 Gissing, *The Odd Women*, 27–8.

33 Anthony M. Ludovici, "The Latest Form of Poisonous Hate," *New Age* n.s. 12, no. 2 (14 November 1912): 8–9.

34 Clarissa Suranyi, "High Fidelity: The Phonograph and Typewriter in Fin-de-siècle Fiction" (PhD diss., University of Western Ontario, 2001).

35 Christopher Keep, "The Cultural Work of the Type-Writer Girl," *Victorian Studies* 40, no. 3 (1997): 414–15.

36 Davy, "'A Cissy Job for Men'," 142.

37 María Paula Bontempo and Graciela A. Queirolo, "Las 'Chicas Modernas' se emplean como dactilógrafas: Feminidad, moda y trabajo en Buenos Aires (1920–1930)," *Bicentenario: Revista de historia de Chile y América* 11, no. 2 (2012): 69.

38 Rayner, *Type-Writer Girl*, 26. The employer is Fingelman and there are anti-Semitic undertones to Appleton's description. See also Victoria Orwell, "The Body Types: Corporeal Documents and Body Politics circa 1900," in Price and Thurschwell, *Literary Secretaries*, 57.

39 Christopher Keep, "Blinded by the Type: Gender and Information Technology at the Turn of the Century," *Nineteenth-Century Contexts* 23, no. 1 (2001): 157.

40 Bernard Marks, *Once Upon a Typewriter: Twelve Secretaries, Twelve Success Stories* (London: Arrow, 1974), 34.

41 Harry Ransom Center, Erle Stanley Gardner (hereafter ESG) papers, box 103, Plot Outlines, Diary etc., no pagination, circa 1943–44.

42 ESG papers, box 294, Gardner to Thayer Hobson, 12 July 1938.

43 Mason's first proposal of marriage was made at the end of *The Case of the Lame Canary* (1937), and the second soon afterwards, but to no purpose, in *The Case of the Substitute Face* (1938).

44 ESG papers, box 294, Gardner to Thayer Hobson 15 March 1938.

45 Susanne Dohrn, "Pioneers in a Dead-end Profession: The First Women Clerks in Banks and Insurance Companies," in Anderson, *White-Blouse Revolution*, 58.

46 Davy, "'A Cissy Job for Men'," 124.

47 Sharon Hartman Strom, *Beyond the Typewriter: Gender, Class, and the Origins of Modern American Office Work, 1900–1930* (Urbana: University of Illinois Press, 1992), 233–4.

48 Davies, *Woman's Place Is at the Typewriter*, 112–25.
49 Fine, *Souls of the Skyscraper*, 87.
50 Allen, *Type-Writer Girl*, 34.
51 Michel Foucault, *Discipline and Punish: The Birth of the Prison* (1975; London: Penguin, 1991, pt. 3; Mary C. Pinard, "Christopher Latham Sholes, the Typewriter, and Women's Economic Emancipation: A Reading of an Image," *Reader* 23 (Spring 1990): 22–35.
52 ESG papers, box 287, Gardner to Jack Simpson, 27 August 1945.
53 ESG papers, box 288, Character descriptions, 15 November 1951.
54 Gissing, *The Odd Women*, 151–3.
55 Ibid., 153.
56 Alys Eve Weinbaum et al., "The Modern Girl as Heuristic Device," in *The Modern Girl Around the World: Consumption: Modernity and Globalization* (Durham, NC: Duke University Press, 2008), 1–24.
57 Gissing, *The Odd Women*, 43.
58 John Harrison, *A Manual of the Type-Writer* (London: Isaac Pitman and Sons, 1888), 9, cited in Keep, "Blinded by the Type," 155.
59 Gardey, *La dactylographe*, 74–5.
60 Sue Walker, "How Typewriters Changed Correspondence: An Analysis of Prescription and Practice," *Visible Language* 18, no. 2 (1984): 102–17; Sue Walker, "Modernity, Method and Minimal Means; Typewriters, Typing Manuals and Document Design," *Journal of Design History* 31, no. 2 (2018): 138–53.
61 Bram Stoker, *Dracula* (1897; London: Penguin, 2003), 250.
62 Jennifer Fleissner, "Dictation Anxiety: The Stenographer's Voice in *Dracula*," in Price and Thurschwell, *Literary Secretaries*, 63–90.
63 Pamela Thurschwell, "Henry James and Theodora Bosanquet: On the Typewriter, *In the Cage*, at the Ouija Board," *Textual Practice* 13, no. 1 (1999): 8.
64 Roland Barthes, "Un rapport presque maniaque avec les instruments graphiques," interview with Jean-Louis de Rambures in *Le Monde*, 27 September 1973, in Roland Barthes, *Le grain de la voix: Entretiens, 1962–1980* (Paris: Seuil, 1981), 172.
65 Keep, "Blinded by the Type," 153–4.
66 Arthur Sullivant Hoffman, ed., *Fiction Writers on Fiction Writing: Advice, Opinions, and a Statement of Their Own Working Methods by More Than One Hundred Writers* (Indianapolis: Bobbs-Merrill, 1923), 411.
67 Ibid., 412. Carr wrote for Mack Sennett, as well as writing magazine stories and cowboy poetry.
68 Arthur Conan Doyle, "A Case of Identity," a short story in *The Adventures of Sherlock Holmes* (London: George Newnes, 1892).
69 Jensen, "Using the Typewriter," 255n4.

70 Keep, "Blinded by the Type," 168.
71 Christie, *The Clocks*, viii.
72 Marion Lamb, *Your First Year of Teaching Typewriting* (Cincinnati, OH: South Western, 1959), 77, cited in Kathleen McConnell, "The Profound Sound of Ernest Hemingway's Typist: Gendered Typewriting as a Solution to the Problems of Communication," *Communication and Critical/Cultural Studies* 5, no. 4 (2008): 336.
73 Keep, "Blinded by the Type," 158.
74 Stoker, *Dracula*, 307 and 332–3.

4. The Modernist Typewriter

1 David Wright, "Subversive Technologies: The Machine Age Poetics of F.T. Marinetti, Ezra Pound, and Charles Olson" (PhD diss., McGill University, 2007), 10.
2 Friedrich A. Kittler, *Gramophone, Film, Typewriter*, trans. Geoffrey Winthrop Young and Michael Wutz (Stanford, CA: Stanford University Press, 1986), 190–3.
3 Carlos Baker, *Ernest Hemingway: A Life Story* (New York: (Charles Scribner's Sons, 1969), 90; Ernest Hemingway, "Mitrailliatrice," *Poetry* 21 (January 1923): 193–5.
4 Henry Lawson, "The Firing Line," in his *When I Was King and Other Verses* (Sydney: Angus & Robertson, 1906).
5 Darren Wershler-Henry, *The Iron Whim: A Fragmented History of Typewriting* (Ithaca, NY: Cornell University Press, 2007), 247.
6 Kathleen Burk, "The Telly Don," *BBC History*, August 2000, 52.
7 Bruce Bliven, Jr., *The Wonderful Writing Machine* (New York: Random House, 1954), 38.
8 Catherine Viollet, "Écriture méchanique, espaces de frappe: Quelques préalables à une sémiologie du dactylogramme," *Genesis* 10 (1996): 199.
9 Ibid., 198.
10 Filippo Tommaso Marinetti's "The Futurist Manifesto" (1909), is translated in James Joll, *Three Intellectuals in Politics* (New York: Pantheon, 1960), 179–84.
11 Marjorie Perloff, *The Futurist Moment: Avant-Garde, Avant Guerre, and the Language of Rupture* (Chicago: University of Chicago Press, 1986), 90–5.
12 Filippo Tommaso Marinetti, "Technical Manifesto of Futurist Literature," in Marinetti, *Selected Poems and Related Prose*, ed. Luce Marinetti (New Haven, CT: Yale University Press, 2002), 77–80.
13 Gabriele D'Annunzio (1863–1938) was a Decadent poet, a war-mongering nationalist, and a precursor of Fascism.
14 "Typographic Revolution and Free Expressive Orthography," in *Futurism: An Anthology*, ed. Lawrence Rainey, Christine Poggi, and Laura Wittman

(New Haven, CT: Yale University Press, 2009), 149. I prefer this translation to several others available. It is taken directly from the Italian, unlike Luce Marinetti's, which has taken a detour via a French version.

15 "Technical Manifesto," 80.

16 For Fortunato Depero's *Luna Park, Esplosione tipografica*, see https://www .amazon.de/Esplosione-Tipografica-Montagne-Fortunato-Kunstdruck/dp /B00YHJY90C.

17 Manuel Fontán del Junco, ed., *Futurist Depero, 1913–1950: Catalogue of an Exhibition at the Fundación Juan March, Madrid, 10 October 2014–18 January 2015* (Madrid: Fundación Juan March, 2014), exhibition item 180. Depero moved to the United States in 1928 and did not return to Italy until after the Second World War.

18 Perloff, *The Futurist Moment*, 58.

19 Günter Berghaus, *Italian Futurist Theatre, 1909–1914* (Oxford: Clarendon, 1998), 249–51; Giacomo Balla, "Onomatopea rumorista Macchina Tipografica," in Giacomo Balla and Fortunato Depero, *Ricostruzione futurista dell'universo* (Milan: Direzione del Movimento Futurista, 1915); Rainey et al., *Futurism*, 430.

20 Berghaus, *Italian Futurist Theatre*, 259.

21 Marinetti, "Geometric and Mechanical Splendour," in *Selected Poems*, 90–2.

22 Wright, "Subversive Technologies," 88.

23 Ibid., 85.

24 Johanna Drucker, *The Visible Word: Experimental Typography and Modern Art, 1909–1923* (Chicago: University of Chicago Press, 1994), 50–9.

25 Ibid., 142.

26 Guillaume Apollinaire, *Calligrammes, poèmes de la paix et de la guerre, 1913–1916* (Paris: Mercure de France, 1918). See also Willard Bohn, *Reading Apollinaire's "Calligrammes"* (New York: Bloomsbury, 2018).

27 Daniel Albright, *Untwisting the Serpent: Modernism in Music, Literature and Other Arts* (Chicago: University of Chicago Press, 2000), 208.

28 See https://www.youtube.com/watch?v=g2LJ1i7222c for a concert performance by Martin Breinschmid.

29 Charles Olson, *Projective Verse* (New York: Totem, n.d. [1959?]), 9.

30 Ezra Pound, *The Letters of Ezra Pound, 1907–1941*, ed. D.D. Paige (London: Faber & Faber, 1950), 418, letter from Rapallo, February 1939.

31 James Laughlin, *Pound as Wuz: Essays and Lectures on Ezra Pound* (St Paul, MN: Graywolf, 1987), 6–7.

32 Ezra Pound, *Pound/Lewis: The Letters of Ezra Pound and Wyndham Lewis*, ed. Timothy Materer (New York: New Directions, 1985) 104, Pound to Wyndham Lewis, 10 September 1917.

33 Seungyeok Kweon, "Technologized Materiality in Modernist Poetics" (PhD diss., State University of New York at Buffalo, 2001), 215–18, citing

"Directions and Suggestions to Printer," Ezra Pound Papers, 74:3357, Beinecke Library, Yale University.

34 Pound, "A Prison Letter," *Paris Review* 28 (Summer–Fall 1962): 17.

35 Daniel Matore, "Cummings's Typewriter Language: The Typography of *Tulips & Chimneys*," *Textual Practice* 31, no. 7 (2017): 1519.

36 E.E. Cummings, *Selected Letters of E.E. Cummings*, ed. F.W. Dupee and George Stade (London: André Deutsch, 1972), 140–1, letter to Aunt Jane, 11 March 1935; Matore, "Cummings's Typewriter Language," 1510–11.

37 Lawrence Rainey, *Revisiting "The Waste Land"* (New Haven, CT: Yale University Press, 2005).

38 T.S. Eliot, *The Letters of T.S. Eliot*, vol. 1, *1898–1922*, rev. ed., ed. Valerie Eliot and Hugh Haughton (London: Faber & Faber, 2009), letters of 22 May 1919 and 22 February 1920.

39 Kweon, "Technologized Materiality," 47.

40 Eliot, *Letters*, 706–7, letter to John Quinn, London, 19 July 1922. Quinn was an Irish-American lawyer and patron of modernist writers who bought drafts of *The Waste Land* from Eliot and bequeathed them to the New York Public Library.

41 Ibid., 158, letter of 21 August 1916.

42 Baker, *Ernest Hemingway*, 32.

43 Charles Fenton, *The Apprenticeship of Ernest Hemingway: The Early Years* (New York: Farrar, Straus and Young, 1954).

44 Diane Gilbert Madsen, "'To Pound a Vicious Typewriter': Hemingway's Corona #3," *Hemingway Review* 32, no. 2 (Spring 2013): 109–11. A 1924 portable Corona No. 3 is demonstrated at https://www.youtube.com/watch?v=3JPeozDv_ME, viewed 26 September 2019.

45 Ernest Hemingway, *Ernest Hemingway: Selected Letters, 1917–1961*, ed. Carlos Baker (New York: Granada, 180), letter from Schruns, circa 24 December 1925.

46 Baker, *Ernest Hemingway*, 167 and 199.

47 Hemingway, *Selected Letters*, 792, letter to Bernard Berenson, La Finca Vigía, 14 October 1952.

48 Baker, *Ernest Hemingway*, 652.

49 Hemingway, *Selected Letters*, 500, letter from La Finca Vigía, 25 February 1944.

50 Ibid., 408, letter from Key West, 28 May 1934.

51 Ibid., 467, letter to Maxwell Perkins, Marseilles, 5 May 1938.

52 Baker, *Ernest Hemingway*, 217.

53 Ibid., 472–3.

54 Hemingway, *Selected Letters*, 677, letter to John Dos Passos, La Finca Vigía, 17 September 1949.

55 Jennifer Latson, "5 Times Ernest Hemingway Cheated Death," *Time*, 21 July 2015, http://time.com/3961119/birthday-ernest-hemingway-history-death/.

56 George Plimpton, "Ernest Hemingway: The Art of Fiction no. 21," *Paris Review* 18 (Spring 1958), https://www.theparisreview.org/interviews/4825/ernest-hemingway-the-art-of-fiction-no-21-ernest-hemingway.

57 Hemingway, *Selected Letters*, 700, letter to Harvey Breit, La Finca Vigía, 9 July 1950.

58 Ibid., 45, letter to Grace Hall Hemingway, Chicago, 21 January 1921.

59 Ibid., 63, letter to Howell Jenkins, Paris, 20 March 1922.

60 Ibid., 34, letter from Toronto, 16 February 1920.

61 Ibid., 237, letter to Maxwell Perkins, Paris, 6 December 1926.

62 Ibid., 281, letter from Kansas City, Missouri, circa 27 July 1928.

63 Ibid., 358, letter from Key West, 15 April 1942.

5. The Distancing Effect: The Hand, the Eye, the Voice

1 Béatrice Fraenkel, "La signature: Du signe à l'acte," *Sociétés et représentations* 25, no. 1 (2008): 21, and the same author's "Actes d'écriture: Quand écrire c'est faire," *Langage et société* 121–2 (2007): 101–12.

2 Fraenkel, "La signature," 13–15, and see Béatrice Fraenkel, *La signature, genèse d'un signe* (Paris: Gallimard, 1992).

3 Friedrich A. Kittler, *Gramophone, Film, Typewriter*, trans. Geoffrey Winthrop Young and Michael Wutz (Stanford, CA: Stanford University Press, 1999), 199 and 210.

4 Friedrich A. Kittler, *Discourse Networks, 1800/1900*, trans. Michael Meteer and Chris Cullens (Stanford, CA: Stanford University Press, 1990).

5 Ibid., 195.

6 Michael Wood, "Paul Auster: The Art of Fiction no. 178," *Paris Review* 121 (Fall 2003), http://www.theparisreview.org/interviews/121/the-art-of-fiction-no-178-paul-auster, read 25 May 2018.

7 Katherine Mansfield, *The Collected Letters of Katherine Mansfield*, vol. 1, *1903–1917*, ed. Vincent O'Sullivan and Margaret Scott (Oxford: Oxford University Press, 1984), 27, Mansfield to Martha Putnam, October 1907.

8 "Me and My Typewriter," *Writer's Digest* 61 (January 1981): 31–2, for these two comments.

9 Jack London, *John Barleycorn*, 1913, ed. John Sutherland (Oxford: Oxford University Press, 2009), 134–5.

10 Mark Seltzer, *Bodies and Machines* (New York: Routledge, 1992), 3–4.

11 King Camp Gillette, *The People's Corporation* (Boston: Ball, 1924), 152, as cited in Seltzer, *Bodies and Machines*, 130.

12 Catherine Viollet, "Écriture méchanique, espaces de frappe: Quelques préalables à une sémiologie du dactylogramme," *Genesis* 10 (1996): 204.

13 Frances de Groen, *Xavier Herbert: A Biography* (St Lucia: University of Queensland Press, 1998), 91. The handwriting is Herbert's, and the only surviving manuscript is in the Australian National Library, Canberra.

14 Miles Franklin, *My Congenials: Miles Franklin and Friends in Letters*, vol. 1, *1879–1938*, ed. Jill Roe (Sydney: Angus & Robertson, 1993), 74, letter of 8 May 1912.

15 Ibid., 76, letter of December 1912.

16 Viollet, "Écriture méchanique," 202.

17 Alex Goody, *Technology, Literature and Culture* (Cambridge: Polity, 2011), 109–10.

18 Jean Devanny, *Point of Departure: The Autobiography of Jean Devanny*, ed. Carole Ferrier (St Lucia: University of Queensland Press, 1986), 83.

19 IBM Office Products Division, "The Typewriter: An Informal History" (August 1977), http://www-03.ibm.com/ibm/history/exhibits/modelb /modelb_informal.html, read 5 March 2014.

20 Roger Laufer, "La machine pour écrire," in *Machines à écrire. Des claviers et des puces: La traversée du siècle*, ed. Monique Peyrière (Paris: Autrement, 1994), 120–30.

21 Kittler, *Gramophone, Film, Typewriter*, 198–200, citing Martin Heidegger, *Parmenides* (Bloomington: Indiana University Press, 1942–3), 80–6.

22 Hermann Hesse, "Die Schreibmaschine," *März* 4 (1908): 377–8.

23 Isaac Pitman, *Pitman's Typewriter Manual: A Practical Guide to Commercial, Literary, Legal, Dramatic and All Classes of Typewriting Work*, 6th ed. (London: Pitman, 1911), 8.

24 Denis O'Driscoll, "Les Murray: The Art of Poetry, no. 89," *Paris Review* 173 (Spring 2005), http://www.theparisreview.org/interviews/5508/the -art-of-poetry-no-89-les-murray, read 28 February 2014.

25 Viollet, "Écriture méchanique," 205.

26 Wood, "Paul Auster."

27 Viollet, "Écriture méchanique," 204.

28 Ibid., 202.

29 Ibid., 204.

30 David Marr, *Patrick White: A Life* (Sydney: Random House, 2008), 374.

31 Viollet, "Écriture méchanique," 206.

32 James Edwin Miller Jr., *T.S. Eliot: The Making of an American Poet, 1888–1922* (University Park, PA: Penn State University Press, 2005), 260, letter to Conrad Aiken, 21 August 1916.

33 Theodora Bosanquet, *Henry James at Work, with Excerpts from Her Diary and an Account of Her Professional Career*, ed. Lyall H. Powers (Ann Arbor: University of Michigan Press, 2006), 34–5.

34 Ibid.

35 Leon Edel, *Henry James: A Life* (London: Collins, 1987), 229–30 and 263.

36 H. Montgomery Hyde, *Henry James at Home* (London: Methuen, 1969), 112.
37 Henry James, *Letters*, vol. 3, *1883–1895*, ed. Leon Edel (London: Macmillan, 1981), 23–4, James to Richard Watson Gilder, 1 February 1884, and 77, to J.R. Osgood, 18 April 1885. Three volumes of James's correspondence were published by Macmillan between 1974 and 1981, henceforth referred to as the London edition. The Belknap Press of Harvard University published four volumes, up to 1916, and these are henceforth referred to as the US edition. Macmillan subsequently published a fourth volume, which was a copy of the Belknap Press edition. See, more recently, *The Complete Letters of Henry James*, ed. Michael Anesko and Greg W. Zacharias, with Katie Sommer (Lincoln: University of Nebraska Press, 2006–), which includes many letters not published by Leon Edel.
38 James, *Letters*, vol. 3 (London edition), 271, James to Grace Norton, 12 March 1890.
39 Edel, *Henry James*, 456.
40 Henry James, *Letters*, vol. 4, *1895–1916*, ed. Leon Edel (Cambridge, MA: Belknap, 1984) (US edition), 95, letter of 26 December 1898.
41 James, *Letters*, vol. 4 (US edition), 712, James to Jessie Allen, 6 May 1914.
42 Ibid., 75, letter of 20 April 1898.
43 H. Montgomery Hyde, *Henry James at Home* (London: Methuen, 1969), 148–55.
44 Ibid., 150.
45 Ibid., 147.
46 Ibid., 155.
47 Edel, *Henry James*, 635.
48 Bosanquet, *Henry James at Work*, 32–3.
49 James, *Letters*, vol. 4 (US edition), 589, James to Bosanquet, 27 October 1911.
50 Ibid., 468, James to William James, 17 October 1907.
51 Seltzer, *Bodies and Machines*, 195.
52 The original garden house was destroyed by a bomb during the Second World War. The room in Lamb House currently labelled as his study is not where James originally wrote.
53 Bosanquet, *Henry James at Work*, 32–3.
54 Marshall McLuhan, *Understanding Media: The Extensions of Man* (London: Abacus, 1974), 277.
55 Bosanquet, *Henry James at Work*, 34–5; Kittler, *Gramophone, Film, Typewriter*, 216.
56 Bosanquet, *Henry James at Work*, 37.
57 Edel, *Henry James*, 541; Bosanquet, *Henry James at Work*, 5.
58 Hyde, *Henry James at Home*, 152.
59 Matthew Schilleman, "Typewriter Psyche: Henry James's Mechanical Mind," *Journal of Modern Literature* 36, no. 3 (Spring 2013): 15.

60 Bosanquet, *Henry James at Work*, 33–4.

61 Ibid., 34–5.

62 Schilleman, "Typewriter Psyche," 18–19.

63 James, *Letters*, vol. 3 (London edition), 301–2, James to Scudder, 5 October 1890.

64 Howard Gardner, "On Becoming a Dictator," *Psychology Today* 14, no. 7 (December 1980): 14–19.

65 Fabio L. Vericat, "Her Master's Voice: Dictation, the Typewriter, and Henry James's Trouble with the Speech of American Women," *South Atlantic Review* 80, nos 1–2 (2015): 14.

66 Bosanquet, *Henry James at Work*, 18.

67 Lee Honeycutt, "Literacy and the Writing Voice: The Intersection of Culture and Technology in Dictation," *Journal of Business and Technical Communication* 18, no. 3 (July 2004): 294–327, citing Quintilian, *Institutes of Oratory: Or, Education of an Orator* (*Institutio Oratoria*), trans. J.S. Watson, vol. 2 (London: Bell, 1903).

68 Paul Saenger, *Space between Words: The Origins of Silent Reading* (Stanford, CA: Stanford University Press, 1997).

69 Bosanquet, *Henry James at Work*, 36.

70 Mark Twain, "The First Writing-Machines," in *The Complete Essays of Mark Twain Now Collected for the First Time*, ed. Charles Neider (Garden City, NY: Doubleday, 1963), 324.

71 Marshall McLuhan, *The Gutenberg Galaxy: The Making of Typographical Man* (Toronto: University of Toronto Press, 1962).

72 McLuhan, *Understanding Media*, 278–9.

73 Honeycutt, "Literacy and the Writing Voice," 320.

74 Harry Ransom Center, Erle Stanley Gardner (hereafter ESG) papers, box 219, General Correspondence, Gardner to Barnum and Flagg, 7 March 1958.

75 Ibid., Gardner to Business Office Outfitters, San Diego, 4 August 1966.

76 Ibid., IBM Executary belt correspondence, memo to Thayer Hobson and Helen King, 8 July 1963.

77 ESG papers, box 616, *The Color of Life*, new, unfinished 1969 version, 130.

78 Ibid.

6. The Romantic Typewriter

1 Giulia Giuffré, *A Writing Life: Interviews with Australian Women Writers* (Sydney: Allen & Unwin, 1990), 155.

2 Hans Georg Schenk, *The Mind of the European Romantics: An Essay in Cultural History* (London: Constable, 1966), 5–6.

3 Gerald Nicosia, *Memory Babe: A Critical Biography of Jack Kerouac* (Berkeley: University of California Press, 1994), chronicles many of these relationships.

4 James Gillespie Blaine, *Reciprocity: An Essay from the Spirit World* (Boston: Jos. M. Wade, 1896).

5 John Kendrick Bangs, *The Enchanted Type-Writer* (New York: Harper, 1899), 11. Some commentators have erroneously identified this work as a collection of short stories. It is in fact a short novel of 171 pages.

6 Beth London, "Secretary to the Stars: Mediums and the Agency of Authorship," in *Literary Secretaries / Secretarial Culture*, ed. Leah Price and Pamela Thurschwell (Aldershot, UK: Ashgate, 2005), 91–110.

7 Pamela Thurschwell, "Henry James and Theodora Bosanquet: On the Typewriter, *In the Cage*, at the Ouija Board," *Textual Practice* 13, no. 1 (1999): 11.

8 Cited in Pamela Thurschwell, *Literature, Technology and Magical Thinking, 1880–1920* (Cambridge: Cambridge University Press, 2001), 20.

9 "Me and My Typewriter," *Writer's Digest* 61 (January 1981): 32.

10 Ibid. My emphasis.

11 Enid Blyton, *The Story of My Life* (London: Pitkins, n.d. [1952?]), 71.

12 Robert Druce, *This Day Our Daily Fictions: An Enquiry into the Multi-Million Bestseller Status of Enid Blyton and Ian Fleming* (Amsterdam: Rodopi, 1992), 15.

13 Lucy Mangan, "How Utterly, Splendidly Ripping," *Guardian*, 20 August 2008, 26–7.

14 Imogen Smallwood, *A Childhood at Green Hedges* (London: Methuen, 1989), 123.

15 Druce, *This Day Our Daily Fictions*, 37.

16 Lucy Mangan, untitled article in *Guardian* (Family Section), 25 January 2008, n.p., in Seven Stories (National Centre for Children's Books), Newcastle-upon-Tyne, Enid Blyton Archive (hereafter EBA), SR/03/02, newspaper cuttings collected by Sheila Ray.

17 Sheila G. Ray, *The Blyton Phenomenon: The Controversy Surrounding the World's Most Successful Writer* (London: André Deutsch), 1982.

18 Barbara Stoney, *Enid Blyton* (London: Hodder and Stoughton, 1974), 164.

19 George Greenfield, *Enid Blyton* (Stroud, UK: Sutton, 1998), 101.

20 According to the *Independent*, 19 August 2008, 10, in EBA, SR/03/02, newspaper cuttings collected by Sheila Ray.

21 EBA, EB/02/01/01/04, Diary, 8 January 1927.

22 Bob Mullan, *The Enid Blyton Story* (London: Boxtree, 1987), 29.

23 EBA, EB/02/01/01/04, Diary, 7 March 1927.

24 EBA, EB/02/01/01/05, Diary, 10 January 1928, dispelling the enduring myth that she invariably wrote correspondence in longhand ("Worked all a.m. at typing letters").

25 EBA, EB/02/01/01/07, Diary, 18 January 1930.

26 Greenfield, *Enid Blyton*, 67–8.

27 Blyton, *Story of My Life*, 91.

28 EBA, EB/02/01/01/14, Diary, 8, 11, and 12 May 1936.
29 EBA, EB/02/01/01/15, Five-year diary, 5 February 1937, and EB/02/01/01/04, Diary, October–December 1927.
30 Brian Alderson, "A Long, Cool Look at the Controversial Miss Blyton," *Times* (London), 18 September 1974, in EBA, SR/03/01/01, Scrapbook no. 1.
31 Dalya Alberge, "Enid Blyton's Letters Offer Glimpse of Writing Process," *Times* (London), 8 October 1994, 2, in EBA, SR/03/02, newspaper cuttings collected by Sheila Ray.
32 Blyton, *Story of My Life*, 62.
33 Stoney, *Enid Blyton*, 134–5.
34 David Rudd, "The Mystery of the Undermind ... A Closer Look at Enid's Creativity – Part 2," *The Enid Blyton Book and Ephemera Collectors Society* 23 (March 1996): 4–7.
35 Stoney, *Enid Blyton*, 206.
36 Ibid., cit. 135.
37 Blyton *Story of My Life*, 89.
38 Stoney, *Enid Blyton*, 211.
39 Alberge, "Enid Blyton's Letters," 2. McKellar subsequently wrote *Imagination and Thinking: A Psychological Analysis* (London: Cohen & West, 1957).
40 Druce, *This Day Our Daily Fictions*, 24–5.
41 EBA, EB/02/01/01/15, Five-year diary, 3 December 1940.
42 David Rudd, "The Mystery of the Undermind ... A Closer Look at Enid's Creativity – Part 1," *The Enid Blyton Book and Ephemera Collectors Society* 22 (February 1996): 12–16.
43 Blyton, *The Story of My Life*, 91.
44 Ibid., 103.
45 Rudd, "The Mystery of the Undermind ... Part 1," 12–16.
46 Ann Charters, ed., *The Portable Beat Reader* (London: Penguin, 1992), 57–9.
47 Tim Hunt, *Kerouac's Crooked Road: Development of a Fiction* (Berkeley: University of California Press, 1981), 112–13.
48 Jack Kerouac, *Atop an Underwood: Early Stories and Other Writings*, ed. Paul Marion (New York: Viking Penguin, 1999), 3. *Atop an Underwood* itself was dated 1941.
49 Kerouac, "From Background," in *Atop an Underwood*, 5.
50 Kerouac, "A Play I Want to Write," in *Atop an Underwood*, 28–9.
51 Kerouac, "Howdy," in *Atop an Underwood*, 165–6.
52 Kerouac, "Credo," in *Atop an Underwood*, 153–4.
53 Kerouac, "Atop an Underwood: Introduction," in *Atop an Underwood*, 133.
54 Kerouac, "Today," in *Atop an Underwood*, 167–8.
55 Catherine Mary Nash, "Technology in the Work of Jack Kerouac and William S. Burroughs" (PhD diss., University of Nottingham, 2008), 16.
56 John Clellon Holmes, *Nothing More to Declare* (London: André Deutsch, 1968), 78.

57 Nicosia, *Memory Babe*, 234.

58 Nash, "Technology in the Work of Jack Kerouac," 34.

59 Jack Kerouac, *Selected Letters, 1940–1956*, ed. Ann Charters (New York: Viking, 1995), 315, Kerouac to Neal Cassady, 22 May 1951.

60 Nicosia, *Memory Babe*, 348.

61 Allen Ginsberg, *Deliberate Prose: Selected Essays, 1952–1995*, ed. Bill Morgan (New York: Harper, 2000), 342.

62 Hunt, *Kerouac's Crooked Road*, 112–13; Darren Wershler-Henry, *The Iron Whim: A Fragmented History of Typewriting* (Ithaca, NY: Cornell University Press, 2007), 241–2.

63 Jack Kerouac, *Selected Letters, 1957–1969*, ed. Ann Charters (New York: Viking Penguin, 1999), 461.

64 Todd F. Tietchen, *Techno-Modern Poetics: The American Literary Avant-Garde at the Start of the Information Age* (Iowa City: Iowa University Press, 2018), 50.

65 Kerouac, *Selected Letters, 1940–1956*, 226, Kerouac to Frank Morley, 27 July 1950.

66 Hunt, *Kerouac's Crooked Road*, 112–13.

67 Kerouac, *Selected Letters, 1940–1956*, 356, Kerouac to Allen Ginsberg, 18 May 1952.

68 Ibid., 401, according to Ann Charters.

69 Ibid., 451, Kerouac to Alfred Kazin, 27 October 1954.

70 Kerouac, *Selected Letters, 1957–1969*, 11, Kerouac to Sterling Lord, 4 March 1957.

71 Marshall McLuhan, *Understanding Media: The Extensions of Man* (London: Abacus, 1974), 279.

72 Ted Berrigan, "Jack Kerouac: The Art of Fiction no. 41," *Paris Review* 43 (Summer 1968), http://www.theparisreview.org/interviews/4260/the-art-of-fiction-no-41-jack-kerouac, read 21 February 2018.

73 Ibid.

74 Nash, "Technology in the Work of Jack Kerouac," 104.

75 Ibid., 175.

76 Kerouac, *Selected Letters, 1957–1969*, 395; Tietchen, *Techno-Modern Poetics*, 152n45.

77 Nicosia, *Memory Babe*, 573.

78 Ibid., 682.

79 Berrigan, "Jack Kerouac."

80 Nicosia, *Memory Babe*, 588.

81 Pati Hill, "Truman Capote: The Art of Fiction no. 17," *Paris Review* 16 (Spring–Summer 1957), https://www.theparisreview.org/interviews/4867/truman-capote-the-art-of-fiction-no-17-truman-capote, read 21 February 2018.

7. Manuscript and Typescript

1 Christiane Amanpour and Eliza Mackintosh, "J.K. Rowling Wrote a Secret Manuscript on a Party Dress," interview with J.K. Rowling, CNN, 10 July 2017, edition.cnn.com/2017/07/10/world/amanpour-j-k-rowling -interview/index.html, read 26 January 2018.

2 Elizabeth L. Eisenstein, *The Printing Press as an Agent of Change: Communications and Global Transformation in Early Modern Europe* (Cambridge: Cambridge University Press, 1979).

3 Marshall McLuhan, *The Gutenberg Galaxy: The Making of Typographical Man* (Toronto: University of Toronto Press, 1962).

4 Roger Chartier, "The Printing Revolution: A Reappraisal," in *Agent of Change: Print Culture Studies after Elizabeth L. Eisenstein*, ed. Sabrina Alcorn Baron, Eric N. Lindquist, and Eleanor F. Shevlin (Amherst: University of Massachusetts Press, 2007), 398; Harold Love, *Scribal Publication in Seventeenth-Century England* (Oxford: Clarendon, 1993).

5 Margaret J.M. Ezell, "The Laughing Tortoise: Speculations on Manuscript Sources and Women's Book History," *English Literary Renaissance* 38, no. 2 (2008): 334.

6 Sigurður Gylfi Magnússon and Davíð Ólaffson, "'Barefoot Historians': Education in Iceland in the Early Modern Period," in *Writing Peasants: Studies on Peasant Literacy in Early Modern Northern Europe*, ed. Klaus-Joachim Lorenzen-Schmidt and Bjørn Poulsen (Aarhus, DK: Landbohistorisk selskab, 2002), 175–209; and see S.G. Magnússon and D. Ólaffson, *Minor Knowledge and Microhistory: Manuscript Culture in the Nineteenth Century* (London: Routledge, 2017).

7 Matthew James Driscoll, *The Unwashed Children of Eve: The Production, Dissemination and Reception of Popular Literature in Post-Reformation Iceland* (Enfield Lock, UK: Hisarlik, 1997), 75–132.

8 Marc Myers, "Jackie Collins and a Home That Brings a Painting to Life," *Wall Street Journal*, 27 February 2014, https://jackiecollins.com/press /test/, read 29 January 2018.

9 Donald F. Mackenzie, "Speech-Manuscript-Print," in his *Making Meaning: "Printers of the Mind" and Other Essays*, ed. Peter D. McDonald and Michael F. Suarez, SJ (Amherst, MA: University of Massachusetts Press), 2002), 248.

10 Tony Cross, "Proust the PR Man Revealed in Rare Swann's Way Sale" *rfi*, 31 October 2017, http://en.rfi.fr/culture/20171031-proust-pr-man -revealed-rare-swanns-way-sale, read 29 January 2018.

11 See "The Roy Davids Collection," on the Bonhams' site, https://bonhams .com/press_release/13025, read 20 January 2018. I have not been able to track down the price eventually realized by this manuscript.

12 Ernest Hemingway, *Selected Letters, 1917–1961*, ed. Carlos Baker (New York: Granada, 1981), 270, Hemingway to Maxwell Perkins, Gstaad, 15 January 1928. The mention of his eye going bad is a reference to eye injury caused by his child, who had stuck a finger in Hemingway's eye, cutting the pupil.

13 Ibid., 77, Hemingway to Ezra Pound, Chamby-sur-Montreux, 13 January 1923; Carlos Baker, *Ernest Hemingway: A Life Story* (New York: Charles Scribner's Sons, 1969), 103.

14 Yann Potin, "Le prix de l'écrit," *Genèses* 105 (December 2016): 3–7. In 2015, the company, indicted for fraud, went into liquidation.

15 Peter Parker, "From the Cutting Room Floor," *Literary Review* 470 (November 2018): 1.

16 Lothar Müller, *White Magic: The Age of Paper*, trans. Jessica Spengler (Cambridge: Polity, 2014), 202–3.

17 Dan Crowe, ed., *How I Write: The Secret Lives of Authors* (New York: Rizzoli, n.d. [2007?]), 20–3.

18 Gerald Clarke, "P.G. Wodehouse: The Art of Fiction no. 60," *Paris Review* 64 (Winter 1975), https://www.theparisreview.org/interviews/3773/p-g-wodehouse-the-art-of-fiction-no-60-p-g-wodehouse, read 21 February 2018.

19 University of Roehampton, Special Collections and Archives, Richmal Crompton Collection, RC/1/1/1/1/6 – Plot notes and RC/2/6/5 – Notes and memoranda.

20 John Curran, *Agatha Christie's Secret Notebooks: Fifty Years of Mysteries in the Making* (London: HarperCollins), 2009.

21 Ibid., 255.

22 Janet Morgan, *Agatha Christie: A Biography* (London: Collins, 1984), 377; and see Wikipedia's 2020 "List of Best-selling Fiction Authors," https://en.wikipedia.org/wiki/List_of_best-selling_fiction_authors.

23 Laura Thompson, *Agatha Christie: An English Mystery* (London: Headline Review, 2007).

24 Ibid., 306 and 359.

25 Curran, *Agatha Christie's Secret Notebooks*, 55.

26 Morgan, *Agatha Christie*, 166 and 200.

27 Curran, *Agatha Christie's Secret Notebooks*, 44.

28 John O'Connell, "Agatha Christie's Secret Notebooks by John Curran" (book review), *Guardian*, 26 September 2009, https://www.theguardian.com/books/2009/sep/26/agatha-christie-secret-notebooks-review, read 21 February 2018.

29 Curran, *Agatha Christie's Secret Notebooks*, 68–9.

30 Ibid., 251.

31 Ibid., 196–7 and 206–7.

32 Ibid., 112–15.

33 Ibid., 237–8.

34 Ibid., 94. The underlining is Christie's. Text in square brackets was added by John Curran.

35 Crowe, *How I Write*, 116.

36 Beverley Eley, *Ion Idriess* (Sydney: HarperCollins, 1995), 118.

37 Ibid., 282.

38 Ibid., 289.

39 Sarah Kinson, "Why I Write: Barbara Taylor Bradford," *Guardian*, 22 October 2007, https://www.theguardian.com/books/2007/oct/22/whyiwrite, read 21 February 2018.

40 "Ten Rules for Writing Fiction (Part Two)," *Guardian*, 20 February 2010, http://www.theguardian.com/books/2010/feb/20/10-rules-for-writing-fiction-part-two, read 18 August 2016.

41 "Me and My Typewriter," *Writer's Digest* 61 (January 1981): 28.

42 Ibid., 30.

43 Wallace L. Chafe, "Integration and Involvement in Speaking, Writing and Oral Literature," in *Spoken and Written Language: Exploring Orality and Literacy*, ed. Deborah Tannen (Norwood, NJ: Ablex, 1982), 36–7 and 198.

44 Dennis Wheatley, *The Time Has Come ... The Memoirs of Dennis Wheatley: Officer and Temporary Gentleman, 1914–1919* (London: Hutchinson, 1978), 151.

45 George Plimpton, "John le Carré: The Art of Fiction no. 149," *Paris Review* 143 (Summer 1997), https://www.theparisreview.org/interviews/1250/john-le-carre-the-art-of-fiction-no-149-john-le-carre, read 21 February 2018.

46 Pati Hill, "Truman Capote: The Art of Fiction no. 17," *Paris Review* 16 (Spring–Summer 1957), https://www.theparisreview.org/interviews/4867/truman-capote-the-art-of-fiction-no-17-truman-capote, read 21 February 2018.

47 Andrew Ross, "Master of the Secret World: John Le Carré on Deception, Storytelling and American Hubris," *Salon*, 21 October 1996.

48 Adam Sisman, *John Le Carré: The Biography* (London: Bloomsbury, 2015), 303, 316, 352.

49 Ibid., 235.

50 Ibid., 290, interview with *Town*, probably in 1965.

51 Matthew J. Bruccoli and Judith S. Baughman, eds., *Conversations with John Le Carré* (Jackson: University Press of Mississippi, 2004), 113, interview with *Der Spiegel* in 1989.

52 James Cameron, "Schoolmaster Who Came In From the Cold," in Bruccoli and Baughman, *Conversations*, 24 (from *Daily Telegraph Magazine*, 28 June 1974).

53 "The Fictional World of Espionage: Interview with Leigh Crutchley," in Bruccoli and Baughman, *Conversations*, 6 (from *The Listener* 75 [14 April 1966]).

54 Pierre Assouline, "Spying on a Spymaker," in Bruccoli and Baughman, *Conversations*, 88 (from *World Press Review* 33 [August 1986]).
55 Bodleian Library, John le Carré Archive, A12, *The Tailor of Panama*, MS 333.
56 Ibid., MSS 333, 337, 357.
57 Ibid., MS 360. Since the papers are grouped into bundles of several chapters, each of which contain overlapping drafts, and since the book's overall structure changes in the course of the text's development, a precise calculation of the number of drafts produced for any single passage is not straightforward. Hence, I give an estimate.
58 John le Carré Archive, A10, *The Night Manager*, MSS 217, 223, 226, 233.
59 John le Carré Archive, A12, *The Tailor of Panama*, MS 333, 3 June 1995.
60 Ibid., MS 333, typed draft 8 June 1995.
61 Ibid., MS 357, 21 March 1996.
62 John le Carré, *The Tailor of Panama* (London: Penguin, 2017), 1.
63 The digital archive donated by Salman Rushdie to Emory University may be an exception. The problem of reading documents recorded by obsolete technologies still presents a challenge for archivists.

8. Georges Simenon: The Man in the Glass Cage

1 Université de Liège, Chateau de Colonster, Fonds Simenon, n.d; illustrated in Alain Bertrand, *Georges Simenon* (Lyon: La Manufacture, 1988), n.p.
2 Pierre Assouline, *Simenon* (Paris: Gallimard, 1996), 175–87.
3 Ibid., 367.
4 Ibid., 685–6.
5 Georges Simenon, *Quand j'étais vieux* (Paris: Presses de la Cité, 1970), 375, entry of 16 August 1961.
6 Véronique Rohrbach, "L'ordinaire en partage: Le courier des lecteurs à Georges Simenon" (doctoral diss., Université de Lausanne, 2015), 9. He dropped to no. 17 on UNESCO's list for the period 1979–2008 (http://www.unesco.org/xtrans/bsstatexp.aspx?crit1L=5&nTyp=min&topN=50, read 30 September 2019).
7 Tigy Simenon, *Souvenirs* (Paris: Gallimard, 2004), 65. At one time or another, Simenon owned several Royals, an Olivetti Lettera, and eventually an IBM Selectric no. 1 (https://site.xavier.edu/polt/typewriters/typers.html, read 30 September 2019).
8 Fonds Simenon; reproduced in Bertrand, *Georges Simenon*, n.p.
9 Antoine Lilti, *Figures publiques: L'invention de la célébrité, 1750–1850* (Paris: Fayard, 2015) published in English as *The Invention of Celebrity* (Cambridge: Polity, 2017).
10 Véronique Rohrbach, "Simenon, un auteur et ses lecteurs: Une économie de grandeur," *COnTEXTES*, published online 14 December 2013, n. 22, http://contextes.revues.org/5760, read 19 September 2016.

11 Dominique Kalifa, *L'encre et le sang: Récits de crimes et société à la Belle Époque* (Paris: Fayard, 1995), 34.

12 Rohrbach, "L'ordinaire en partage," 87.

13 Patrick Marnham, *The Man Who Wasn't Maigret: A Portrait of Georges Simenon* (London: Bloomsbury, 1992), 100–1.

14 Judith Lyon-Caen, *La lecture et la vie: Les usages du roman au temps de Balzac* (Paris: Tallandier, 2006); James Smith Allen, *In the Public Eye: A History of Reading in Modern France, 1800–1940* (Princeton, NJ: Princeton University Press, 1991).

15 Rohrbach, "L'ordinaire en partage," 38 and 270.

16 Ibid., 53.

17 Ibid., 114–18.

18 Ibid., 351.

19 Rohrbach, "Simenon," para. 22.

20 Rohrbach, "L'ordinaire en partage," 131–8 and 190.

21 Ibid., 274.

22 Ibid., 277.

23 Simenon was cleared of charges of collaboration in 1949.

24 Fenton Bresler, *The Mystery of Georges Simenon: A Biography* (London: Heinemann, 1983), 168.

25 Bertrand, *Georges Simenon*, 184–5.

26 Assouline, *Simenon*, 532–3 and 683–4.

27 Bresler, *The Mystery of Georges Simenon*, 103.

28 Georges Simenon, *Pedigree* (Paris: Presses de la Cité, 1948).

29 Simenon, *Quand j'étais vieux*.

30 Georges Simenon, *Mémoires intimes* (Paris: France-Loisirs, 1981).

31 Assouline, *Simenon*, especially 12–14.

32 Bertrand, *Georges Simenon*, 201–2.

33 Brendan Gill, "Profiles: Out of the Dark," *New Yorker* 28 (24 January 1953): 48.

34 Bresler, *The Mystery of Georges Simenon*, 192–3.

35 Fonds Simenon, "Presse sur Simenon, Français – Généralités, 1939–1949," François Fontvielle in *Libération-Soir*, 15 July 1945.

36 Assouline, *Simenon*, 156, 193, and 367.

37 Simenon, *Quand j'étais vieux*, 16.

38 Claudine Gothot-Mersch, "Le travail de l'écrivain à la lumière des dossiers et manuscrits du fonds Simenon," in C. Gothot-Mersch et al., *Lire Simenon: Réalité/ Fiction/Écriture* (Brussels: Labor, 1980), 87.

39 Fonds Simenon, Enveloppes jaunes, 1956–1962, *Maigret voyage*.

40 Simenon, *Mémoires intimes*, 457–8.

41 Fonds Simenon, Enveloppes jaunes, *Les Anneaux de Bicêtre* (1963).

42 *L'Express*, 1337 (21–27 February 1977): 130; Bresler, *The Mystery of Georges Simenon*, 4; Rudi Chelminski, "Georges Simenon Has Earned His

Retirement," *People Magazine*, 28 January 1980: 80–4, www.trussel.com /maig/people80.htm, read 13 March 2014.

43 Simenon, *Quand j'étais vieux*, 375, entry of 16 August 1961.

44 Bresler, *The Mystery of Georges Simenon*, 242–9.

45 Assouline, *Simenon*, 856.

46 André Parinaud, *Connaissance de Georges Simenon*, tome 1, *Le secret du romancier suivi des entretiens avec Simenon* (Paris: Presses de la Cité, 1957), 403.

47 Fonds Simenon, Presse sur Simenon, Articles, 1929–1938, "Tête de Turc: Georges Simenon," *Fantasio* 645 (16 December 1933).

48 Rohrbach, "L'ordinaire en partage," 216, letter to a reader (in English), 24 March 1953.

49 Ibid.

50 Bertrand, *Georges Simenon*, 194.

51 Marnham, *The Man Who Wasn't Maigret*, 142.

52 Parinaud, *Connaissance de Georges Simenon*, 403.

53 Simenon, *Quand j'étais vieux*, 337, entry of 16 May 1961.

54 Parinaud, *Connaissance de Georges Simenon*, 384.

55 Carvel Collins, "Georges Simenon: The Art of Fiction no. 9," *Paris Review* (Summer 1955), http://www.theparisreview.org/interviews/5020/the -art-of-fiction-no-9-georges-simenon, read 14 March 2016.

56 Parinaud, *Connaissance de Georges Simenon*, 384.

57 Gothot-Mersch, "Le travail de l'écrivain," 98.

58 Fonds Simenon, Enveloppes jaunes, 1938–55.

59 Fonds Simenon, Enveloppes jaunes, 1963–66.

60 Fonds Simenon, Enveloppes jaunes, 1938–55; see, for example, *Cécile est morte* (1942).

61 Richard Cobb, "Maigret in Retirement," *Times Literary Supplement*, 17 January 1975, 53.

62 Gothot-Mersch, "Le travail de l'écrivain," 96.

63 Bertrand, *Georges Simenon*, includes the texts of these interviews as "Simenon sur le gril."

64 Gothot-Mersch, "Le travail de l'écrivain," 112–13, reproduces some of them.

65 Rohrbach, "L'ordinaire en partage," 220. Emphasis in original.

66 Parinaud, *Connaissance de Georges Simenon*, 399–400.

67 Assouline, *Simenon*, 802–6.

68 Ibid., 841.

69 Ibid., 807.

70 Simenon, *Quand j'étais vieux*, 158, entry of 1 December 1960.

71 Collins, "Georges Simenon."

72 Fonds Simenon, Presse sur Simenon, Français – Généralités, "Georges Simenon Avoue," *Opéra*, 26 March 1952.

73 Jacques Dubois and Benoît Denis, "Introduction," in *Georges Simenon: Romans*, 2 vols, ed. Dubois and Denis (Paris: Gallimard–La Pléiade, 2003), 1: xviii.

74 Simenon, *Quand j'étais vieux*, 375, entry of 16 August 1961.

75 Simenon, *Mémoires intimes*, 168–9.

76 Ibid., 421; Simenon, *Quand j'étais vieux*, 158, 375, 432, etc.

77 Simenon, *Quand j'étais vieux*, 158, entry of 1 December 1960.

78 Assouline, *Simenon*, 717–18.

79 Simenon, *Quand j'étais vieux*, 14, entry of 25 June 1960.

80 Fonds Simenon, Presse sur Simenon, Français – Généralités, 1955–1957, Marie Brun, "Georges Simenon dans sa 'cellule'," *Nice-Matin*, 3 September 1955. The brands of these machines were unspecified.

81 Simenon, *Quand j'étais vieux*, 398, entry of 18 November 1961.

82 Ibid., 387–8, entry of 24 September 1961.

83 Assouline, *Simenon*, 694.

84 Ibid., 897–9.

85 Simenon, *Mémoires intimes*, 420–1.

86 Ibid., 420–1.

87 Assouline, *Simenon*, 717–18.

88 Gothot-Mersch, "Le travail de l'écrivain," 99.

89 Ibid., 100–2.

90 Jacques Dubois and Benoît Denis, "Préface" to *Georges Simenon: Pedigree et autres romans* (Paris: Gallimard–La Pléiade, 2009), ix–xxiii.

91 Rohrbach, "L'ordinaire en partage," 66.

92 Ibid., 75.

93 Dubois and Denis, "Introduction," lxxxix.

94 Gaston Gallimard and Jean Paulhan, *Correspondance, 1919–1968*, ed. Laurence Brisset (Paris: Gallimard-nrf, 2011), 117.

95 Jean Paulhan, "Les *Anneaux de Bicêtre*," in *Simenon*, ed. Francis Lacassin and Gilbert Sigaux (Paris: Plon, 1973), 280–1.

96 Cobb, "Maigret in retirement," 53.

97 Georges Simenon and André Gide, "*... sans trop de pudeur": Correspondance, 1938–1950*, ed. Dominque Fernandez and Benoît Denis (Paris: Omnibus, 1999), 66.

98 Ibid., 186.

99 Ibid., 185–7.

100 Pierre Assouline, "En 1964, un violent réquisitoire contre le livre de poche," *Le Monde des livres*, 2 October 2008, http://www.lemonde.fr/livres/article/2008/10/02/en-1964-un-violent-requisitoire-contre-le-livre-de-poche_1102135_3260.html, read 18 July 2017. The debate is discussed and contextualized by Douglas Smith, "The Burning Library: The Paperback Revolution and the End of the Book in 1960s France," *French Studies* 72, no. 4 (2018): 539–56.

9. Erle Stanley Gardner: The Fiction Factory

1 David Arnold, *Everyday Technology: Machines and the Making of India's Modernity* (Chicago: University of Chicago Press, 2013), 111. Gandhi nevertheless owned typewriters and employed stenographers in his South African years, when he produced pamphlets and a not-for-profit newspaper using a hand-operated printing press. See Isabel Hofmeyr, *Gandhi's Printing Press: Experiments in Slow Reading* (Cambridge, MA: Harvard University Press, 2013).

2 Nathan Deuel, "The Cruel Wit of Evelyn Waugh," *Atlantic*, 1 May 2003, https://www.theatlantic.com/entertainment/archive/2003/05/the-cruel-wit-of-evelyn-waugh/378538/, read 3 July 2017.

3 Arthur Sullivant Hoffman, ed., *Fiction Writers on Fiction Writing: Advice, Opinions, and a Statement of Their Own Working Methods by More Than One Hundred Writers* (Indianapolis: Bobbs-Merrill, 1923), 412.

4 Dorothy B. Hughes, *The Case of the Real Perry Mason* (New York: William Morrow, 1978), 306; Francis L. Fugate and Roberta B. Fugate, *Secrets of the World's Best-Selling Writer: The Storytelling Techniques of Erle Stanley Gardner* (New York: William Morrow, 1980), 13.

5 Harry Ransom Center, Erle Stanley Gardner (hereafter ESG) papers, box 294, article by Joseph Henry Jackson for *Saturday Review*, June 1938.

6 ESG papers, box 287, Thayer Hobson to Gardner, 23 December 1943.

7 ESG papers, box 288, Freeman Lewis to Thayer Hobson, 1 June 1951.

8 ESG papers, box 438, Gardner to H.C. North, 27 March 1925.

9 Fugate and Fugate, *Secrets of the World's Best-Selling Writer*, 51.

10 Erin A. Smith, *Hard-Boiled: Working-Class Readers and Pulp Magazines* (Philadelphia: Temple University Press, 2000), 19.

11 Ibid., 79.

12 Ibid., 27.

13 ESG papers, box 533, *Secrets of the World's Best-Selling Writer*, Grace Naso to Francis Fugate, 25 June 1979.

14 Smith, *Hard-Boiled*, 37–9, on Chandler's 1944 article in *Atlantic Monthly*.

15 ESG papers, box 439, Gardner to Joe Shaw, 7 April 1930.

16 ESG papers, box 105, Notebook "Writing Techniques for Articles, Plot Notes, etc.," 95–8.

17 ESG papers, box 183, Gardner to Jane Hardy, 23 April 1935.

18 Jennifer Nolan, "Reading 'Babylon Revisited' as a *Post* Text: F. Scott Fitzgerald, George Horace Lorimer and the *Saturday Evening Post* Audience," *Book History* 20 (2017): 353.

19 Smith, *Hard-Boiled*, 33.

20 ESG papers, box 183, Gardner to Jane Hardy, 30 April 1934.

21 Fugate and Fugate, *Secrets of the World's Best-Selling Writer*, 153.

22 ESG papers, box 184, Gardner to Jane Hardy, 8 April 1936.
23 Fugate and Fugate, *Secrets of the World's Best-Selling Writer*, 199.
24 ESG papers, box 184, Gardner to Jane Hardy, 10 December 1935.
25 ESG papers, box 287, Gardner to Thayer Hobson, 16 March 1945.
26 Ibid., 30 October 1951.
27 Ibid., 3 October 1951.
28 ESG papers, box 294, Gardner to Ben Hibbs, 21 October 1937.
29 ESG papers, box 184, Gardner to Jane Hardy and Thayer Hobson, 1 July 1935. This formula has been successfully applied in many successful westerns, including, for example, *The Magnificent Seven.*
30 ESG papers, box 288, Gardner to Thayer Hobson, 21 January 1952.
31 ESG papers, box 523, Inventory of Erle Stanley Gardner Library.
32 ESG papers, box 183, Gardner to Jane Hardy, 16 April 1934.
33 ESG papers, box 102, Plot Notebooks, "Notes on Story Technique."
34 ESG papers, box 293, Gardner to Marie Freid, 16 December 1935.
35 ESG papers, box 104, Plot Notebooks, see untitled loose-leaf A4 black-bound notebook, with comments on *The Case of the Buried Clock.*
36 ESG papers, box 102, Plot Notebooks, "Plot Outlines," n.p., and box 103, Plot Notebooks, "Local Color – Background Notes (1926)," n.p.
37 ESG papers, box 105, Plot Notebooks, "Writing Techniques for Articles," 11.
38 Ibid., from Hamilton Craigie in *Writer's Digest*, 137–43.
39 ESG papers, box 103, Plot Notebooks, "Plot Notes – Story Development," 13 February 1936.
40 ESG papers, box 103, Plot Notebooks, "Local Color – Background Notes (1926)," n.p.
41 ESG papers, box 103, Plot Notebooks, "Plot Notes – Story Development," July 1936, n.p.
42 Fugate and Fugate, *Secrets of the World's Best-Selling Writer*, 55.
43 ESG papers, box 533, *Secrets of the World's Best-Selling Writer*, Gardner to George Sutton, 28 June 1923, and box 615, *The Color of Life*, 187.
44 ESG papers, box 438, Gardner to H.C. North, 30 May 1934.
45 ESG papers, box 183, Gardner to Bob Hardy, 19 October 1925.
46 ESG papers, box 439, Gardner to Willis Wing, 19 February 1946.
47 ESG papers, box 615, *The Color of Life*, 188–9.
48 ESG papers, box 438, Gardner to Captain Shaw, 18 June 1927.
49 ESG papers, box 438, Gardner to H.C. North, 13 October 1923.
50 ESG papers, box 293, Autobiographical sketch, Gardner to Thayer Hobson, 30 October 1934.
51 ESG papers, box 616, *The Color of Life*, new unfinished version, 127.
52 ESG papers, box 293, Gardner to Thayer Hobson, 20 December 1932.
53 Ibid., 9 August 1933.

54 ESG papers, box 530–1, Dorothy Hughes biography correspondence, Jean Gardner to Dorothy Hughes, 21 November 1974.

55 ESG papers, box 293, Gardner to Thayer Hobson, 29 March 1934.

56 ESG papers, box 530–1, Dorothy Hughes biography correspondence, Jean Gardner to Dorothy Hughes, 19 June 1975.

57 Ibid.

58 ESG papers, box 287, Gardner to Thayer Hobson, 3 May 1945.

59 ESG papers, box 615, *The Color of Life*, 220.

60 ESG papers, box 184, Gardner to Jane Hardy, 28 September 1935.

61 ESG papers, box 530–1, Dorothy Hughes biography correspondence, Jean Gardner to Dorothy Hughes, 24 October 1974.

62 ESG papers, box 183, Gardner to Jane Hardy, 26 June and 8 October 1934.

63 ESG papers, box 287, Gardner to Thayer Hobson, 22 September 1941.

64 ESG papers, box 615, *The Color of Life*, 230.

65 ESG papers, box 523, A to Z Inventory of Equipment.

66 Daniel Karlin, "The Case of the Capable Fingers: A Della Street Mystery," in *Literary Secretaries / Secretarial Culture*, ed. Leah Price and Pamela Thurschwell (Aldershot, UK: Ashgate, 2005), 111–28.

67 ESG papers, box 294, Gardner to Thayer Hobson, 8 October 1937.

68 ESG papers, box 183, Gardner to Bob Hardy, 14 April 1926, and box 193, Gardner to Thayer Hobson, 3 December 1932.

69 ESG papers, box 616, *The Color of Life*, new unfinished version, 131.

70 ESG papers, box 290, Frederick M. Schlater to Barmore P. Gambrell, 22 January 1958.

71 Hughes, *The Case of the Real Perry Mason*, 23.

72 ESG papers, box 114, Daybooks.

73 ESG papers, box 183, Gardner to Jane Hardy, 10 January 1935.

74 ESG papers, box 293, Thayer Hobson to Gardner, 26 May 1933. Edgar Wallace was a prolific English thriller-writer.

75 ESG papers, box 287, Gardner to Thayer Hobson, 13 January 1951.

76 ESG papers, box 615, *The Color of Life*, 1.

77 ESG papers, box 530–1, Dorothy Hughes biography correspondence, Jean Gardner to Dorothy Hughes, 19 June 1975.

78 ESG papers, box 183, Gardner to Jane Hardy, 7 June 1934.

79 ESG papers, box 439, Gardner to Joe Shaw, 7 April 1930.

80 ESG papers, box 183, Gardner to Jane Hardy, 19 June 1934.

10. Domesticating the Typewriter

1 Sandra M. Gilbert and Susan Gubar, *The Madwoman in the Attic: The Woman Writer and the Nineteenth-Century Literary Imagination* (New Haven, CT: Yale University Press, 1979); Sandra M. Gilbert and Susan

Gubar, *No Man's Land: The Place of the Woman Writer in the Twentieth Century*, vol. 1, *The War of the Words* (New Haven, CT: Yale University Press, 1988); Mary Poovey, *The Proper Lady and the Woman Writer: Ideology as Style in the Works of Mary Wollstonecraft, Mary Shelley, and Jane Austen* (Chicago: University of Chicago Press, 1984); Nina Auerbach, *Communities of Women: An Idea in Fiction* (Cambridge, MA: Harvard University Press, 1978); Mary Eagleton, *Figuring the Woman Author in Contemporary Fiction* (Basingstoke, UK: Palgrave Macmillan, 2005), 138–44.

2 Poovey, *The Proper Lady*, 245.

3 Gilbert and Gubar, *The Madwoman in the Attic*, 64–81; Poovey, *The Proper Lady*, 35–47.

4 Agatha Christie, *An Autobiography* (New York: Dodd, Mead, 1977).

5 Catherine Cookson, *Plainer Still: A New Personal Anthology* (London: Corgi, 1996), 67.

6 Virginia Woolf, *A Room of One's Own* (1929; Cambridge: Cambridge University Press, 1955), 102.

7 Bob Mullan, *The Enid Blyton Story* (London: Boxtree, 1987), 16.

8 June Prance, "An Interview with Barbara Taylor Bradford," *British Digest Illustrated* (Winter 1980), 24–6, in Brotherton Library Special Collections, in Barbara Taylor Bradford papers (hereafter BTB papers), BC MS 20c Bradford 3, Press cuttings, box 1.

9 Imogen Smallwood, *A Childhood at Green Hedges* (London: Methuen, 1989).

10 Bessie Baughn, "A Substantial Success," in *San Francisco Recorder-Progress*, 10 November 1984, BTB papers, BC MS 20c Bradford 3, Press cuttings, box 1.

11 Seven Stories (National Centre for Children's Books), Newcastle-upon-Tyne, Enid Blyton Archive (hereafter EBA), EB/02/01/01/04, 1927 diary, see January entries.

12 Béatrice Didier, *Le journal intime* (Paris: Presses universitaires de France, 1976), 79–81.

13 Blake Morrison, "Why Do Writers Drink?" *Guardian*, 20 July 2013, http://www.theguardian.com/books/2013/jul/20/why-do-writers-drink-alcohol, read 18 August 2016.

14 Woolf, *A Room of One's Own*, 13.

15 Giulia Giuffré, *A Writing Life: Interviews with Australian Women Writers* (Sydney: Allen & Unwin, 1990), 5.

16 Ibid., 159.

17 David Foster, *Self Portraits* (Canberra: National Library of Australia, 1991), 62.

18 Until 2010, a replica of Gardner's study could be visited at the University of Texas. The exhibit has now been dismantled, but a virtual memory of it is available at http://www.hrc.utexas.edu/collections/performingarts/holdings/personaleffects/gardner/study/, viewed 14 April 2018.

19 Photo available at the Classic Typewriter Page, http://site.xavier.edu/polt/typewriters/blyton.jpg, viewed 15 January 2018.

20 EBA, EB/02/01/01/03, Diary, 5 January and 19 February 1926.

21 EBA, EB/02/01/01/15, Five-year diary, 20 and 25 October 1938.

22 Auerbach, *Communities of Women*, ch. 2.

23 Stoney, *Enid Blyton*, 20–7.

24 Smallwood, *Childhood at Green Hedges*, 65–70.

25 Stoney, *Enid Blyton*, 216–20.

26 Smallwood, *Childhood at Green Hedges*, 9, including note added by Gillian Baverstock.

27 Cookson, *Plainer Still*, 69.

28 For more biographical detail, see Mary Cadogan, *The Woman behind William: A Life of Richmal Crompton* (London: Macmillan, 1993).

29 Madeleine Harmsworth, "William and the Old Lady of Beechworth," *Daily Mirror*, 20 November 1968, 16–17, in University of Roehampton, Special Collections and Archives, Richmal Crompton Collection (hereafter RCC), RC1/9/8.

30 Dan O'Neill, "Conquering William Just Refuses to Grow Old," *Guardian*, 20 April 1965, in RCC, RC/1/9/8. This was a common error: in Mary Shelley's novel, Frankenstein was the scientist, not the monster.

31 Jane McVeigh, "Understanding Literary Diatexts: Approaching the Archive of Richmal Crompton, the Creator of 'Just William' Stories," *European Journal of Life Writing* 5 (2016), reproduced on p. 12.

32 Ibid.

33 Michael Moynihan, "Uncivilised Yuman Bein'," *Sunday Times*, 18 December 1966, in RCC, RC5/1/1.

34 Sue Francis, "*Just William* Creator Still Busy at 78," *Yorkshire Evening Post*, 6 December 1968, in RCC, RC/1/9/8.

35 RCC, RC2/6/5/2c.

36 Christie, *Autobiography*, 192–3.

37 Laura Thompson, *Agatha Christie: An English Mystery* (London: Headline Review, 148); Janet Morgan, *Agatha Christie: A Biography* (London: Collins, 1984), ch. 6.

38 Christie, *Autobiography*, 347–8.

39 Ibid., 348.

40 John O'Connell, "Agatha Christie's Notebooks by John Curran," *Guardian*, 26 September 2009, https://www.theguardian.com/books/2009/sep/26, read 22 January 2018.

41 Christie, *Autobiography*, 320.

42 Ibid., 284.

43 Ibid., 443–4.

44 Morgan, *Agatha Christie*, 292.

45 Christie, *Autobiography*, 479.
46 Ibid., 277–8.
47 Erin A. Smith, *Hard-Boiled: Working-Class Readers and Pulp Magazines* (Philadelphia: Temple University Press, 2000), 38–9.
48 Thompson, *Agatha Christie*, 130.
49 Morgan, *Agatha Christie*, ch. 11; Thompson, *Agatha Christie*, 220–1; Christie's autobiography is completely silent on this episode.
50 Christie, *Autobiography*, 365.
51 Ibid., 444.
52 Ibid., 442.
53 Billie Figg, "The White Rose Blooms Again," *Guardian*, 18 March 1983, 12, BTB papers, BC MS 20c Bradford 3, Press cuttings box 1.
54 Carl Maves, "Woman of Substance Could Describe the Author," *Times Tribune*, 8 November 1984, BTB papers BC MS 20c Bradford 3, Press cuttings box 1.
55 Elaine Bissell, "Barbara Bradford Counts Her Millions," *Gannett Westchester Newspapers*, 29 May 1983, BTB papers, BC MS 20c Bradford 3, Press cuttings box 1.
56 Philip Finn, "A Woman of £20m Substance," *Daily Express*, 3 January 1985, 9, BTB papers, BC MS 20c Bradford 3, Press cuttings box 1.
57 Kathe Robin, "Barbara Taylor Bradford," *Romantic Times*, Fall 1984, 34–6, BTB papers, BC MS 20c Bradford 3, Press cuttings box 1.
58 Val Hennessy, "Why a Woman of Substance Keeps Working," unknown magazine, n.d., 61–2, BTB papers, BC MS 20c Bradford 3, Press cuttings box 1.
59 Robin, "Barbara Taylor Bradford," 34–6.
60 Kathy Larkin, "A Room of My Own," *Daily News*, 25 November 1984, 6, BTB papers, BC MS 20c Bradford 3, Press cuttings box 1.
61 Judith W. Winne, "It's 'Now' for Barbara Taylor Bradford," *Camden Courier-Post*, 22 May 1983, 1–3, and Candy Schulman, "Barbara Taylor Bradford's Acts of Will," *Writer's Digest*, June 1987, 36–8, both in BTB papers, BC MS 20c Bradford 3, Press cuttings box 1.
62 Prance, "An Interview with Barbara Taylor Bradford," 24–6.
63 Maves, "Woman of Substance."
64 Prance, "An Interview with Barbara Taylor Bradford," 24–6.
65 BTB papers, BC MS 20c Bradford 5, TSS of *Cavendon Hall*, folders 1 and 2.
66 For example, Sharon Krum, "At Home in Manhattan," *Hello* 832 (7 September 2004): 4–10, BTB papers, BC MS 20c Bradford 3, Press cuttings box 2.
67 Finn, "A Woman of £20m Substance," 9.
68 BTB papers, BC MS 20c Bradford 5, TSS of *Cavendon Hall*, folder 2, message to Linda, 1 July 2013.

69 Catherine Cookson, *Our Kate* (London: Macdonald, 1969), and her *Plainer Still*, 38–9, 315.

70 BTB papers, BC MS Bradford 20c: 2 (a), *Woman of Substance*, box 3: examples of spelling errors include "disparigingly," "mediaevel," "racously," and so on.

11. The End of the Typewriter Century and Post-Digital Nostalgia

1 Robert J. Samuelson, "Requiem for the Typewriter," *Washington Post*, 12 July 1995, https://www.washingtonpost.com/archive/opinions/1995/07/12/requiem-for-the-typewriter, read 9 April 2018; "What's a Typewriter, Mommy?" *Time* 140, no. 5 (3 August 1992): 25.

2 Siobhan Lyons, "Beyond Luddism: Typewriters and the Return of Pre-Digital Writing," paper presented to the Literature and Technology conference, Australasian Association of Literature, Western Sydney University, July 2016, https://www.academia.edu/27033886/Beyond_Luddism_Typewriters_and_the_Return_of_Pre-Digital_Writing, 6, read 4 January 2017.

3 Wilfred A. Beeching, *Century of the Typewriter* (London: Heinemann, 1974), 127.

4 "Me and My Typewriter," *Writer's Digest* 61 (January 1981): 32 (Krantz); Paul Auster and Sam Messer, *The Story of My Typewriter* (New York: Distributed Art Publishers, 2002), 15.

5 Ronald John Donovan, "A Writer's Guide to Typewriters," *Writer's Digest* 61 (January 1981): 20–7.

6 Andrew Tobias, "My Typewriter," *Esquire* 91 (5 June 1979): 93.

7 AnnMarie Brennan, "Olivetti: A Work of Art in the Age of Immaterial Labour," *Journal of Design History* 28, no. 3 (2015): 235–53.

8 Marc Fisher, "The Typewriter Reaches the End of the Line," *Washington Post*, 6 July 1995, https://www.washingtonpost.com/archive/lifestyle/1995/07/06/the-typewriter-reaches-the-end-of-the-line, read 9 April 2018.

9 Robin Pagnamenta, "Clack, Clack, Ding! Bell Tolls for the Typewriter," *Times* (London), 23 April 2011, 59.

10 Eugene Kwibuka, "Rwanda's Last Typewriter Users," *New Times* (Rwanda), 9 March 2013, http://www.newtimes.co.rw/section/Printer/2013-03-09/90922, read 10 May 2017.

11 Matthew G. Kirschenbaum, *Track Changes: A Literary History of Word Processing* (Cambridge, MA: Belknap, 2016), 47, 71, 101, and 210–13.

12 Wendell Berry, *Why I Am Not Going to Buy a Computer* (London: Penguin, 2018), with Inkeles's letter on 5–6. The exchange originally appeared in *Harper's Magazine* 277, no. 1663 (December 1988): 6–10.

13 Joe Moran, "Typewriter, You're Fired! How Writers Learned to Love the Computer," *Guardian*, 28 August 2015, http://www.theguardian.com/books/2015/aug/28/how-amstrad-word-processor-encouraged-writers-use-computers, read 9 April 2018.

14 Sarah Kinson, "Why I Write: Barbara Taylor Bradford" (interview), *Guardian*, 22 October 2007, https://www.theguardian.com/books/2007/oct/22/whyiwrite, read 9 April 2018; Linda Richards, "Interview with Barbara Taylor Bradford," *January Magazine*, n.d., https://www.januarymagazine.com/profiles/taylorbradford.html, read 22 September 2017.

15 David Germain, "63rd Golden Globe Awards," *Seattle Post-Intelligencer*, 16 January 2006, https://www.seattlepi.com/ae/movies/article/63rd-Golden-Globe-Awards-Housewives-and-1192936, read 9 April 2018.

16 Patricia Cohen, "No Country for Old Typewriters: A Well-Used One Heads to Auction," *New York Times*, 1 December 2009, C1.

17 Tom Hanks, "I Am TOM. I Like to TYPE. Hear That?" *New York Times*, 3 August 2013, http://www.nytimes.com/2013/08/04/opinion/sunday/i-am-tom-i-like-to-type-hear-that.html?_r=0, read 9 April 2018.

18 S. Lyons, "Beyond Luddism," 3.

19 Richard Polt, *The Typewriter Revolution: A Typist's Companion for the 21st Century* (Woodstock, VT: Countryman, 2015), 7–8. See also Polt's website "The Classic Typewriter Page," at http://site.xavier.edu/polt/typewriters/index.html.

20 Polt, *Typewriter Revolution*, 18–19 and 52.

21 Carla Wilson, "Typewriter Notes, Papery Treasures at New Lower Johnson Store," *Times Colonist* (Victoria, BC), 15 March 2013, http://www.timescolonist.com/business/typewriter-notes-papery-treasures-at-new-lower-johnson-store-1.92300, read 19 April 2018.

22 Polt, *Typewriter Revolution*, 7–8.

23 *Harlequin Creature* website, at http://www.harlequincreature.org, read 9 April 2018; Polt, *Typewriter Revolution*, 238.

24 Ashlea Halpern, "The Analog Underground," *New York Magazine*, 11 July 2011, http://nymag.com/shopping/features/analog-2011-7/, and her "Analog Renaissance," *New York Magazine*, 3 July 2011, http://nymag.com/shipping/features/analog-renaissance-2011-7, both read 9 April 2018.

25 Polt, *Typewriter Revolution*, 122.

26 S. Lyons, "Beyond Luddism," 2.

27 See http://izvestia.ru/news/553314; Ian Cobain, "Foreign Office Hoarding 1m Historic Files in Secret Archive," *Guardian*, 18 October 2013, https://www.theguardian.com/politics/2013/oct/18/foreign-office-historic-files-secret-archive, read 9 April 2018; Rahul Bedi, "Indian High Commission Returns to Typewriters," *Telegraph* (London), 27 September 2013, https://www.telegraph.co.uk/news/worldnews/asia/india

/10339111/Indian-High-Commission-returns-to-typewriters.html, read 9 April 2018.

28 Allan Hall, "Typewriter Sales Boom in Germany," *Daily Mail* (Australia), 22 July 2014, http://www.dailymail.co.uk/news/article-2701392 /Typewriter-sales-boom-Germany-thousands-basics-bid-avoid-U-S-spies -wake-NSA-allegations, read 10 May 2017.

29 Roger Rosenblatt, "The Last Page in the Type-writer," *Time* 121 (16 May 1983).

30 Carmen Bugan, *Burying the Typewriter: Childhood under the Eye of the Secret Police* (London: Picador, 2012), 4, 83, 106.

31 "Ten Rules For Writing Fiction, Part Two," *Guardian*, 20 February 2010, www.theguardian.com/books/2010/feb/20/10-rules-for-writing-fiction -part-two, read 18 August 2016.

32 Alison Boulton, "'It's a Remington Typewriter in a Smartphone World': Baroness Amos on UN Reform," *Oxford Today*, 12 June 2016, http://www. oxfordtoday.ox.ac.uk/interviews/%E2%80%98its-remington-typewriter -smartphone-world-baroness-amos-un-reform#, read 8 April 2018.

33 Behrouz Boochani, *No Friend but the Mountains: Writing from Manus Prison* (Sydney: Picador, 2018).

34 David Arnold, *Everyday Technology: Machines and the Making of India's Modernity* (Chicago: University of Chicago Press, 2013).

35 Fernand Braudel, *Capitalism and Material Life, 1400–1800* (London: Fontana, 1974), translation of *Civilisation matérielle et capitalisme* (Paris: Armand Colin, 1967).

36 Jonathan Rose, "Rereading the English Common Reader: A Preface to the History of Audiences," *Journal of the History of Ideas* 53, no. 1 (1992): 47–70.

Bibliography

Primary Sources – Archives

Australia

National Library of Australia, NLA ms9149, Gordon Clive Bleeck papers

Belgium

Université de Liège, Chateau de Colonster, Fonds Simenon
Enveloppes jaunes, 1931–66 (5 boxes)
Presse sur Simenon – Français, Généralités, 1935–89

United Kingdom

Bodleian Library, Oxford, John le Carré Literary Archive
A10, *The Night Manager*
A12, *The Tailor of Panama*
Brotherton Library, Leeds University, Barbara Taylor Bradford papers
BC MS 20c Bradford 2 (a), "A Woman of Substance," boxes 1–3
BC MS 20c Bradford 3, Press cuttings, boxes 1–2
BC MS 20c Bradford 5, "Cavendon Hall," corrected typescript
BC MS 20c Bradford 6, "The Cavendon Women," corrected typescript
BC MS 20c Bradford 7, "The Cavendon Luck," corrected typescript
Seven Stories (National Centre for Children's Books), Newcastle-upon-Tyne, Enid Blyton Archive
EB/02/01/01/01 to 16, Diaries, 1924–63
EB/02/01/05, Personal papers
SR/02/02 to 04, Sheila Ray papers, essays, and articles
SR/03/01 to 02, Sheila Ray papers, scrapbooks, and press cuttings

University of Roehampton, London, Special Collections and Archives, Richmal Crompton Collection
RC/1/1/1/1, Plot notes and handwritten ideas
RC/1/1/1/2/1, Handwritten drafts of William stories
RC/1/9, Articles, book reviews, and news cuttings
RC/1/11, Notes on the craft of writing
RC/2/6/5, Notes and memoranda
RC/5/1/1, Press cuttings

United States

Harry Ransom Center, Austin TX, Erle Stanley Gardner papers
Boxes 101–5, Plot notebooks and pocketbooks, 1926–69
Box 106, Plot Robot Index
Boxes 107–9, Miscellaneous notebooks
Box 114, Daybooks, 1946–54
Boxes 183–4, Correspondence with Bob and Jane Hardy, 1927–46
Box 219, General correspondence – Office supplies
Boxes 287–94, Correspondence with Thayer Hobson, 1932–60
Boxes 438–9, *Black Mask* correspondence, 1923–42
Box 523, Notebooks
Boxes 530–1, Dorothy Hughes biography correspondence, 1973–9
Box 533, *Secrets of the World's Bestselling Writer*
Boxes 615–16, *The Color of Life*

Primary Sources — Published

Allen, Grant [Olive Pratt Rayner, pseud.]. *The Type-Writer Girl*. London: C. Arthur Pearson, 1897.
Amanpour, Christiane, and Eliza Mackintosh. "J.K. Rowling Wrote a Secret Manuscript on a Party Dress." Interview with J.K. Rowling. CNN, 10 July 2017. http://edition.cnn.com/2017/07/10/world/amanpour-j-k-rowling-interview/index.html, consulted on 26 January 2018.
Apollinaire, Guillaume. *Calligrammes, poèmes de la paix et de la guerre 1913–1916*. 1918. Paris: Gallimard-nrf, 1948.
Auster, Paul, and Sam Messer. *The Story of My Typewriter*. New York: Distributed Art Publishers, 2002.
Baker, Arthur M. *How to Succeed as a Stenographer or Typewriter*. New York: Fowler and Wells, 1888.
Balla, Giacomo, and Fortunato Depero. *Ricostruzione futurista dell'universo*. Milan: Direzione del Movimento Futurista, 1915.
Bangs, John Kendrick. *The Enchanted Type-Writer*. New York: Harper, 1899.

Barthes, Roland. "Un rapport presque maniaque avec les instruments graphiques." Interview with Jean-Louis de Rambures, *Le Monde*, 27 September 1973. In Roland Barthes, *Le grain de la voix: Entretiens, 1962–1980*, 170–4. Paris: Seuil, 1981.

Berrigan, Ted. "Jack Kerouac: The Art of Fiction No. 41." *Paris Review* 43 (Summer 1968). http://www.theparisreview.org/interviews/4260/the-art-of-fiction-no-41-jack-kerouac, read 21 February 2018.

Berry, Wendell. *Why I Am Not Going to Buy a Computer*. 1988. London: Penguin, 2018.

Bertrand, Alain. *Georges Simenon*. Lyon: La Manufacture, 1988.

Blaine, James Gillespie. *Reciprocity: An Essay from the Spirit World*. Boston: Jos. M. Wade, 1896.

Blyton, Enid. *The Story of My Life*. London: Pitkins, n.d. [1952].

Bosanquet, Theodora. *Henry James at Work, with Excerpts from Her Diary and an Account of Her Professional Career*. Edited by Lyall H. Powers. Ann Arbor: University of Michigan Press, 2006.

Bruccoli, Matthew J., and Judith S. Baughman, eds. *Conversations with John le Carré*. Jackson: University Press of Mississippi, 2004.

Bugan, Carmen. *Burying the Typewriter: Childhood under the Eye of the Secret Police*. London: Picador, 2012.

Burroughs, William S. "The Technology of Writing." In *The Adding Machine: Collected Essays*. London: Calder, 1985.

Charters, Ann, ed. *The Portable Beat Reader*. London: Penguin, 1992.

Christie, Agatha. *An Autobiography*. New York: Dodd, Mead, 1977.

– *The Clocks*. 1964. New York: HarperCollins, 2011.

Clarke, Gerald. "P.G. Wodehouse: The Art of Fiction no. 60." *Paris Review* 64 (Winter 1975). https://www.theparisreview.org/interviews/3773/p-g-wodehouse-the-art-of-fiction-no-60-p-g-wodehouse, read 21 February 2018.

Collins, Carvel. "Georges Simenon: The Art of Fiction no. 9." *Paris Review* 9 (Summer 1955). http://www.theparisreview.org/interviews/5020/the-art-of-fiction-no-9-georges-simenon, read 14 March 2016.

Cookson, Catherine. *Our Kate*. London: Macdonald, 1969.

– *Plainer Still: A New Personal Anthology*. London: Corgi, 1996.

Cummings, E.E. *Selected Letters of E.E. Cummings*. Edited by F.W. Dupree and George Stade. London: André Deutsch, 1972.

Curran, John. *Agatha Christie's Secret Notebooks: Fifty Years of Mysteries in the Making*. London: HarperCollins, 2009.

Devanny, Jean. *Point of Departure: The Autobiography of Jean Devanny*. Edited by Carole Ferrier. St Lucia: University of Queensland Press, 1986.

Dickens, Charles. *David Copperfield*. Ware, UK: Wordsworth Classics, 2000.

Du Perry, Jean. See Georges Simenon.

Eliot, Thomas Stearns. *The Letters of T.S. Eliot*. Volume 1, *1898–1922*. Rev. ed. Edited by Valerie Eliot and Hugh Haughton. London: Faber & Faber, 2009.

Fleming, Fergus, ed. *The Man with the Golden Typewriter: Ian Fleming's James Bond Letters*. London: Bloomsbury, 2015.

Fontán del Junco, Manuel, ed. *Futurist Depero, 1913–1950: Catalogue of an Exhibition at the Fundación Juan March, Madrid, 10 October 2014–18 January 2015*. Madrid: Fundación Juan March, 2014.

Foster, David. *Self Portraits*. Canberra: National Library of Australia, 1991.

Franklin, Miles. *My Congenials: Miles Franklin and Friends in Letters*. Volume 1. *1879–1938*. Edited by Jill Roe. Sydney: Angus and Robertson, 1993.

Gallimard, Gaston, and Jean Paulhan. *Correspondance, 1919–1968*. Edited by Laurence Brisset. Paris: Gallimard-nrf, 2011.

Gardner, Erle Stanley. *The Case of the Terrified Typist*. 1956. London: Pan, 1964.

Germain, David, "63rd Golden Globe Awards." *Seattle Post-Intelligencer*, 16 January 2006, https://www.seattlepi.com/ae/movies/article/63rd-Golden-Globe-Awards-Housewives-and-1192936, read 9 April 2018.

Gill, Brendan. "Profiles: Out of the Dark." *New Yorker* 28 (24 January 1953): 35–49.

Gissing, George. *The Odd Women*. Oxford: Oxford University Press, 2008.

Giuffré, Giulia. *A Writing Life: Interviews with Australian Women Writers*. Sydney: Allen & Unwin, 1990.

Hammett, Dashiell. *The Maltese Falcon*. New York: Knopf, 1930.

Hemingway, Ernest. *Ernest Hemingway: Selected Letters, 1917–1961*. Edited by Carlos Baker. New York: Granada, 1981.

– "Mitrailliatrice." *Poetry* 21 (January 1923): 193–5.

Hesse, Hermann. "Die Schreibmaschine." *März* 4 (1908): 377–8.

Hill, Pati. "Truman Capote: The Art of Fiction no. 17." *Paris Review* 16 (Spring–Summer 1957). https://www.theparisreview.org/interviews/4867/truman-capote-the-art-of-fiction-no-17-truman-capote, read 21 February 2018.

Hoffman, Arthur Sullivant, ed. *Fiction Writers on Fiction Writing: Advice, Opinions, and a Statement of Their Own Working Methods by More Than One Hundred Writers*. Indianapolis: Bobbs-Merrill, 1923.

James, Henry. *Letters*. 4 vols. Edited by Leon Edel. Cambridge. MA: Belknap, 1974–84.

Janin, Jules. "Les influences de la plume de fer en literature." 1831. *Revue de Paris* 93 (December 1836): 292–302.

Kerouac, Jack. *Atop an Underwood: Early Stories and Other Writings*. 1941. Edited by Paul Marion. New York: Viking Penguin, 1999.

Kerouac, Jack. *Selected Letters, 1940–1956*. Edited by Ann Charters. New York: Viking, 1995.

– *Selected Letters, 1957–1969*. Edited by Ann Charters. New York: Viking, 1999.

Kinson, Sarah. "Why I Write: Barbara Taylor Bradford." *Guardian*, 22 October 2007. https://www.theguardian.com/books/2007/oct/22/whyiwrite, read 21 February 2018.

Lawson, Henry. "The Firing Line." In *When I Was King and Other Verses*. Sydney: Angus & Robertson, 1906.

Le Carré, John. *The Tailor of Panama*. 1996. Penguin, 2017.

London, Jack. *John Barleycorn*. 1913. Edited by John Sutherland. Oxford: Oxford University Press, 2009.

Mansfield, Katherine. *The Collected Letters of Katherine Mansfield*. 5 vols. Edited by Vincent O'Sullivan and Margaret Scott. Oxford: Oxford University Press, 1984–2008.

Marinetti, Filippo Tommaso. "The Futurist Manifesto." 1909. Translated by James Joll in his *Three Intellectuals in Politics*, 179–84. New York: Pantheon, 1960.

– *Selected Poems and Related Prose*. Edited by Luce Marinetti. New Haven, CT: Yale University Press, 2002.

Marks, Bernard. *Once Upon a Typewriter: Twelve Secretaries, Twelve Success Stories*. London: Arrow, 1974.

"Me and My Typewriter." *Writer's Digest* 61 (January 1981): 28–32.

O'Driscoll, Denis. "Les Murray: The Art of Poetry, no. 89." *Paris Review* 173 (Spring 2005). http://www.theparisreview.org/interviews/5508/the-art-of-poetry-no-89-les-murray, read 28 February 2014.

Olson, Charles. *Projective Verse*. New York: Totem, n.d. [1959?].

Palmer, Nettie. *Nettie Palmer: Her Private Journal "Fourteen Years," Poems, Reviews and Literary Essays*. Edited by Vivian Smith. St Lucia: University of Queensland Press, 1988.

Parinaud, André. *Connaissance de Georges Simenon*. Tome 1, *Le secret du romancier suivi des entretiens avec Simenon*. Paris: Presses de la Cité, 1957.

Pitman, Isaac. *Pitman's Typewriter Manual: A Practical Guide to Commercial, Literary, Legal, Dramatic and All Classes of Typewriting Work*. 6th ed. London: Pitman, 1911.

Plimpton, George. "Ernest Hemingway: The Art of Fiction no. 21." *Paris Review* 18 (Spring 1958). https://www.theparisreview.org/interviews/4825/ernest-hemingway-the-art-of-fiction-no-21-ernest-hemingway, read 20 April 2018.

– "John le Carré: The Art of Fiction no. 149." *Paris Review* 143 (Summer 1997). https://www.theparisreview.org/interviews/1250/john-le-carre-the-art-of-fiction-no-149-john-le-carre, read 21 February 2018.

Pound, Ezra. *The Letters of Ezra Pound, 1907–1941*. Edited by D.D. Paige. London: Faber & Faber, 1950.

– *Pound/Lewis: The Letters of Ezra Pound and Wyndham Lewis*. Edited by Timothy Materer. New York: New Directions, 1985.

- "A Prison Letter." *Paris Review* 28 (Summer–Fall 1962): 17.
Rainey, Lawrence, Christine Poggi, and Laura Wittman, eds. *Futurism: An Anthology*. New Haven, CT: Yale University Press, 2009.
Rayner, Olive Pratt. See Grant Allen.
Richards, Linda. "Interview with Barbara Taylor Bradford." *January Magazine*, n.d. https://www.januarymagazine.com/profiles/taylorbradford.html, read 22 September 2017.
Sainte-Beuve, Charles-Augustin. "De la littérature industrielle." 1839. In *Portraits contemporains*. Vol. 2: 444–71. Paris: Calmann-Lévy, 1888.
Simenon, Georges. *Mémoires intimes*. Paris: France-Loisirs, 1981.
- *Quand j'étais vieux*. Paris: Presses de la Cité, 1970.
- [Jean du Perry, pseud.]. *Le roman d'un dactylo*. Paris: Ferenczi, n.d. [1924?].
Simenon, Georges, and André Gide. *"... sans trop de pudeur". Correspondance, 1938–1950*. Edited by Dominique Fernandez and Benoît Denis. Paris: Omnibus, 1999.
Stoker, Bram. *Dracula*. 1897. London: Penguin, 2003.
"Ten Rules For Writing Fiction, Part Two." *Guardian*, 20 February 2010. www.theguardian.com/books/2010/feb/20/10-rules-for-writing-fiction-part-two, read 18 August 2016.
Twain, Mark. "The First Writing-Machines." in *The Complete Essays of Mark Twain Now Collected for the First Time*. Edited by Charles Neider, 324–6. Garden City, NY: Doubleday, 1963.
Wheatley, Dennis. *The Time Has Come ... The Memoirs of Dennis Wheatley, Officer and Temporary Gentleman, 1914–1919*. London: Hutchinson, 1978.
White, Patrick. *Flaws in the Glass*. London: Vintage, 1981.
Wood, Michael. "Paul Auster: The Art of Fiction no. 178." *Paris Review* 121 (Fall 2003). http://www.theparisreview.org/interviews/121/the-art-of-fiction-no-178-paul-auster.
Yolen, Jane. "I Am a Typewriter." *The Writer* 94 (January 1981): 9.

Secondary Sources

Adler, Michael H. *The Writing Machine*. London: George Allen & Unwin, 1973.
Albright, Daniel. *Untwisting the Serpent: Modernism in Music, Literature and Other Arts*. Chicago: University of Chicago Press, 2000.
Anderson, Gregory, ed. *The White-Blouse Revolution: Female Office-workers since 1870*. Manchester: Manchester University Press, 1988.
Arnold, David. *Everyday Technology: Machines and the Making of India's Modernity*. Chicago: University of Chicago Press, 2013.
Assouline, Pierre. "En 1964, un violent réquisitoire contre le livre de poche." *Le Monde des livres*, 2 October 2008. http://www.lemonde.fr/livres/article/2008/10/02/en-1964-un-violent-requisitoire-contre-le-livre-de-poche_1102135_3260.html, read 18 July 2017.

– *Simenon*. Paris: Gallimard, 1996.

Auerbach, Nina. *Communities of Women: An Idea in Fiction*. Cambridge MA: Harvard University Press, 1978.

Baker, Carlos. *Ernest Hemingway: A Life Story*. New York: Charles Scribner's Sons, 1969.

Baron, Sabrina Alcorn, Eric N. Lindquist, and Eleanor F. Shevlin, eds. *Agent of Change: Print Culture Studies after Elizabeth L. Eisenstein*. Amherst, MA: University of Massachusetts Press, 2007.

Bedi, Rahul. "Indian High Commission Returns to Typewriters." *Telegraph*, 27 September 2013. https://www.telegraph.co.uk/news/worldnews/asia/india/10339111/Indian-High-Commssion-returns-to-typewriters.html, read 9 April 2018.

Beeching, Wilfred A. *Century of the Typewriter*. London: Heinemann, 1974.

Benjamin, Walter. "The Work of Art in the Age of Mechanical Reproduction." 1936. In *Illuminations*. Edited by Hannah Arendt, translated by Harry Zohn, 217–51. New York: Shocken, 1985.

Berghaus, Günter. *Italian Futurist Theatre, 1909–1914*. Oxford: Clarendon, 1998.

Biro, Matthew. Review of Friedrich Kittler, *Gramophone, Film, Typewriter* in *Clio* 29, no. 4 (2000): 485–90.

Bliven, Bruce, Jr. *The Wonderful Writing Machine*. New York: Random House, 1954.

Bohn, Willard. *Reading Apollinaire's "Calligrammes."* New York: Bloomsbury, 2018.

Bon, François. "Plume d'oie, plume de fer." In *Le tiers livre*. (n.d.). www.tierslivre.net, read 22 July 2016.

Bontempo, María Paula, and Graciela A. Queirolo. "Las 'Chicas Modernas' se emplean como dactilógrafas: feminidad, moda y trabajo en Buenos Aires (1920–1930)." *Bicentenario: Revista de historia de Chile y América* 11, no. 2 (2012): 51–76.

Boulton, Alison. "'It's a Remington Typewriter in a Smartphone World': Baroness Amos on UN Reform." *Oxford Today*, 12 June 2016. http://www.oxfordtoday.ox.ac.uk/interviews/%E2%80%98its-remington-typewriter-smartphone-world-baroness-amos-un-reform#, read 8 April 2018.

Bowles, Hugo. *Dickens and the Stenographic Mind*. Oxford: Oxford University Press, 2019.

Brennan, AnnMarie. "Olivetti: A Work of Art in the Age of Immaterial Labour." *Journal of Design History* 28, no. 3 (2015): 235–53.

Bresler, Fenton. *The Mystery of Georges Simenon: A Biography*. London: Heinemann, 1983.

Brisset, Laurence. *La Nouvelle Revue Française de Jean Paulhan*. Paris: Gallimard, 2003.

Bukatman, Scott. "Gibson's Typewriter." In "Flame Wars: The Discourse of Cyberculture," special issue of *South Atlantic Quarterly* 92, no. 4 (Fall 1993): 627–45.

Burk, Kathleen. "The Telly Don." *BBC History*, August 2000, 52–3.

Cadogan, Mary. *The Woman Behind William: A Life of Richmal Crompton.* London: Macmillan, 1993.

Cameron, S. Brooke. "Sister of the Type: The Feminist Collective in Grant Allen's *The Type-Writer Girl.*" *Victorian Literature and Culture* 40 (2012): 229–44.

"The Case of QWERTY vs Maltron." *Time* 117, no. 3 (26 January 1981): 57.

Chartier, Roger. *Forms and Meanings: Texts, Performances and Audiences.* Philadelphia: University of Pennsylvania Press, 1995.

Chelminski, Rudi. "Georges Simenon Has Earned His Retirement." *People Magazine*, 28 January 1980, 80–4. www.trussel.com/maig/people80.htm, read 13 March 2014.

Cobain, Ian. "Foreign Office Hoarding 1m Historic Files in Secret Archive." *Guardian*, 18 October 2013. https://www.theguardian.com/politics/2013/oct/18/foreign-office-historic-files-secret-archive, read 9 April 2018.

Cobb, Richard. "Maigret in Retirement." *Times Literary Supplement*, 17 January 1975, 53.

Cohen, Patricia. "No Country for Old Typewriters: A Well-Used One Heads for Auction." *New York Times*, 30 November 2009. http://www.nytimes.com/2009/12/01/books/01typewriter.html?_r=0, read 8 August 2016.

Contreras, Russell. "Vintage Typewriters Gain Fans amid 'digital burnout'." *Wand17*, 15 June 2017. www.wandtv.com/story/35660854/vintage-typewriters-gain-fans-amid-digital-burnout, read 16 June 2017.

Cross, Tony. "Proust the PR Man Revealed in Rare Swann's Way Sale." *rfi*, 31 October 2017. http://en.rfi.fr/culture/20171031-proust-pr-man-revealed-rare-swanns-way-sale, read 29 January 2018.

Crowe, Dan, ed. *How I Write: The Secret Lives of Authors.* New York: Rizzoli, n.d. [2007?].

Current, Richard N. *The Typewriter and the Men Who Made It.* Urbana: University of Illinois Press, 1954.

David, Paul A. "Clio and the Economics of QWERTY." *American Economic Review* 75, no. 2 (1985): 332–7.

Davies, Margery W. *Woman's Place Is at the Typewriter: Office Work and Office Workers, 1870–1930.* Philadelphia: Temple University Press, 1982.

Davis, Dwight D.W. "An Analysis of Student Errors on the Universal and Dvorak-Dealey Simplified Keyboard." MA thesis, University of Washington, 1935.

Davy, Teresa. "'A Cissy Job for Men: A Nice Job for the Girls': Women Shorthand Typists in London, 1900–1939." In *Our Work, Our Lives, Our Words: Women's History and Women's Work.* Edited by Lenore Davidoff and Belinda Westover, 124–44. Basingstoke, UK: Macmillan, 1986.

DeMott, Robert. *Steinbeck's Typewriter: Essays on His Art*. Troy, NY: Whitston, 1996.

Derrida, Jacques. *Papier machine: Le ruban de machine à écrire et autres réponses*. Paris: Galilée, 2001.

Diamond, Jared. "The Curse of QWERTY," *Discover* 18, no. 4 (April 1997): 34–42.

Donovan, Ronald John. "A Writer's Guide to Typewriters." *Writer's Digest* 61 (January 1981): 20–7.

Driscoll, Matthew James. *The Unwashed Children of Eve: The Production, Dissemination and Reception of Popular Literature in Post-Reformation Iceland*. Enfield Lock, UK: Hisarlik, 1997.

Druce, Robert. *This Day Our Daily Fictions: An Enquiry into the Multi-Million Bestseller Status of Enid Blyton and Ian Fleming*. Amsterdam: Rodopi, 1992.

Drucker, Johanna. *The Visible Word: Experimental Typography and Modern Art, 1909–1923*. Chicago: University of Chicago Press, 1994.

Dubois, Jacques, and Benoît Denis, eds. *Georges Simenon: Pedigree et autres romans*. Paris: Gallimard–La Pléiade, 2009.

– eds. *Georges Simenon, Romans*. 2 vols. Paris: Gallimard–La Pléiade, 2003.

Eagleton, Mary. *Figuring the Woman Author in Contemporary Fiction*. Basingstoke, UK: Palgrave-Macmillan, 2005.

Edel, Leon. *Henry James: A Life*. London: Collins, 1987.

Eisenstein, Elizabeth L. *The Printing Press as an Agent of Change: Communications and Global Transformations in Early Modern Europe*. Cambridge: Cambridge University Press, 1979.

Eley, Beverley. *Ion Idriess*. Sydney: HarperCollins, 1995.

Ezell, Margaret J.M. "The Laughing Tortoise: Speculations on Manuscript Sources and Women's Book History." *English Literary Renaissance* 38, no. 2 (2008): 331–55.

Fenton, Charles. *The Apprenticeship of Ernest Hemingway: The Early Years*. New York: Farrar, Straus and Young, 1954.

Figg, Billie. "The White Rose Booms Again." *Guardian*, 18 March 1983, 12.

Fine, Lisa M. *The Souls of the Skyscraper: Female Clerical Workers in Chicago, 1870–1930*. Philadelphia: Temple University Press, 1990.

Fisher, Marc. "The Typewriter Reaches the End of the Line." *Washington Post*, 6 July 1995. https://www.washingtonpost.com/archive/lifestyle/1995/07/06/the-typewriter-reaches-the-end-of-the-line, read 9 April 2018.

Ford, Thomas. "Poetry's Media." *New Literary History* 44, no. 3 (Summer 2013): 449–69.

Foulke, Arthur Toye. *Mr. Typewriter: A Biography of Christopher Latham Sholes*. Boston MA: Christopher, 1961.

Fraenkel, Béatrice. "Actes d'écriture: Quand écrire c'est faire." *Langage et société* 121–2 (2007): 101–12.

– *La signature, genèse d'un signe.* Paris: Gallimard, 1992.

– "La signature: Du signe à l'acte." *Sociétés et représentations* 25, no. 1 (2008): 13–23.

Fugate, Francis L., and Roberta B. Fugate. *Secrets of the World's Best-Selling Writer: The Storytelling Techniques of Erle Stanley Gardner.* New York: William Morrow, 1980.

Gardey, Delphine. *La dactylographe et l'expéditionnaire: Histoire des employés du bureau, 1890–1930.* Paris: Belin, 2001.

– *Écrire, calculer, classer: Comment une révolution de papier a transformé les sociétés contemporaines.* Paris: La Découverte, 2008.

Gardner, Howard. "On Becoming a Dictator." *Psychology Today* 14, no. 7 (December 1980): 14–19.

Gilbert, Sandra M., and Susan Gubar. *The Madwoman in the Attic: The Woman Writer and the Nineteenth Century Literary Imagination.* New Haven, CT: Yale University Press, 1979.

– *No Man's Land: The Place of the Woman Writer in the Twentieth Century.* Vol. 1, *The War of the Words.* New Haven. CT: Yale University Press, 1988.

Goehring, Viola Elsie. "Comparison of the Typewriting Achievements of Students Trained on the 'Universal' and the 'Dvorak-Dealey Simplified' Typewriter Keyboards." MA thesis, University of Washington, 1933. Ann Arbor MI: University Microfilms, 1961.

Goody, Alex. *Technology, Literature and Culture.* Cambridge: Polity, 2011.

Gothot-Mersch, Claudine, Jacques Dubois, Jean-Marie Klinkenberg, Danièle Racelle-Latin, and Christian Delcourt. *Lire Simenon: Réalité/Fiction/Écriture.* Brussels: Labor, 1980.

Gray, Jessica. "Typewriter Girls in Turn-of-the-Century Fiction." *English Literature in Transition* 58, no. 4 (2015): 486–502.

Greenfield, George. *Enid Blyton.* Stroud, UK: Sutton, 1998.

Groen, Frances de. *Xavier Herbert: A Biography.* St Lucia: University of Queensland Press, 1998.

Hall, Allan. "Typewriter Sales Boom in Germany." *Mailonline (Daily Mail)*, 22 July 2014. www.dailymail.co.uk/news/article-2701392, read 10 May 2017.

Halpern, Ashlea. "The Analog Renaissance." *New York Magazine*, 3 July 2011. http://nymag.com/shipping/features/analog-renaissance-2011-7, read 9 April 2018.

– "The Analog Underground." *New York Magazine*, 11 July 2011. http://nymag.com/shopping/features/analog-2011-7, read 9 April 2018.

Hanks, Tom. "I am TOM. I like to TYPE. Hear That?" *New York Times*, 3 August 2013. http://www.nytimes.com/2013/08/04/opinion/sunday/i-am-tom-i-like-to-type-hear-that,html?_r=0, read 9 April 2018.

Holmes, John Clellon. *Nothing More to Declare*. London: André Deutsch, 1968.

Honeycutt, Lee. "Literacy and the Writing Voice: The Intersection of Culture and Technology in Dictation." *Journal of Business and Technical Communication* 18, no. 3 (July 2004): 294–327.

Howard, Seymour. "The Steel Pen and the Modern Line of Beauty." *Technology and Culture* 26, no. 4 (1985): 785–98.

Hughes, Dorothy B. *The Case of the Real Perry Mason*. New York: William Morrow, 1978.

Hunt, Tim. *Kerouac's Crooked Road: Development of a Fiction*. Berkeley: University of California Press, 1981.

Hyde, H. Montgomery. *Henry James at Home*. London: Methuen, 1969.

IBM Office Products Division. "The Typewriter: An Informal History." August 1977. http://www-03.ibm.com/ibm/history/exhibits/modelb/modelb_informal.html, read 5 March 2014.

Jensen, Joli. "Using the Typewriter: Secretaries, Reporters, Authors, 1880–1930." *Technology in Society* 10 (1988): 255–66.

Johnston, Alva. *The Case of Erle Stanley Gardner*. New York: William Morrow, 1947.

Kalifa, Dominique. *L'encre et le sang: Récits de crimes et société à la Belle Époque*. Paris: Fayard, 1995.

Keep, Christopher. "Blinded by the Type: Gender and Information Technology at the Turn of the Century." *Nineteenth-Century Contexts* 23, no. 1 (2001): 149–73.

– "The Cultural Work of the Typewriter Girl." *Victorian Studies* 40 (1997): 401–26.

Kennedy, Randy. "Cormac McCarthy's Typewriter Brings $254,500 at Auction." *New York Times*, 4 December 2009. https://artsbeat.blogs.nytimes.com/2009/12/04, read 9 May 2017.

Kenner, Hugh. *The Mechanic Muse*. New York: Oxford University Press, 1987.

Kirschenbaum, Matthew. "The Book-Writing Machine." *Slate*, 1 March 2013. http://www.slate.com/articles/arts/books/2013/03/len_deighton_s_bomber_the_first_book_ever_written_on_a_word_processor.single.html, read 25 February 2018.

– *Track Changes: A Literary History of Word Processing*. Cambridge, MA: Belknap, 2016.

Kittler, Friedrich A. *Discourse Networks, 1800/1900*. Translated by Michael Meteer and Chris Cullens. Stanford, CA: Stanford University Press, 1990.

– *Gramophone, Film, Typewriter*. Translated by Geoffrey Winthrop Young and Michael Wutz. Stanford, CA: Stanford University Press, 1999.

Krebs, Albin. "The Fiction Factory" (Obituary of Erle Stanley Gardner). *New York Times*, 12 March 1970. https://www.nytimes.com/1970/03/12/archives/the-fiction-factory-erle-stanley-gardner-author-of-the-perry-mason.html, read 11 May 2018.

Kweon, Seunghyeok. "Technologized Modernity in Modernist Poetics." PhD diss., State University of New York at Buffalo, 2001.

Kwibuka, Eugene. "Rwanda's Last Typewriter Users." *New Times* (Rwanda), 9 March 2013. http://www.newtimes.co.rw/section/ Printer/2103-03-09/90922, read 10 May 2017.

Lacassin, Francis, and Gilbert Sigaux, eds. *Simenon*. Paris: Plon, 1973.

Laughlin, James. *Pound as Wuz: Essays and Lectures on Ezra Pound*. St Paul, MN: Graywolf, 1987.

Leclerc, Yvan. "Les 'animalités de l'homme' plume." *Revue Flaubert* 10 (2010). http://flaubert.univ-rouen.fr/revue/article.php?id=70, read 22 July 2016.

LeGallee, Julie. "Typewriters: Are Computers Driving Them to Pasture?" *Office* 118, no. 2 (April 1993): 16.

Liebowitz, Stan, and Stephen E. Margolis. "Typing Errors." *Reason* 28, no. 2 (June 1996): 28–35.

Love, Harold. *Scribal Publication in Seventeenth-Century England* Oxford: Clarendon, 1993.

Ludovici, Anthony M. "The Latest Form of Poisonous Hate." *New Age*, n.s. 12, no. 2 (14 November 1912): 8–9.

Lyons, Martyn. *A History of Reading and Writing in the Western World*. Basingstoke, UK: Palgrave Macmillan, 2010.

– "Qwertyuiop: How the Typewriter Influenced Writing Practices. *Quaerendo* 44, no. 4 (2014): 219–40.

Lyons, Martyn, and Rita Marquilhas, eds. *Approaches to the History of Written Culture: A World Inscribed*. Cham, CH: Springer International / Palgrave, 2017.

Lyons, Siobhan. "Beyond Luddism: Typewriters and the Return of Pre-Digital Writing." Paper presented to the Literature and Technology conference, Australasian Association of Literature, Western Sydney University, July 2016, https://www.academia.edu/27033886/Beyond_Luddism_ Typewriters_and_the_Return_of_Pre-Digital_Writing, read 4 January 2017.

Mackenzie, Donald F. *Making Meaning: "Printers of the Mind" and Other Essays*. Edited by Peter D. McDonald and Michael F. Suarez, SJ. Amherst, MA: University of Massachusetts Press, 2002.

Madsen, Diane Gilbert. "'To Pound a Vicious Typewriter': Hemingway's Corona #3." *Hemingway Review* 32, no. 2 (Spring 2013): 109–21.

Maffioletti, Marco. *L'impresa ideale tra fabbrica e comunità: Una biografia intellettuale di Adriano Olivetti*. Rome: Collana Intangibili-Fondazione Adriano Olivetti, 2016.

Magnússon, Sigurður Gylfi, and Davíð Ólaffson. "'Barefoot Historians': Education in Iceland in the Early Modern Period." In *Writing Peasants: Studies on Peasant Literacy in Early Modern Northern Europe*. Edited by

Klaus-Joachim Lorenzen-Schmidt and Bjorn Poulsen, 175–209. Aarhus, DK: Landbohistorisk selskab, 2002.

– *Minor Knowledge and Microhistory: Manuscript Culture in the Nineteenth Century.* London: Routledge, 2017.

Magoun, Alex. Review of Friedrich Kittler, *Gramophone, Film, Typewriter.* In *Technology and Culture* 42, no. 1 (2001): 174–6.

Mangan, Lucy. "How Utterly, Splendidly Ripping." *Guardian*, 20 August 2008, 26–7.

Mares, Geo. Carl. *The History of the Typewriter: Being an Illustrated Account of the Origin, Rise and Development of the Writing Machine.* London: Guilbert Pitman, 1909.

Marnham, Patrick. *The Man Who Wasn't Maigret: A Portrait of Georges Simenon.* London: Bloomsbury, 1992.

Marr, David. *Patrick White: A Life.* Sydney: Random House, 2008.

Matore, Daniel. "Cummings's Typewriter Language: The Typography of *Tulips & Chimneys*." *Textual Practice* 31, no. 7 (2017): 1509–31.

McAleer, Joseph. *Popular Reading and Publishing in Britain, 1914–1950* Oxford: Clarendon, 1992.

McConnell, Kathleen F. "The Profound Sound of Ernest Hemingway's Typist: Gendered Typewriting as a Solution to the Problems of Communication." *Communication and Critical/Cultural Studies* 5, no. 4 (2008): 325–43.

McLuhan, Marshall. *The Gutenberg Galaxy: The Making of Typographical Man.* Toronto: University of Toronto Press, 1962.

– *Understanding Media: The Extensions of Man.* London: Abacus, 1974.

McVeigh, Jane. "Understanding Literary Diatexts: Approaching the Archive of Richmal Crompton, the Creator of 'Just William' Stories." *European Journal of Life Writing* 5 (2016): 2–22.

Melvin, Sheila. "How Chinese Typewriters Led Way to Predictive Text on Smartphones." *Caixin Online Society and Culture*, 26 March 2016. http://english.caixin.com/2016-03-26/100924780.html, read 18 August 2016.

Messenger, Robert. "Typing Writers: An Endangered Species (But Not Yet Extinct)." *Canberra Times*, 14 February 2009.

Miller, James Edwin, Jr. *T.S. Eliot: The Making of an American Poet, 1888–1922.* University Park: Pennsylvania State University Press, 2005.

Monaco, Cynthia. "The Difficult Birth of the Typewriter." *Harvard Business Review* 67, no. 2 (March 1989): 214–15.

Moran, Joe. "Typewriter, You're Fired! How Writers Learned to Love the Computer." *Guardian*, 28 August 2015. http://www.theguardian.com/books/2015/aug/28/how-amstrad-word-processor-encouraged-writers-use-computers, read 9 April 2018.

Morgan, Janet. *Agatha Christie: A Biography.* London: Collins, 1984.

Morrison, Blake. "Why Do Writers Drink?" *Guardian*, 20 July 2013. http://
www.theguardian.com/books/2013/jul/20/why-do-writers-drink-alcohol,
read 18 August 2016.

Mullan, Bob. *The Enid Blyton Story*. London: Boxtree, 1987.

Mullaney, Thomas S. *The Chinese Typewriter: A History*. Cambridge, MA: MIT
Press, 2017.

Müller, Lothar. *White Magic: The Age of Paper*. Translated by Jessica Spengler.
Cambridge: Polity, 2014.

Myers, Marc. "Jackie Collins and a Home That Brings a Painting to Life." *Wall
Street Journal*, 27 February 2014. https://jackiecollins.com/press/test/, read
29 January 2018.

Nash, Catherine Mary. "Technology in the Work of Jack Kerouac and William
S. Burroughs." PhD diss., University of Nottingham, 2008.

Nicosia, Gerald. *Memory Babe: A Critical Biography of Jack Kerouac*. Berkeley:
University of California Press, 1994.

Nolan, Jennifer. "Reading 'Babylon Revisited' as a *Post* Text: F. Scott
Fitzgerald, George Horace Lorimer, and the *Saturday Evening Post*
Audience." *Book History* 20 (2017): 351–73.

Nolan, William F. *The* Black Mask *Boys: Masters in the Hard-Boiled School of
Detective Fiction*. New York: William Morrow, 1985.

O'Connell, John. "Agatha Christie's Secret Notebooks by John Curran."
Guardian, 26 September 2009. https://www.theguardian.com/books/2009/
sep/26/agatha-christie-secret-notebooks-review, read 21 February 2018.

Olsén, Jan Eric. "Vicariates of the Eye: Blindness, Sense Substitution, and
Writing Devices in the Nineteenth Century." *Mosaic: A Journal for the
Interdisciplinary Study of Literature* 46, no. 3 (2013): 75–91.

O'Neil, Tim. "Typewriter Interest Growing among Young People." *St Louis
Post-Dispatch*, 20 October 2013.

Pagnamenta, Robin. "'Clack, Clack, Ding!' Bell Tolls for the Typewriter." *Times*
(London), 23 April 2011, 59.

Parikka, Jussi, and Paul Feigelfeld. "Friedrich Kittler: E-Special Introduction."
Theory, Culture and Society 32, nos 7–8 (2015): 349–58.

Perloff, Marjorie. *The Futurist Moment: Avant-Garde, Avant Guerre and the
Language of Rupture*, Chicago: University of Chicago Press, 1986.

Peyrière, Monique. *Machines à écrire: Des claviers et des puces – la traversée du
siècle*. Paris: Autrement, 1994.

Pinard, Mary C. "Christopher Latham Sholes, the Typewriter, and Women's
Economic Emancipation: A Reading of an Image." *Reader* 23 (Spring 1990):
22–35.

Pinch, Trevor J., and Wiebe E. Bijker. "The Social Construction of Facts and
Artefacts: Or How the Sociology of Science and the Sociology of Technology

Might Benefit Each Other." *Social Studies of Science* 14, no. 3 (August 1984): 399–441.

Polt, Richard. *The Typewriter Revolution: A Typist's Companion for the 21st Century*. Woodstock, VT: Countryman, 2015.

Poovey, Mary. *The Proper Lady and the Woman Writer: Ideology as Style in the Works of Mary Wollstonecraft, Mary Shelley and Jane Austen*. Chicago: University of Chicago Press, 1984.

Potin, Yann. "Le prix de l'écrit." *Genèses* 105 (December 2016): 3–7.

Price, Leah, and Pamela Thurschwell, eds. *Literary Secretaries / Secretarial Culture*. Aldershot, UK: Ashgate, 2005.

Rainey, Lawrence S. "Eliot among the Typists: Writing *The Waste Land*." *Modernism/ Modernity* 12, no. 1 (January 2005): 27–84.

– *Revisiting "The Waste Land."* New Haven, CT: Yale University Press, 2005.

Ray, Sheila G. *The Blyton Phenomenon*. London: André Deutsch, 1982.

Rehr, Darryl C. "QWERTY-DVORAK: 'The Keyboard Wars'." *Office* 111, no. 4 (April 1990): 12–19.

Reuveni, Gideon. *Reading Germany: Literature and Consumer Culture in Germany before 1933*. New York: Berghahn, 2006.

Rohrbach, Véronique. "'Cher auteur': Quand les lecteurs 'ordinaires' écrivent à Simenon." *Cahiers de l'Herne* (2013): 220–5.

– "L'ordinaire en partage: Le courier des lecteurs à Georges Simenon." Doctoral diss., Université de Lausanne, 2015.

– "Simenon, un auteur et ses lecteurs: Une économie de la grandeur." *COnTEXTES*, Varia, published online 14 December 2013. http://contextes. revues.org/5760, read 19 September 2016.

Rose, Jonathan. "Rereading the *English Common Reader*: A Preface to the History of Audiences." *Journal of the History of Ideas* 53, no. 1 (1992): 47–70.

Rosenblatt, Roger. "The Last Page in the Typewriter." *Time* 121 (16 May 1983).

Rotella, Elyce J. *From Home to Office: U.S. Women at Work, 1870–1930*. Ann Arbor, MI: UMI Research Press, 1981.

Rudd, David. "The Mystery of the Undermind ... A Closer Look at Enid's Creativity." *Enid Blyton Book and Ephemera Collectors Society* 22 (February 1996): 12–16, and 23 (March 1996): 4–7.

Saenger, Paul. *Space between Words: The Origins of Silent Reading*. Stanford, CA: Stanford University Press, 1997.

Samuelson, Robert J. "Requiem for the Typewriter." *Washington Post*, 12 July 1995. https://www.washingtonpost.com/archive/opinions/1995/07/12/ requiem-for-the-typewriter/b3e634a4-6473-4e72-9022-1e1ee2b135a4/?utm_ term=.a23e15e52d94, read 22 April 2018.

Schilleman, Matthew. "Typewriter Psyche: Henry James's Mechanical Mind." *Journal of Modern Literature* 36, no. 3 (Spring 2013): 14–30.

Seltzer, Mark. *Bodies and Machines*. New York: Routledge, 1992.

Sisman, Adam. *John le Carré: The Biography*. London: Bloomsbury, 2015.

Smallwood, Imogen. *A Childhood at Green Hedges*. London: Methuen, 1989.

Smith, Douglas. "The Burning Library: The Paperback Revolution and the End of the Book in 1960s France." *French Studies* 72, no. 4 (2018): 539–56.

Smith, Erin A. *Hard-Boiled: Working-Class Readers and Pulp Magazines*. Philadelphia: Temple University Press, 2000.

Solan, Matthew. "Tracking Down Typewriters." *Poets and Writers*, September–October 2009, 31–3.

Stoddard, Roger E. "Morphology and the Book from an American Perspective." *Printing History* 17 (1987): 2–14.

Stoney, Barbara. *Enid Blyton: The Biography*. London: Hodder & Stoughton, 1974.

Strom, Sharon Hartman. *Beyond the Typewriter: Gender, Class, and the Origins of Modern American Office Work, 1900–1930*. Urbana: University of Illinois Press, 1992.

Suranyi, Clarissa. "High Fidelity: The Phonograph and Typewriter in Fin-de-siècle fiction." PhD diss., University of Western Ontario, 2001.

Tannen, Deborah, ed. *Spoken and Written Language: Exploring Orality and Literacy*. Norwood, NJ: Ablex, 1982.

Thompson, Laura. *Agatha Christie: An English Mystery*. London: Headline Review, 2007.

Thurschwell, Pamela. "Henry James and Theodora Bosanquet: On the Typewriter, *In the Cage*, at the Ouija Board." *Textual Practice* 13, no. 1 (1999): 5–23.

– *Literature, Technology and Magical Thinking, 1880–1920*. Cambridge: Cambridge University Press, 2001.

Tietchen, Todd F. *Techno-Modern Poetics: The American Literary Avant-Garde at the Start of the Information Age*. Iowa City: Iowa University Press, 2018.

Tobias, Andrew. "My Typewriter." *Esquire* 91 (5 June 1979): 93.

Trofimova, Evija. *Paul Auster's Writing Machine: A Thing to Write With*. London: Bloomsbury, 2014.

Vericat, Fabio L. "Her Master's Voice: Dictation, the Typewriter, and Henry James's Trouble with the Speech of American Women." *South Atlantic Review* 80, nos 1–2 (2015): 1–23.

Viollet, Catherine. "Écriture méchanique, espaces de frappe: Quelques préalables à une sémiologie du dactylogramme." *Genesis* 10 (1996): 193–208.

Walker, Sue. "How Typewriters Changed Correspondence: An Analysis of Prescription and Practice." *Visible Language* 18, no. 2 (Spring 1984): 102–17.

– "Modernity, Method and Minimal Means: Typewriters, Typing Manuals and Document Design." *Journal of Design History* 31, no. 2 (2018): 138–53.

Wershler-Henry, Darren. *The Iron Whim: A Fragmented History of Typewriting*. Ithaca, NY: Cornell University Press, 2007.

"What's a Typewriter, Mommy?" *Time* 140, no. 5 (3 August 1992): 25.

Wicke, Jennifer. "Vampiric Typewriting: *Dracula* and Its Media." *English Literary History* 59 (1992): 467–93.

Williams, R. John. "The *Technê* Whim: Lin Yutang and the Invention of the Chinese Typewriter." *American Literature* 82, no. 2 (2010): 389–419.

Wilson, Carla. "Typewriter Notes, Papery Treasures at New Lower Johnson Store." *Times Colonist* (Victoria, BC), 15 March 2013. http://www.timescolonist.com/business/typewriter-notes-papery-treasures-at-new-lower-johnson-store-1.92300, read 22 April 2018.

Woolf, Virginia. *A Room of One's Own*. 1929. Cambridge: Cambridge University Press, 1995.

Wright, David. "Subversive Technologies: The Machine Age Poetics of F.T. Marinetti, Ezra Pound and Charles Olson." PhD diss., McGill University, 2007.

Index

Adler typewriters, 39
Adventure magazine, 63–4
alcohol, 83, 142, 149, 177
all-finger technique, 40–1
Allen, Grant, *The Type-Writer Girl*, 56, 57, 59
analog underground, 24, 197
Anderson, Leroy, composer, 76
Apollinaire, Guillaume, 22, 68, 74, 75, 76–7
Apple Macintosh, 13, 46, 132
Arnold, David, historian, 7, 199, 206n57, 209n2, 230n1
Auster, Paul, 3, 88, 92, 192, 203n3
automatic writing, 99, 106–8, 111, 113, 119, 200

Balla, Giacomo, 72. *See also* futurism
Bangs, John Kendrick, *The Enchanted Type-Writer*, 107, 220n5
Barthes, Roland, 62–3
Benjamin, Walter, 5
Berry, Wendell, 195–6
Black Mask magazine, 156, 157–9, 163
Bleeck, Gordon Clive, 16, 18, 19
Blickensderfer typewriters, 38, 44, 88, 193

Blyton, Enid, 16, 18, 22, 23, 65, 69, 106, 108, 109–13, 119, 120, 174, 175, 177, 178–82, 183, 187, 190
Bosanquet, Theodora, 65, 94, 96–9, 100, 107, 201
Bradford, Barbara Taylor, 3, 16, 17, 21, 23, 130, 174, 175, 177, 178, 187–9, 190, 196, 201
Breslin, Catherine, 3
Burroughs, William, 19

Caligraph typewriters, 41–2
Capote, Truman, 6, 119, 131
Cato, Nancy, 105, 178–9
celebrity, literary, 16, 18, 19, 137, 138–41, 154, 168, 177, 189, 190
Chandler, Raymond, 158, 159, 186
Christie, Agatha, 16, 19, 20, 21, 23, 54, 58, 65, 124–9, 135, 158, 172, 174, 175, 177, 178, 179–81, 182, 183–7, 189, 190, 201
 – *The Clocks*, 54, 65, 201
 – *The Mysterious Affair at Styles*, 125, 183, 186
 – *One, Two, Buckle My Shoe*, 128
 – *Ten Little Niggers*, 128
 – *Mrs McGinty's Dead*, 128–9
 – *The Mystery of the Blue Train*, 186

Clift, Charmian, 179
Collins, Jackie, 123
Cookson, Catherine, 172, 174, 177, 178, 182–3, 190, 200
Corona typewriters, 38, 40, 82, 88, 167, 187, 193, 201
correctability, 39, 90, 92, 131–5, 136, 184, 189, 191, 192, 193, 200
Crompton, Richmal, 16, 23, 125–6, 177–8, 182–4, 187, 189, 190
cummings, e.e., 22, 68, 76, 79–80, 85, 102

Deighton, Len, 13–15, 191
DeMott, Robert, literary critic, 4
Densmore, James, 31, 32, 33, 37, 45, 48
Depero, Fortunato, 71, 74, 214nn16, 17. See also futurism
Derrida, Jacques, 5
Devanny, Jean, 19, 91
Dickens, Charles, David Copperfield, 43
dictation, 4, 5, 13, 16, 22, 23, 41, 63, 78, 83–4, 87, 89, 90, 94–104, 107, 108, 112, 117, 131, 165, 167, 168, 169, 176, 179, 185, 200, 201
distancing effect, 12–13, 22, 50, 64–5, 86–104, 105, 119, 165, 195, 200
domestic environment, 24, 127–8, 170, 172, 173, 175, 177, 178–82, 184, 185, 190
Doyle, Arthur Conan, A Case of Identity, 64
Dracula, 62, 65
Dubus, Andre, 130
Dumas, Alexandre, 6–7
Dvorak keyboard, 45–8

Eisenstein, Elizabeth, historian, 7, 122
electronic surveillance, 24, 191, 198
Eliot, George, 173
Eliot, T.S., 9, 13, 21, 22, 68, 76, 80–1, 93
everyday technologies, 7, 20, 199

fan mail, 18, 58, 139–41, 152, 164
film, 10, 17, 20, 127, 141
Flaubert, Gustave, 6, 114
Fleming, Ian, 3, 18
Foucault, Michel, 59, 124
Foucault, Pierre, 27
Fraenkel, Béatrice, historian, 86–7
Franklin, Miles, 4, 90
futurism, 22, 67, 69–74, 76, 81, 85, 87, 200

Gallimard, publisher, 138, 151–4
Gardner, Erle Stanley, 16, 19, 20–1, 23, 53, 58–60, 98, 103–4, 128, 155–71, 177, 179, 200, 201, 233n18; fiction factory, 23, 155, 157, 162, 164–8, 169, 170, 171; Perry Mason stories, 53, 58, 59–61, 156, 159, 160–1, 163, 164, 166, 168, 171, 211n43; plot notebooks, 162, 163, 169
– The Case of the Green-Eyed Sister, 169
– The Case of the Grinning Gorilla, 169
– The Case of the Stuttering Bishop, 162, 163
– The Case of the Terrified Typist, 53, 162, 166
– The Case of the Velvet Claws, 162, 168
– The Shrieking Skeleton, 164
Gide, André, 142, 150, 153–4
Gissing, George, The Odd Women, 55–7, 60, 61, 63
Glidden, Carlos, 31, 32, 33, 34, 48
Gutenberg, Johannes, 7, 11, 31

Hammett, Dashiell, 53, 158, 159, 161, 170; The Maltese Falcon, 53, 54, 161
handwriting, 5, 12, 16, 19, 23, 32, 40, 61, 66, 82, 86, 87, 90, 91, 95, 99,

110, 117, 120, 121–36, 145, 146, 149, 150, 164, 175, 183, 184, 185, 187, 188, 196, 200, 220n24
Hansen, Hans Malling, 28–9. *See also* writing ball
Heidegger, Martin, 12, 91
Hemingway, Ernest, 4, 22, 38, 68, 81–5, 123–4, 158, 174, 177, 194, 224n12
Herbert, Xavier, 90
Hermes typewriters, 3, 4, 40, 196
Hesse, Hermann, 91, 99
Hugo, Victor, 6, 139
hunt-and-peck technique, 41, 69, 88, 164

IBM, 13–15, 88, 103, 167, 188, 190, 191, 192
Iceland, 122
Ideal keyboard, 44
Idriess, Ion, 130
Imperial typewriters, 40, 110, 193
India, 7, 44, 95, 193–4, 198, 199, 206n57, 209n2
industrialisation of literature, 64, 135, 151, 168, 171

James, Henry, 16, 22, 65, 89, 93–104, 107–8, 114, 201, 218n52
Janin, Jules, 6

Kerouac, Jack, 6, 15, 16, 22, 65, 106, 108, 114–20, 194
Kirschenbaum, Matthew, media historian, 7, 8, 15, 195
Kittler, Friedrich, 9, 10–13, 22, 28, 68, 87, 93

Lawson, Henry, 68
Le Carré, John, 15, 16, 23, 131, 132–5, 136; *The Night Manager*, 132, 133; *The Tailor of Panama*, 133–5

Le Clézio, J.M.G., 15, 93, 98
literary agents, 19, 58, 59, 109, 110, 123, 135, 156, 159, 163, 168, 170, 174, 182, 183, 200
London, Jack, 88–9
Longley, Margaret, typist, 40–1

machine-gun analogies, 22, 68–9, 84, 199
Mallarmé, Stéphane, *Un Coup de Dés*, 74
Maltron keyboard, 44
Mansfield, Katherine, 88
manuscript culture, 5, 23, 121–4, 125, 136. *See also* handwriting
Marinetti, Filippo Tommaso. *See* futurism
McCarthy, Cormac, 197
McGurrin, Frank, typist, 40–1, 42, 43
McKellar, Peter, psychologist, 111–13
McLuhan, Marshall, 5, 97, 102, 104, 118, 122, 200
McMurtry, Larry, 3, 196
Messud, Claire, 129–30, 136
modernist literature, 15, 22, 67–85, 200
Murdoch, Iris, 196
Murray, Les, 92

"New Woman," 22, 56, 60, 199
Nietzsche, Friedrich, 9, 12, 13, 15, 21, 28–9

office work, 20–1, 52–4, 55–63, 65–6, 165–6, 194, 200–1
Offut, Andrew J., 130
Oliver typewriters, 38, 49, 97, 193
Olivetti typewriters, 38, 39, 93, 193, 197; Valentine, 193
Olson, Charles, 76–8
Olympia typewriters, 3, 4, 38, 198, 203n3
orality, return to, 5, 78, 97, 99–104, 118

Palmer, Nettie, 8–9
paper, 10, 27, 28, 32, 35, 42, 71, 80,
      90, 91, 97, 107, 108, 115, 117, 125,
      133–4, 149, 157, 159, 183, 184,
      195–7; carbon, 27, 30; coloured,
      133–5; reloading, 42, 106, 107,
      115, 117; sensuality of, 129, 136;
      size, 27, 40, 115, 117, 130, 184;
      wartime shortage of, 17, 160
paperback revolution, 17, 154, 156
Parade, 76
Paris Review, 16, 84, 118, 119
pens, 6, 8, 27, 51, 155; quill pens, 6–7,
      30, 50, 51, 95
piano analogies, 22, 27, 29, 35, 36, 45,
      52, 61, 68–9, 84, 97, 199
Pirandello, Luigi, 100–2, 184
Pitman shorthand system, 43, 52, 64,
      65, 92, 175
Pound, Ezra, 68, 73, 78–9, 80, 81, 84
Pratt's Pterotype, 29–30, 31, 35
Proulx, Annie, 130
Proust, Marcel, 123, 147, 184, 195
Provost, Gary, 8
pseudonyms, 18, 19, 134, 156, 158,
      174, 185
pulp fiction, 8, 15, 16, 17–20, 63, 64,
      144, 151–4, 156, 157–61, 169,
      199, 200

Quintilian, 99–100, 103
QWERTY keyboard, 26, 41, 43–8

radio, 17, 19, 139, 146, 156, 157, 160,
      167, 183
Ravizza, Giuseppe, inventor, 27, 30
Remarque, Erich Maria, 17
Remington typewriters, 21, 27, 30,
      33, 34, 35–6, 37–42, 43, 45, 47, 48,
      68, 69, 93, 95, 96, 97, 99, 175, 192,
      193, 199, 201

Roche, Denis, 69
Roland, Betty, 178
romantic typewriter, 13, 22, 89,
      105–20, 200, 201
Rowling, J.K., 109, 121, 123, 124
Royal typewriters, 3, 39, 40, 82, 88,
      138, 185, 196, 201

Sagan, Françoise, 69
Sainte-Beuve, literary critic, 6, 64
Saturday Evening Post, 157, 159, 160
Schwalbach, Matthias, machinist, 31,
      32, 48
Scientific keyboard, 26
Self, Will, 125
sewing machines, 7, 33, 35–6, 61, 199
Sholes, Christopher Latham, 25, 26,
      30–4, 35, 37, 39, 44, 45, 46, 48
shorthand, 21, 32, 40, 42–3, 49, 52, 54,
      56, 63, 65, 94, 104, 107, 149, 165,
      166, 177, 184, 187
signatures, 35, 64, 66, 86–7
Simenon, Georges, 9, 16, 17, 19,
      20, 23, 50, 53, 137–54, 177, 181;
      enveloppes jaunes, 143, 147, 148,
      149, 181; literary establishment,
      19, 152–4; *romans durs*, 144, 152;
      writing rituals, 23, 146, 148–9
Smith, Zadie, 198
Smith-Corona typewriters. *See*
      Corona typewriters
Soule, Samuel, inventor, 31, 32, 48
speed of typing, 5, 8, 9, 23, 27, 32, 35,
      36, 40–2, 45, 50, 59, 61, 63–6, 68,
      69, 82–3, 105, 108, 110–11, 113,
      114–15, 117, 199, 131, 138, 143,
      144, 151, 152, 154, 156, 168–9,
      170, 171, 193, 200, 201
Steinbeck, John, 3–4
stenography. *See* shorthand
Sue, Eugène, 6, 139

Taub, Louis, typist, 41
Taylor, A.J.P., historian, 68–9
technological determinism, 7
television, 17, 19, 20, 58, 60, 126, 139, 156, 157, 160, 161, 168, 183
textual genesis, 15, 80
Thompson, Hunter S., 3
Thurber, Charles, 27, 28, 30
Tolstoy, Leo, 109, 175–7
touch-typing, 27, 40, 41, 45, 62, 64, 69, 150
Turri, Pellegrino, 27
Twain, Mark, 13, 15, 34–5, 38, 40, 63, 91, 100, 108, 191
typewriter, death of, 24, 191, 193–4, 197
typewriter, electric, 15, 39, 45, 63, 69, 156, 164–5, 167, 188, 190, 192–3
typewriter, invention of, 11, 21, 25–34, 35, 36, 41, 48
typewriter, noiseless, 26, 38
typewriter, portability of, 27, 36, 38, 39, 69, 165, 179, 185, 192, 193, 208n40
typewriter, price of, 33, 37, 38, 192
typewriter, purchase of, 19, 34–5, 175
typewriter, stigma of, 6–7, 96, 155, 170
"typewriter girl," 21, 22, 49, 54–63, 65–6, 199
typewriter as prosthetic device, 11, 21, 26, 27, 28, 30, 48
typewriter racing, 41–2

typewriters, Chinese, 44–5, 209n61
typists, female, 3, 11, 20–1, 22, 36, 42, 49–59, 60, 61, 63, 65, 67, 69, 80, 96, 100, 131, 132, 135, 140, 150, 172, 175. See also "typewriter girl"

Underwood typewriters, 37, 39, 40, 42, 82, 83, 91, 102, 114, 115, 184, 193, 201

Viollet, Catherine, historian, 7, 15
visibility, problem of, 28, 33, 36–9, 91

Waugh, Evelyn, 155
Weyergans, François, 90
Wheatley, Dennis, 131
White, Patrick, 4, 93
Wodehouse, P.G., 125
women as authors, 172–90
Woolf, Virginia, 174, 178, 179
word processors, 4, 8, 13, 14, 15, 24, 39, 69, 135, 136, 191–5. See also Apple Macintosh
writing ball, 21, 28–9
writing technologies, 5, 6, 7, 9, 10, 13, 15, 24, 155, 189

Yolen, Jane, 19
Yost, George Washington, 33, 106

Zolotow, Maurice, 108

Studies in Book and Print Culture

General Editor: Leslie Howsam

1 Hazel Bell, *Indexers and Indexes in Fact and Fiction*
2 Heather Murray, *Come, Bright Improvement! The Literary Societies of Nineteenth-Century Ontario*
3 Joseph A. Dane, *The Myth of Print Culture: Essays on Evidence, Textuality, and Bibliographical Method*
4 Christopher J. Knight, *Uncommon Readers: Denis Donoghue, Frank Kermode, George Steiner, and the Tradition of the Common Reader*
5 Eva Hemmungs Wirtén, *No Trespassing: Authorship, Intellectual Property Rights, and the Boundaries of Globalization*
6 William A. Johnson, *Bookrolls and Scribes in Oxyrhynchus*
7 Siân Echard and Stephen Partridge, eds, *The Book Unbound: Editing and Reading Medieval Manuscripts and Texts*
8 Bronwen Wilson, *The World in Venice: Print, the City, and Early Modern Identity*
9 Peter Stoicheff and Andrew Taylor, eds, *The Future of the Page*
10 Jennifer Phegley and Janet Badia, eds, *Reading Women: Literary Figures and Cultural Icons from the Victorian Age to the Present*
11 Elizabeth Sauer, *"Paper-contestations" and Textual Communities in England, 1640–1675*
12 Nick Mount, *When Canadian Literature Moved to New York*
13 Jonathan Earl Carlyon, *Andrés González de Barcia and the Creation of the Colonial Spanish American Library*
14 Leslie Howsam, *Old Books and New Histories: An Orientation to Studies in Book and Print Culture*
15 Deborah McGrady, *Controlling Readers: Guillaume de Machaut and His Late Medieval Audience*
16 David Finkelstein, ed., *Print Culture and the Blackwood Tradition*
17 Bart Beaty, *Unpopular Culture: Transforming the European Comic Book in the 1990s*
18 Elizabeth Driver, *Culinary Landmarks: A Bibliography of Canadian Cookbooks, 1825–1949*

19 Benjamin C. Withers, *The Illustrated Old English Hexateuch, Cotton Ms. Claudius B.iv: The Frontier of Seeing and Reading in Anglo-Saxon England*

20 Mary Ann Gillies, *The Professional Literary Agent in Britain, 1880–1920*

21 Willa Z. Silverman, *The New Bibliopolis: French Book-Collectors and the Culture of Print, 1880–1914*

22 Lisa Surwillo, *The Stages of Property: Copyrighting Theatre in Spain*

23 Dean Irvine, *Editing Modernity: Women and Little-Magazine Cultures in Canada, 1916–1956*

24 Janet Friskney, *New Canadian Library: The Ross-McClelland Years, 1952–1978*

25 Janice Cavell, *Tracing the Connected Narrative: Arctic Exploration in British Print Culture, 1818–1860*

26 Elspeth Jajdelska, *Silent Reading and the Birth of the Narrator*

27 Martyn Lyons, *Reading Culture and Writing Practices in Nineteenth-Century France*

28 Robert A. Davidson, *Jazz Age Barcelona*

29 Gail Edwards and Judith Saltman, *Picturing Canada: A History of Canadian Children's Illustrated Books and Publishing*

30 Miranda Remnek, ed., *The Space of the Book: Print Culture in the Russian Social Imagination*

31 Adam Reed, *Literature and Agency in English Fiction Reading: A Study of the Henry Williamson Society*

32 Bonnie Mak, *How the Page Matters*

33 Eli MacLaren, *Dominion and Agency: Copyright and the Structuring of the Canadian Book Trade, 1867–1918*

34 Ruth Panofsky, *The Literary Legacy of the Macmillan Company of Canada: Making Books and Mapping Culture*

35 Archie L. Dick, *The Hidden History of South Africa's Book and Reading Cultures*

36 Darcy Cullen, ed., *Editors, Scholars, and the Social Text*

37 James J. Connolly, Patrick Collier, Frank Felsenstein, Kenneth R. Hall, and Robert Hall, eds, *Print Culture Histories Beyond the Metropolis*

38 Kristine Kowalchuk, *Preserving on Paper: Seventeenth-Century Englishwomen's Receipt Books*

39 Ian Hesketh, *Victorian Jesus: J.R. Seeley, Religion, and the Cultural Significance of Anonymity*

40 Kirsten MacLeod, *American Little Magazines of the Fin de Siècle: Art, Protest, and Cultural Transformation*

41 Emily Francomano, *The Prison of Love: Romance, Translation and the Book in the Sixteenth Century*

42 Kirk Melnikoff, *Elizabethan Publishing and the Makings of Literary Culture*

43 Amy Bliss Marshall, *Magazines and the Making of Mass Culture in Japan*

44 Scott McLaren, *Pulpit, Press, and Politics: Methodists and the Market for Books in Upper Canada*

45 Ruth Panofsky, *Toronto Trailblazers: Women in Canadian Publishing*

46 Martyn Lyons, *The Typewriter Century: A Cultural History of Writing Practices*

Ingram Content Group UK Ltd.
Milton Keynes UK
UKHW011815210323
418937UK00001B/37

9 781487 525736